BabyTalk

BabyTalk

Strengthen Your Child's Ability to Listen,

Understand, and Communicate

DR. SALLY WARD

Ballantine Books • New York

A Ballantine Book
Published by The Ballantine Publishing Group
Copyright © 2001 by Dr. Sally Ward

www.randomhouse.com/BB/

Library of Congress Cataloging-in-Publication Data

Ward, Sally.
Babytalk : strengthen your child's ability to listen, understand, and communicate /
Sally Ward.—1st. ed.
p.   cm.
ISBN 0-345-43707-1
1. Language acquisition—Parent participation.   2. Children—Language.   I. Title.
P118.5 .W37 2001
401'.93—dc21
00-063102

Manufactured in the United States of America

Cover design by Dreu Pennington-McNeil
Cover photo © Laurence Monneret/Stone

Designed by Ann Gold

First Edition: May 2001

10 9 8 7 6 5 4 3 2 1

Contents

Introduction: My Story

I have always loved words, and this, together with a strong interest in language and an inclination to work directly with people, led me toward a career in speech and language therapy. Speech and language therapy is concerned with the treatment of the full range of people with communication difficulties, from adults who have had a stroke to babies affected by cleft palate. I was educated in London and then married and went to Manchester. There I pursued further studies in the area of audiology—the diagnosis and management of hearing and listening problems.

Soon after, I had three children of my own, a daughter and two sons, who taught me a great deal about language and communication development in the succeeding few years.

I worked part-time in Manchester, in what is now the Mancunian Community National Health Service Trust, setting up a preschool parent guidance service for hearing-impaired children, and also working in clinics with children who had a wide range of speech and language problems. I was subsequently appointed chief speech and language therapist with responsibility for children with language, hearing, and learning difficulties, and I taught courses on these special areas to speech and language therapists and other professional groups. I was also invited to act as advisor in developmental language disability to the Royal College of Speech and Language Therapists, and

I am consequently able to advise any member of the profession who asks for my help.

I was then awarded a major three-year grant by the North West Regional Health Authority, and the resulting study established an accurate means of detecting infants at risk of language delay in the first year of life. This, together with a related study of the ways in which hearing-impaired, learning-disabled, deaf, and autistic children respond to sound, resulted in the award of my Ph.D. I was soon appointed principal speech and language therapist, with responsibility for all speech and language impaired children within the trust.

In the course of all my work, I had become particularly interested in discovering more about the ways in which listening and attention in young children relate to language development. Along with my colleague Deirdre Birkett, whom I had long respected as an exceptionally skillful speech and language therapist, I carried out regular clinics for preschool children. Deirdre and I learned an enormous amount from each other as we worked to help our young patients talk and communicate. We developed an extremely effective program, based entirely upon the power of parents to help their children's development. We found to our delight that in every instance where the child had a language difficulty or delay, however severe, that was not associated with deafness, autism, neurological damage, or general developmental delay, and a parent was able and willing to spend half an hour a day following our program, the children made excellent progress. They often attained the ability to understand and use language normally expected for their age in just a few weeks or months. The joy on the face of a parent as his or her child begins to communicate remains one of the most rewarding aspects of my professional life. Not surprisingly, Deirdre and I both became, and still remain, totally committed to this method of intervention.

Many of the children we were treating in Manchester came from economically deprived backgrounds. Since then I have had the opportunity to use the program that we developed—now known as the BabyTalk program—with families from many different parts of Great Britain and across the whole social spectrum. The results have been consistently successful.

The BabyTalk Study

Our intervention program was originally developed to help children who were already experiencing language difficulties. It soon became apparent to us that it might be possible to prevent language disability from occurring in the first place, by adapting our techniques for use with very young children. In the course of our screening study, we had visited the homes of 373 ten-month-old infants. Our first observation was that even at this very early stage, the infants were showing great differences in pre-language skills. The infants' environments differed considerably, as did the amount and ways in which they were spoken to, and these factors appeared to relate strongly to their language development. By the time the screening study was completed, we felt that we could pinpoint those babies likely to develop language delay.

I was awarded a second major three-year grant by the North West Regional Health Authority in order to test out this idea. As a result of our screening, we discovered a group of 140 ten-month-old infants who were showing varying degrees of delay in language development, ranging from very mild to profound. These infants were divided into two groups, matched for language development, general development, and social background. One group received the program and the other did not, acting as a control. Over the next four months, Deirdre and I visited the BabyTalk group four times, where we began by discussing with parents a number of aspects of their lives. Such details as background sound and television, the amount the infants were talked to, and the exact ways in which they interacted were all recorded. We then asked the parents to follow the BabyTalk program for half an hour each day.

To our delight we found that, just as we had seen with toddlers at our clinics, the BabyTalk infants made very rapid progress in their language development, and all who had stuck with the program had caught up with their normally developing peers in less than four months. Moreover, their parents told us how much they and the infants had enjoyed the program, which delighted us!

THE BABYTALK CHILDREN
AT THREE YEARS OLD

It was extremely important to know whether the effects of the BabyTalk program would be permanent, so we followed up both groups until they were three years old. We chose this age because traditional language studies have all *begun* at this age and have been followed up over a number of years, some into adulthood. Previous language development research showed that many children with problems at age three continued to have problems with speech and language, and a considerable number also had educational difficulties as a result.[1, 2, 3, 4, 5]

We were astonished by our own results! At age three, 85 percent of the group who had not received the BabyTalk program were still showing language delay, in some cases very severe. By contrast, not only were all but three (all of whom had experienced adverse circumstances in their lives) of those who had received the program up to the normal standard, but many in this inner-city area were showing language development *above* their age level. Some were even using complicated speech and sentence structure normally seen in children of four and a half years. These children were able to understand very long and complex sentences and could express themselves with amazing fluency. One little boy called John, just three, could follow enormously long directions such as "Go and find the thick wax crayons and give them to Billy to hand out to the girls," which normally could only be followed by a child almost two years older. He also had no trouble discussing his interest in dinosaurs in great detail, using words like "extinct." At this stage too, there appeared to be considerable differences in all the children's ability to play, as well as their conversational skills.

These results appeared to indicate that changing environmental factors and the way in which the infants were talked to had a profound effect on preventing language difficulties as well as remediating children who were already falling.[6] We were so excited that we decided to have both groups of children studied again at the age of seven.

THE BABYTALK CHILDREN
AT SEVEN YEARS OLD

We recruited two psychologists and asked them to assess our two groups without revealing which children had received the BabyTalk program and which had not. They used a fully standardized battery of tests, including the intelligence tests most commonly used in England with children at this age.[7, 8, 9]

Once again, the results of this study were astonishing. Only four children (two of those who were behind at three years, plus two more) in the BabyTalk group were showing any delay in language development, compared with twenty in the control group. In fact, the ability of the BabyTalk children both to understand complex sentences and to utilize advanced sentence structures were, on average, one year and three months ahead of the control group. Some of them showed language development typical of ten-and-a-half-year-olds! The reading ability of the BabyTalk children was also on average a year and three months ahead.

The same results were found on a test of vocabulary, which is commonly believed to be the best predictor of intelligence.[10] The most advanced children understood words like "catastrophe," "exhibition," "fragment," and "lecturing," which are not commonly used by children under ten.

The most exciting finding of all was that there was a very considerable difference in general intelligence between the two groups. The average IQ of the group who had received the BabyTalk program was in the top third of the population, and between a third and a quarter of these children were in the intellectually gifted range. In contrast, the average IQ of those who had not received the program was in the bottom third of the population, and only one child was in the gifted range.

These differences were reflected in the results of standardized tests given to children in England at the ages of seven and eleven. All the BabyTalk children reached the target standards or higher, while a third of the other group failed to reach the minimum levels.

There were also noticeable differences between the two groups in emotional and behavioral development, social skills, and ability to concentrate. The psychologists who did the testing made encouraging comments on the test forms of the BabyTalk children like "excellent concentration," "forthcoming and friendly manner," and "he expresses himself easily and effectively." Most of the BabyTalk children appeared to enjoy the testing very much and their parents were also greatly pleased with the results. The expression "He's such a confident communicator now" was often heard. Similar comments were even made by a crew who interviewed some of the children while making a television program about the results. The cameraman was very struck by the way a little boy, once his mother had told him that it was fine to talk to the crew, engaged them in conversation, asking questions about their equipment and comparing it with his father's camera. So impressed were they that they let him make the concluding comments of the TV program!

Conversely, on the test forms of over a third of the control children were comments about the fact that they were easily distracted and needed many breaks to enable them to finish the tasks. Saddest of all, some of the children in that group clearly found the whole situation stressful and greatly feared failure.

In conclusion, our findings, independently tested, led us to realize that the program developed for the prevention of problems would enhance the development of all kinds of children. It was clear that parents could be taught to use the BabyTalk program from their children's birth to give every one the opportunity to develop to his or her maximum potential.

The results of our studies appeared in a number of scientific journals and led to presentations at national and international conferences and a considerable demand for teaching about the screening test and the BabyTalk program, both to speech and language therapists and to other professionals. I am now engaged in further research on the development of attention in infancy, but hope never to stop doing clinical work as well—contact with the children and their parents is still the most rewarding part of my work.

How Language Develops

Despite our knowledge that children whose language development is below the normal standard for their age are at very high risk of educational, social, and emotional problems, we still do not know exactly how helpless newborns essentially master their language in only four years.

The earliest theory[11] of language development explained that a baby makes random sounds, and the adults around him "shape" those sounds by rewarding those closest to words. For example, the baby would frequently babble "mama" at an early age, and every time he did so his mother would appear. He would eventually link the word with her. The great linguist Noam Chomsky, however, rejected this view in the 1950s and 1960s.[12, 13] His theory put forth the idea that children are born with an innate capacity for language learning and when hearing language automatically begin to use what he called a "language acquisition device (LAD)" to help them make sense out of what they hear, and later on to help them to put sentences together for themselves. He considered that the amount of language the child was exposed to and the kind of language the child heard was of little importance. According to Chomsky, we are born with a natural knowledge of grammatical rules. For example, we already know that nouns and verbs agree—that, for instance, "the boy jumps" is correct, as is "the girls jump," but "the boy jump" and "the girls jumps" are not.[14] This theory still assumes that language development is only possible because of this inborn knowledge, and that the amount and kind of speech the baby and little child hears is of little importance. Steven Pinker, another great linguist writing more recently,[15] also holds the view that children have knowledge from the start of life about the different types of words and the parts they play in language. The little child knows, for example, that whatever causes an event is the subject of the sentence. Seeing the cat knock over a vase of flowers and hearing his mother say, "That naughty cat," he rightly assumes that the cat is the cause of the problem and therefore the subject of the sentence.

While there is still no final conclusion about the amount of innate knowledge we're born with, there is a general agreement among experts that some kind of natural mechanism must be in place to explain the amazing speed with which human infants learn language.

The extent to which such mechanisms are sensitive to input from the environment is another matter of considerable debate. Chomsky and Pinker, as we have heard, both claim that environment has little influence over early language, but other much acclaimed researchers[16, 17, 18] stress the vital importance of social interaction and input to the process of language acquisition. Their view is that early language skills are acquired through children's meaningful and active involvement with the people in their lives.

While it is accepted that we are preprogrammed for language in some way, learning to develop this skill is seen as extremely dependent upon the interaction between the child and his environment. The kind of language he hears significantly influences the extent to which the child realizes his potential, as evidenced by studies that examine the relationship between adult input and the rate and nature of speech development. Much of this research was carried out in response to Chomsky's claim that there must be a "language acquisition device" in infants so they can decipher the complex, disorganized, and deviant language of the adults around them. (It appeared that Chomsky may not have had much contact with babies and small children, as most adults instinctively do not speak to infants as they do to their friends!)

Although it is evident that certain language milestones are relatively independent of environmental influences (deaf children begin to babble at the same time as do hearing babies, and the age at first word production is the same in children in both highly stimulating and in deprived backgrounds), there can be little doubt that environmental influences are critical in shaping future language and social development. There is, for instance, a substantial amount of evidence indicating that the quantity of speech addressed to the little child correlates positively with their development. Specifically, the more they are talked to, the more rapidly they learn language.[19, 20] The content of speech has also been shown to have extremely important implications for language learning.[21, 22] Studies also indicate that babies and young children show a marked preference for certain kinds of speech.[23] Indeed, the acquisition of specific vocabulary and grammatical structures seems to be directly related to the input the children receive from their caregivers.[24]

In our own clinical experience and research, we found that modifying the way parents speak to their children has been a crucial factor in their children's dramatic progress, and is consequently an extremely important part of the BabyTalk program.

To summarize, while it does seem very likely that we have an inborn language learning mechanism, there is a substantial body of evidence that the way children are spoken to has considerable bearing on their language development. Biologist E. Lenneberg, writing in the 1960s, summed up this middle position when he stated that "infants are biologically programmed to develop language in the same way as much animal behaviour is programmed. To occur satisfactorily, however, the organism must be intact, and the environment provide an appropriate quantity of the right quality of input.[25] Interestingly, this pattern is seen in other animal species as well. The basic song of the chaffinch, for example, appears to be innate, as it occurs in birds reared in isolation, but the young bird needs to be exposed to singing from adults for the full song to develop.[26] With BabyTalk, I can help you to help your baby to sing his or her fullest song!

Why Things Go Wrong

Language is what distinguishes human beings from the rest of creation, and there can be little doubt as to its importance to our society and culture. Despite this wonderful ability to talk, however, we still often have great difficulties communicating with one another. I was interested to hear from a veterinarian friend the other day that almost all the second opinions she is asked for are not in fact due to a wrong diagnosis, but to a lack of communication between vets and their clients. We went on to speculate about how many wars and other serious conflicts might be due to such simple misunderstandings.

It is clear, therefore, that there can be few things more important than ensuring that our children acquire the very best communication skills that we can give them. Delay in language development, however, is recognized as the most common childhood disability,[27] having been estimated to affect up to 10 percent or more of all seven-year-olds and considerably higher numbers in inner-city localities.[28, 29, 30, 31]

You may be wondering why this is so. Language delay is inevitably associated with learning difficulties, autism, and hearing impairment. It can also result from specific neurodevelopmental problems as in specific language impairment, dyspraxia, and attention deficit hyperactivity disorder (ADHD), which are discussed in appendix 1. Problems with producing speech sounds also result from physical conditions such as cleft palate and damage to the nerve supply to the lips, tongue, and palate.

However, for the many otherwise perfectly normal children—who constitute the largest number of speech- and language-impaired children—Deirdre and I have long been convinced that the delay in language development results from a mismatch between the language addressed to the little child and the actual level either of his use or, more commonly, of his understanding of speech. Adults usually adjust their speech to the age and size of children. Sometimes a child may fall behind his age group, particularly in comprehension—which can occur for a variety of reasons—resulting in miscommunication between parent and child. Periods of intermittent hearing loss associated with colds and ear infections, for example, are extremely common in babyhood and early childhood and can very easily lead to listening difficulties, with consequential effects on comprehension. Prolonged illness in baby or mother also can cause problems, as can many of the stresses and demands of life, such as the need to relocate, maybe to somewhere far away from the support of the wider family.

Isn't Intelligence Fixed at Birth?

Just as there is no absolute conclusion to all the theories regarding language acquisition, there has been a general debate since the eighteenth century as to whether human intelligence is the product of genetic attributes only, or is affected by experience. Scientists agree, however, that a baby does not arrive as a genetically preprogrammed automaton, and they continue to look at the many ways in which genetic predisposition and environmental circumstances interact. It is now known that at twelve weeks after conception, neurons already show coordinated waves of activity, and that these waves actually

> *It is of the greatest importance to recognize that only in the most rare and tragic situations of abuse or severe neglect can language impairment ever be said to be the parents' fault.*
>
> I feel very strongly about this, as I have seen many parents blame themselves for problems that are out of their control.

change the shape of the brain. The same processes that wire the brain before birth drive the astonishingly rapid learning that takes place afterward. An infant's brain has virtually all the nerve cells it will ever have, but at birth the pattern of wiring has not yet been established. Soon after birth the infant begins to receive information through his senses, stimulating neural activity. (A 1997 report summarizes recent work on this subject.[32])

The earliest years, particularly the first three, are a time of huge developmental plasticity, when the completion of neural circuits in the brain depends on appropriate stimulation, which is critical in shaping future intelligence. By the age of two years, the little child's brain has twice the number of synapses and consumes twice the amount of energy as that of an adult! Connections that are made in babyhood and not used are gradually eliminated after the age of ten years.

It is not surprising, therefore, that there is much evidence that lack of stimulation can have the same devastating effect on development as does sensory deprivation. An example can be seen in the tragic lives of the Romanian orphans whose plight came to light in the early 1990s. Various studies showed, in general, that the children, having been deprived of adult stimulation, suffered developmental lag from the age of three months on that could not be reversed.

Other research has also shown the immensely powerful effect of early stimulation on intellectual development. These studies have led to the establishment of the Headstart programs in the United States and similar programs in Europe, which were designed to compensate culturally deprived children. These preschool programs are designed to give the children rich play opportunities and language input. Many of the children show definite intellectual gains. However, it is interesting to note that many involved in running the programs, which start at three years, believe they offer too little too late.

There can be no doubt that there are real differences in inborn intellectual capacity from the beginning. After all, we can't all be Einstein! The evidence is also clear, however, that there is nothing fixed or permanent about intelligence quotient and that in the early stages of life, enormous changes can be made by environmental stimulation. It is possible that the most important of these is in boosting language development. Language is our main vehicle for thought, and therefore language and thought are inevitably linked. Once again, there is no absolute agreement among psychologists as to the degree and nature of this link, but there is certainly a consensus that they are very closely related. Most theorists consider that both intellectual and language development come about from a child exploring the objects, events, and people in his environment. A little child, for example, needs to achieve certain stages of intellectual development for the acquisition of words to be possible. He needs to have a concept that objects continue to exist even when they are out of sight before he can label them. Conversely, intellectual development is clearly greatly facilitated by language. Imagine the very young child trying to figure out where the pieces go in a jigsaw puzzle. An adult giving him words like "Turn it" or "It's too small" will enable him to transfer his learning to another situation. Concept formation is also greatly facilitated by the addition of a verbal label. For example, the baby initially only relates the word "cat" to the family cat, but the use of the word "cat" in other situations soon enables him to generalize the idea to any cat in any situation. Still later, children can use language to plan and discuss their activities before actually embarking upon them. Four-year-olds, for example, can be heard saying things like, "You can have the first turn with this and then I'll have my turn" or "After we've been to the park I think I'll play with my guinea pig."

Language helps us all to remember and to give and receive information. By the age of four and a half, language is fully internalized and can be used as a substitute for action, as it is in adulthood, acting as a shortcut to arriving at solutions to problems. The child is able, for example, to think through how to solve a puzzle before actually trying to do so, mentally working out how he will arrange and move the pieces. Language becomes, in fact, the key to understanding the world, and remains so for life.

The BabyTalk Approach

The BabyTalk program aims to establish the foundations for all later learning. These foundations include not only the understanding and use of language, but also listening, attention, and play activities. Many people do not realize that these skills actually develop in stages and that it is possible to help infants and young children to move easily and effectively through them.

BabyTalk is developmentally appropriate and totally stress-free for both parent and child. Although it is soundly based in extensive clinical experience, linguistic theory, and cutting-edge research, it is also firmly rooted in natural interaction. No artificial teaching situations are ever set up: BabyTalk fits into the normal relaxed pattern of your child's day.

There is currently great concern about the increasing numbers of children with literacy and numeracy problems. I was recently talking to a teacher in a large public school who told me that she had been shocked to hear that more than half the children arriving at her school at the age of eleven were reading below grade level. There is a move to address this growing problem by instigating the very early teaching of numbers, colors, shapes, and the alphabet. This move is highly controversial, and a few educators consider it to be a mistake. There are some indications that this "hothousing" not only stresses the child, but also creates in many children the very problem it seeks to prevent, by engendering anxiety and aversion in children who are not ready for such teaching. In a parallel situation, I have seen many children in my clinics who have been "taught" to say their sounds correctly at an inappropriately early age when they do not understand what is required. These children just get the message that the way in which they try to communicate is not acceptable, and as a result they become anxious, sad, and virtually silent.

> *Don't feel guilty about being a working parent!*

I can think of one little boy called Jasper, just three and a half, whose extremely worried mother brought him to me in order to continue the intensive work on his speech sounds that had been done for the past year in another part of the country. This little chap peered at me from under his bangs and clearly had decided that talking was definitely not on the agenda! His mother reported that he now only spoke at home and was becoming increasingly silent there. She was aware that he hated his speech and language sessions and had obviously become very much aware that he had a speech problem, but she had been assured that that kind of therapy was necessary. I gave her the BabyTalk program and told her to take him home and forget about speech and language therapy. She telephoned me a few weeks later to tell me that to her delight, not only had Jasper's speech sounds sorted themselves out, but she had her delightfully outgoing and chatty little son back again!

Parents following the BabyTalk program do not need to feel anxious or guilty about going to work, or that they need to spend huge amounts of time with their children to ensure their optimal progress. In the highly sensitive early stages of development, a little of the absolutely right stimulus has huge effects. Thirty minutes a day is fine, although you are very likely to find that some of the suggestions will carry over naturally and effortlessly into daily living.

As your child grows up, your role and that of books and play will change in accordance with the child's stage of development. Always remember that your baby's development is fuller and richer for what you are doing, and that you will always know exactly how best to help him. At whatever point you are starting, I hope that you and your child will have fun together.

A Very Important Note for Parents

The stages of normal development have been included in this book so that you can celebrate your little child's development and see how the program matches the levels he has reached, but *not* so that you can "test" him! There are very large variations in normal development, resulting not only from the environment, but also from the baby's genetic inheritance, and from the interplay of different aspects of development. A baby who achieves early mobility, for example, is likely to be slower to acquire words and may also be slower in his play progress. Your child, like all others, will have his own unique pattern of development.

About the Contents of This Book

The book is divided into age bands, four in the first year, three in the second, two in the third, and one in the fourth. Your baby is referred to as "he" or "she" in alternating chapters.

Within each section, the following areas are covered for that stage:

- communication and interaction;
- speech and language development as they pertain to general development;
- listening and attention;
- play;
- reading and toy suggestions.

The BabyTalk program is outlined in detail at each age band. It covers

- how to create the proper environment for your baby's development;
- how much to talk to your child and what to talk about; and
- what to do outside your daily half hour.

The program is illustrated by case studies. You can find answers to questions parents commonly ask in appendix 2.

You will find that some themes run throughout the entire program, and that some of the suggested activities are repeated over several time periods, sometimes with small differences.

You may come upon this book when your little child is leaving or has left babyhood. If he has experienced any of the reasons we have discussed that may have caused a delay in his language development, such as trouble with his ears or prolonged illness, you may notice that his language levels are at a lower level than his age. If this is the case, go to the section of the program that is at the level of his understanding and start there. I hope that you will see a rapid improvement, but please do not hesitate to ask for a referral to speech and language therapy if you are at all concerned.

If your baby or little child is affected by any problems usually associated with language delay—like learning difficulties or autistic spectrum disorder—you will almost certainly have been referred by your pediatrician for speech and language therapy. The BabyTalk program, I believe, will provide additional help, so talk to your speech and language therapist about it.

A friend of mine, who has a four-year-old boy named Bennie with Down's syndrome, asked me if I thought the program would be helpful to him. I replied that I was quite sure that it would be. I explained that instead of following the program section for his actual age, she should observe him for a few days to see how much he was understanding and then start the program at his skill level. She found that the right place to start was at the two-year level, as he was understanding quite a few names of people and objects and some little phrases. She and Bennie loved their times together, and in six months Bennie made six months of progress in his understanding and use of language, which was rather remarkable. His genetic endowment will prevent him from continuing to develop at that rate, but his mother is now confident that he will reach his maximum potential.

LISTENING AND ATTENTION

You may wonder why listening is so important to the program. We live in an increasingly noisy society, and as adults we take for granted the ability to "tune out" background sound and focus on what we wish to listen to, maintaining that focus for as long as we desire. (Just take a moment to stop and listen to all the sounds you have been ignoring!) This ability, like that of controlling and maintaining attention, develops in stages, and recently we've found that more children are failing to acquire it. Large numbers of kids with perfectly normal hearing are showing enormous problems with listening, and clinicians and teachers are beginning to make the connection between learning and language problems and the inability to listen. I was interested to hear from a friend whose eleven-year-old has just started middle school. In his welcome address to parents the principal said that there was one problem shared by all the children, and that problem was *listening*.

Adults can help their children develop the ability to select from the many sounds around them and to keep listening for as long as they wish. The program will explain how to do this.

In this book, attention development is covered for equally important reasons. Many people consider that children (and indeed adults) either do or do not pay attention. In fact, the ability to focus attention and maintain that focus, shifting it as required (particularly in a distracting environment), develops in well-defined stages in early childhood.[33]

In many school-age children, however, this development has not occurred. Teachers increasingly complain that their students are not able to sustain attention to daily activities, particularly in a noisy, busy classroom. Learning can be severely impeded, especially the early stages of language when the child begins to link words with their meanings. It is absolutely vital that the infant and adult be able to share the same focus of attention. Further, attention control is traditionally regarded as a central factor in adult intelligence. The ability to screen out irrelevant or distracting stimuli must be developed at a young age. Trying to "make" children pay attention only makes matters worse. Instead, they need help that will enable them to progress through the normal stages.

The BabyTalk program will tell you how to identify the stage your child has reached and how to enable him to progress to the next.

PLAY

Play also has a very important place in the program. It has often been termed the "work" of childhood, as it is the child's way of learning about the world, developing his social relationships, and expressing himself. Play and language development are inextricably linked, and play is the most wonderful vehicle for the adult to add language use. The child can explore objects and materials and discover new ideas while the adults around him provide the words to go with his activities. Dropping things from a high chair is much more fun when an adult says "Gone!" with a smile each time.

Early adult-child play is also important because it gives adult and baby shared experiences and ideas, providing the basis for future memories and conversation. At later stages, pretend play is powerfully affected by language, the increasing complexity and richness in one leading to similar expansion in the other. As this play develops, language enables the child to playact many daily routines, thereby increasing his understanding of how his world works. At still later stages, language can be used to problem-solve and develop his imagination.

Creative activities are wonderful vehicles for language learning, language again serving to enhance the play. For example, wonderful words can be applied to water play, such as "drip," "drop," and "swish."

Play is another area of development that occurs in well-defined (although overlapping) stages. The BabyTalk program will help you to identify your child's stage and show how to use the play for language input and to facilitate richer and more enjoyable play at each stage. Suggestions for appropriate play materials and toys will be given.

Conclusion

In this book, I will show you how to maximize your child's developmental potential in basically simple ways. You do not need to spend huge amounts of time—as little as thirty minutes a day can make an enormous difference—and above all, you will find that following the program is totally stress-free and fun for both you and your child!

The book is written not only for parents, but also for grandparents and other members of the extended family. It is also for intended nannies, day-care workers, and baby-sitters, and indeed anyone who has the care of young children.

The many years I have spent working in the field of child language have led me to believe that there is no greater gift that you can give your child at the beginning of his life than the ability to communicate. This book will teach you how to maximize this area of development, giving your child the highest possible communication skills.

—Sally Ward
May 2001

BabyTalk

Birth to Three Months

The newborn baby arrives totally helpless and dependent, but nonetheless amazingly well equipped in a number of ways to interact with the adults around him. He shows an emotional inclination toward people from the very start of life and soon engages them in the communication process.

He recognizes his mother's and father's voices on his very first day,[1] from how they sounded while he was in the womb. He also will respond to a television or radio show that has been frequently played in his vicinity![2] (He has in fact been hearing for the past two months, as the auditory system is functional from the seventh month of pregnancy.) The newborn's hearing is not yet as sensitive as that of adults;[3] he shows a reflex turning toward low quiet sounds, which will later be lost.

Within days, he can distinguish recordings of his own cries from those of other babies and can discriminate between the sound of a real baby crying and a computer simulation, crying harder in response to the former. At this stage too, he shows a preference for speech that is high-pitched and very tuneful, with lots of rises and falls.[4, 5] By the age of one month, he is showing interest in listening to a wide range of sounds and will "fixate" on one sound for some time. An extraordinary feature at this stage is that by the age of four weeks, he can distinguish between phonemes, which are the smallest units in the language to signal meaning. This means, for example, that he knows there are two different sounds when he hears the words "pat" and "bat" spoken, although the difference is only a tiny one.[6] By two months, babies can even discriminate male from female voices. It is tempting to conclude that the infant arrives closely attuned to speech, but it is also possible that speech is suited to the innate characteristics of the human condition.

At the same time he is exploring sound, the new baby shows a parallel interest in people. Faces engage his attention, having many of the qualities that he finds most attractive—movement, three dimensions rather than two, contrast between dark and light, and curved lines.[7, 8, 9] By the age of only thirty-six hours, he already shows a preference for watching a video of his mother's face over one of a stranger, demonstrating amazingly rapid learning.[10] He also prefers to watch the movements made by people rather than those made by animals or inanimate objects.[11] The newborn baby has an extraordinary ability—lost a few weeks later—of imitating tongue protrusion and mouth opening.[12] He can also imitate facial expressions of sadness, happiness, and surprise.[13, 14, 15] Nobody quite knows why these abilities exist at this time, or why they disappear.

In the early weeks, the baby cries and produces other vocalizations like hiccups and burps, all related to his bodily functions. Although these sounds are not used to communicate intentionally at this stage, the adults around him respond to his noises, paving the way for true interaction a little later. The baby learns that different behaviors receive different responses. For example, he cries and fusses, and his mother says, "Oh, you want your diaper changed," or he looks toward a toy and she says, "You want to see teddy," as she brings it toward him.

The magical first smile is seen at about six weeks. It is an extremely powerful stimulus to the adults around him, who are prepared to do almost anything up to and including standing on their heads to evoke one! At this stage, the amount he vocalizes and the frequency with which his facial expressions change does not differ according to whether or not he is looking at an adult. He will smile to a range of stimuli, and not only at people.[16] He may now start an interaction sequence with an adult by catching his eye and conclude it

B a b y T a l k

by looking away. Cooing emerges at this time, usually signaling that he is contented.

From the age of eight weeks, the baby's gaze and the little sounds he makes are more frequently directed at adults, and by twelve weeks, he shows a very well established preference for people rather than any other stimulus in his environment. He vocalizes much more to them than to anything else and most of all to his mother.[17] He is now, for the first time, responsive to his mother's facial expressions and tone of voice and can change his own facial expressions. He is more inclined to smile at familiar adults than at strangers.

Over the period of the first three months, babies develop the capacity to produce more and more complex sounds, starting with the vague vowel-like squeaks of the newborn to the more complex expressions of pleasure and occasional vocalizations of two or more different syllables. By three months, he produces the most delightful laughter and will now respond to a smile by smiling back. (Please remember, though, that babies do develop at different rates, and that in the early stages, even whether he was born a week early or late makes a difference.)

In the first three months, social interaction typically occurs between infant and adult, without other objects or events serving as a focus of the interaction. This will be one of the big changes to come in the baby's continued development.

Language and General Development

THE FIRST MONTH

Soon after birth, the baby shows his responsiveness to the adults around him. When he is fussy or crying, he can be quieted by being spoken to, by being picked up, and by eye contact. Nature has arranged things so that he focuses best at the distance he is from his mother's face when he is in her arms.[18] He already shows interest in listening, ceasing his activity as a sound comes nearer. By the end of the first month he will fixate on a nearby sound. He cries frequently, but soon starts to produce some vowel sounds other than crying. His noises are not in any way communicative at this stage, but rather reflect his bodily state. He clearly signals his degree of alertness and comfort with the presence or absence of crying or fussing and will actively seek eye contact with adults.

In terms of general development, he is beginning to make rudimentary attempts to explore his world.[19] He will turn his head toward a light, and although he has no binocular vision as yet, he already perceives that size and shape are constant even though objects are seen from different angles and distances. He can, at this very early stage, discriminate between a cross, a circle, and a triangle.[20]

He has very little control over his body, using jerky and involuntary movements. As is the case in all vertebrates, the general direction of behavioral organization is from head to foot, so that he can hold his head steady for a few seconds if he is supported at the shoulders, but has little control over his legs. He shows some reflex behaviors that will become increasingly purposeful—for example, clenching his hand on contact with a rattle. He shows a complete and coordinated, albeit temporary, walking reflex when he is held upright.

THE SECOND MONTH

In this period, the baby is showing more and more interest in both his environment in general and people in particular. He now often turns his head and looks in the direction of voices and appears to listen intently to anyone speaking. He seems to respond to tone of voice, and by the middle of this month will sometimes smile when he is spoken to. His "voice" is also developing. Cooing emerges during this month. Cooing is quieter and more musical than crying and can be heard when he is content. It consists of a consonant-type sound followed by a vowel-type sound, with occasional repetition. At this stage, the baby may develop special vocalizations signaling hunger, which is the first time his sound has a particular meaning. He will now demand attention by vocal fussing.

He has longer and more defined waking periods. His motor development is dominated by the asymmetrical tonic neck reflex, in which his head is averted to the preferred side, with the arm on that side extended and the opposite one flexed. This position limits his visual field, but his control over his eye muscles is strengthening. He can now turn his head toward a rattle or light and visually follow a moving object, first horizontally and then vertically. He is able to watch a play activity and will sometimes fixate on an object for a long time. His head control is also increasing as he can now lift it when he is lying on his tummy. His developing muscles can be seen at work during his vigorous kicking in the bath.

THE THIRD MONTH

The baby is now showing rapidly increasing interest in speech and regularly looks around for, and successfully locates, speakers. He can differentiate between angry and friendly voices. He tends to watch the lips and mouth rather than the whole face, as if he realizes that that is where these very interesting sounds come from. He shows increasing interest in sounds of all kinds, searching for them persistently with his eyes. He will look, for example, for an opening door, the clatter of cutlery, and the sounds associated with housework. He quiets down to listen to music. He loves it all, pop and classical, but at this stage prefers it to be quiet rather than loud. Best of all is the sound of his mother singing to him.

His sound-making is also developing, in both quantity and quality. He makes noises to himself, occasionally now with two or more different syllables containing a consonant and a vowel, and can be heard to string ten or more little sounds together. He will sometimes produce a long vowel-like sound during or after feeding. By three months, cooing is his main vocal activity, and it can be heard more often when he is contented. He also makes groping movements with his tongue and lips, as if attempting to say words. This happens mostly when he is face to face with an adult. There is a shift from sounds made at the front of the mouth to those made at the back and a big increase in the range of sounds he uses. There are now also lots of expressive noises like chuckles, laughs, and squeals of pleasure. Interactive vocalization is also developing. He sometimes now responds when he is being talked to and will return an adult's glance with cooing accompanied with a smile—a totally irresistible combination. The baby vocalizes more when he is being talked to, and most of all when "speaking to" a familiar adult who is using a lively facial expression. This exciting adult/baby vocal interchange is the true beginning of a lifetime of conversation!

Many of these developments have been made possible by the baby's newly acquired head control and the fact that by the age of three months, he has control of all the twelve muscles responsible for eye movements. He can now lift his head when he is lying on his back and hold it steady when sitting on an adult's knee. He can glance from one object to another, follow a moving object in a circle, and watch something being pulled along nearby.

The asymmetrical tonic neck reflex is losing sway, and many of the early reflexes are being lost. He now enjoys a sitting position, from where he shows ever-increasing interest in the world around him. He is beginning to become aware of familiar situations. He promptly looks at and shows excitement for toys placed in front of him and makes crude reaching movements toward them. He also waves his arms around, bringing them together and playing with his fingers, which he seems just to have noticed. He looks intently at them and can now grasp a rattle if it is placed in his hand. Kicking in the bath is now even more vigorous.

Recent research has shown that contrary to what was previously believed, young babies possess surprisingly advanced awareness of the principles governing the physical world. They appear to know that solid objects should not pass through each other and should not hang in midair without visible support.[21] There is also evidence that the infant by three months of age can understand the existence of hidden objects.[22] The mystery remains as to why babies don't use this knowledge, not searching for hidden objects until they are eight to nine months—the age at which it was previously thought babies understood the existence of hidden objects.

We also now know that infants begin to form concepts from birth. By three months, if shown, for example, a series of pictures of horses, they are able to form a concept of a horse that excludes other animals, including zebras.[23]

BabyTalk

The newborn has become a surprisingly competent little scientist in three short months.

You are now at the end of the first three months, and you are likely to find that your baby is

- chuckling and laughing when you play with him, making it very evident how much he enjoys this;
- cooing and making a number of different sounds containing a vowel and a consonant;
- beginning occasionally to make sounds back to you when you talk to him (conversation is beginning!);
- showing you that he is very interested in speech by looking around for speakers and watching their lips and mouths;
- showing interest in other nonhuman sounds, like those associated with domestic activities; and
- demonstrating his enjoyment in listening to music.

Listening Ability

The ability to listen, to focus on what we hear, begins at birth and develops in stages. It has a long road to maturity, and is possibly the most neglected and underrated developmental skill. Yet it is a vital underpinning to language and intellectual development. Listening is also one of the areas most sensitive to environmental influences.

As we have already explained, a baby at birth listens to and shows recognition of sounds such as his mother's and father's voices, which he has been able to hear for the past two months in utero. Evidence that he is listening is also given by his reflex turning toward low quiet sounds[24] and his cessation of activity at times when a new sound occurs near him. He initially shows undifferentiated responses to the many noises in his environment, as very few sounds as yet have any meaning for him. (Imagine not being able to distinguish the rattle of a cup on a saucer from the scrape of a key in the lock.) Within a few weeks, however, he begins to notice the sounds that are important to him, such as the those connected with feeding. He can only do this at first when the sounds are very close to him, but as the links between the noises and their sources become more secure, he begins to be able to recognize them at greater distances.

The infant is primed for interaction, and his listening abilities and their development reflect this. We've heard how in the first months he looks for speakers and is quieted by a soothing voice, and how by four weeks he has the amazing ability to distinguish between phonemes. In the second and third months he's most interested in voices, but also in music and all the other sounds in his environment as well. At this stage he has, however, no ability at all to focus on foreground sound and tune out background. This inability has very important implications for the BabyTalk program.

Attention Span

When speaking of an infant's "attention," it's important to examine two features. The first is that the span is extremely short. The second is that the baby has no mechanism at all for coping with distractions.

In the first month, watch the way he will look at a toy only for a brief few seconds. Similarly, he will fixate only momentarily on your face, and when you are feeding him, you will be able to catch his eye only briefly.

There are changes in the second month. He develops the ability to sustain attention for a short time, first to an attractive object moving horizontally, and then a week or so later to one moving vertically. You'll notice how he becomes immobile, gazing with great intensity at something that has caught his interest. He may also look at you intently, although still quite briefly. He will now be giving attention to all the voices around him, and not only to those most familiar to him.

The third month sees the very beginnings of the baby's ability to control his attention. He can now for the first time shift his focus from one object to another, although at this stage only in brief glances. He can now watch for a short time an interesting object moving in a circle, and also one pulled along by a string. He is showing more sustained attention to people, gazing at speakers' mouths and enjoying watching people moving about. By the end of this time, he is just beginning to be able to direct his gaze to where someone else is looking—the first precursor to the vital language learning ability of sharing joint attention with an adult.

Play

HOW TO INTERACT

Play at this period, as at all stages, combines beautifully with language exercises. It is based entirely upon adult-baby interaction, and it does not yet involve external objects. Your baby will cleverly trigger you into the activities he finds most fun and rewarding. Adults, therefore, are virtually the only playthings babies need at this time.

In the newborn period, physical play with him is hugely enjoyable. Pat his feet, gently tickle his face, allow his fingers to curl around yours, count toes, and gently rub your forehead on his tummy. All these activities, in tandem with verbal input, serve to stimulate the baby and maintain the best level of arousal to enable him to explore his environment with all his senses. Play, even in these early weeks, is important in forming a trusting relationship. Building up a repertoire of shared intentions, activities, and knowledge between you and your baby provides an essential basis for language development at a later time.

After a few weeks, your baby will begin to require things to look at and listen to, and toward the end of this period, to hold. Look for mobiles with sharp color contrasts, particularly black and white, which can be very interesting to look at. Simple bells and other musical toys are good to have around to stimulate listening skills.

By three months, your baby will enjoy waving a rattle if you put it into his hand and will start to reach toward objects. Brightly colored toys that are easy to handle and safe to chew will be popular. Have a variety of textures on hand, though a simple cloth can be one of the very best toys at this stage. The baby's mouth is his main means of exploration, but he will also start to look at objects that are farther away now and likes to see different things. He will love music and singing and will also relish opportunities to kick and move relatively free from clothing. He needs time to play alone with his toys as well as lots of play with you and other adults.

TELEVISION AND VIDEOS

We are going to talk about television quite a lot in the course of the program. It has become a very prominent part of our society, and it can be of enormous value to children at certain stages, helping them to learn and opening up many facets of the world to them that would otherwise be closed. It can, however, also impede development, particularly in the very early stages of life.

As we have seen, infants and young children have a wonderful propensity for communication and interaction and can make enormous strides with amazing rapidity in the early months and years. For this to happen, however, it is necessary for the baby to have a responsive communicative partner, and the television can in no way fulfill this role.

Though infants as young as a few weeks can become mesmerized by the bright moving colors on the TV, babies require many hands-on opportunities to explore and understand the world around them. Please do not be tempted to use the television to stop your baby from fussing or crying.

Cause for Concern

We have talked about the wide range of normal development, but as parents, we all want to know as soon as possible when there are indications that our children may have a problem. Below are circumstances in which it would be advisable to seek professional advice about your baby or little child's language development. (Please remember, though, that rapid progress in one area can result in a temporary delay in another.)

It is important to recognize that no checklist can be a substitute for a professional opinion. If you are in any doubt, even if the reason for your concern is not mentioned here, do take your baby or little child to see a speech and language therapist as soon as possible.

There could be cause for concern

- if your baby does not smile;
- if he is not quieted by a voice or by being picked up;
- if he does not coo with little vowel sounds;
- if he never turns toward a light or the sound of a rattle; or
- if he does not cry when a feeding is due.

The BabyTalk Program

Here you are, home with your miraculous new baby, exalted, knowing your life is changed forever, sharing every parent's desire to do the best for your precious little being. But you're exhausted. No need to worry. As we have seen, it is clear that new babies are far from passive partners in the interaction process, but instead bring an enormous amount to the party.

Nature has arranged matters so that as adults we are biologically triggered to respond to infants with appropriate communicative and interactive input at this stage. Many aspects of baby care, of course, need to be learned, but interestingly, in the very early stages, we seem to know all about communication. While other child-rearing practices differ greatly in almost all cultures, the biologically triggered responses to language are the same. Sadly, this is not the case at later stages, when we all need to learn what to do and how to do it.

In the first few months, provided that some important conditions are met, you'll easily master the techniques. We will discuss these conditions, and for the rest, we'll describe what you will almost certainly find to be happening.

THE RIGHT TIME

Half an hour a day

The most important criterion to the program is to establish half an hour a day to be one-on-one with your baby. It is a time when you can be totally focused on each other and gain the maximum benefit from the learning activities. Unfortunately, it is too easy to fill our lives with other things so that time is sometimes difficult to arrange on a daily basis, particularly with children who are not first in the family. It really is worth going to almost any lengths to arrange your schedule for BabyTalk.

Best mood

At this stage, the program can be done by extending feeding and diaper changing rather than setting aside specific times. This time together will give you a wonderful opportunity to get to know each other, for you to see the world from his viewpoint and to become fully aware of his amazing abilities.

THE RIGHT PLACE

Your playtime environment

The next essential, which again will run throughout the whole program, is establishing an environment that is quiet and as free from distraction as possible. This means no television, videos, radio, or music (although these will all have their place at other times and in other situations). It is also important to have as little chance as possible of other people coming in and out. As we have seen, attention will develop in small, subtle ways, but it can only do so in an environment relatively free from distractions. The playroom is probably not the best place. Perhaps the nursery or another quiet bedroom can provide the optimum conditions.

> *Make sure the room is quiet for some of the time.*

Remove distractions

Listening is the beginning of the long developmental path toward structuring the auditory field—to develop the ability to focus on a particular foreground sound and "tune out" background noise. Babies need a much greater difference between background and foreground sound than do adults in order to be able to begin to do this. So close the windows and take the phone off the hook, if you can.

Go it alone

At this stage, the magical ability to discriminate between phonemes—those sounds that differentiate meaning, like the first sounds in "pin" and "bin"—is developing. Evidence suggests that the environment be structured in such a way that these discriminative abilities have a chance to operate. The baby must have plenty of opportunities to hear speech very clearly. This means that there must be times when the infant is listening to one adult speaking to him in an otherwise quiet environment. A background of adults talking to one another is not helpful to this process. The implication of this is that although it would be lovely for different adults in your baby's life to enjoy the program with him, it is very important that they do so at different times. BabyTalk is a one-on-one process.

HOW TO TALK WITH YOUR BABY

Let your voice be heard

Start talking to your child on day one! There is a considerable body of research evidence that shows that the quantity of speech addressed to children relates strongly to their language development.[25, 26] You can't start too soon.

Talk to him a lot!

Of course he won't understand what you are saying yet, but your voice communicates your feelings about him clearly enough. It is one of the most powerful facilitators to the mutual bonding experience, one that is essential to mental health. We have seen already how effective sound is in soothing the baby, but it is also one of the only means to signal your responsiveness to him. Speaking communicates that you acknowledge him not only as a unique human being, but also as a social creature with lots to bring to the party!

Make it interesting

What you talk about really does not matter at all at this stage, although it will be very important indeed later on. Talk to him about whatever is happening, or what is on your mind. You might say, for example, "It's our playtime. You're looking at teddy." I remember very clearly telling my daughter all about the landmarks of the route on our way home from the hospital where she had been born! Alternatively you might say something like "I do like this green paper with animals on it that we chose for your nursery—I hope you will too!"

In the quiet times when you are alone together, try these BabyTalk activities:

• Use short simple sentences, which are very tuneful. You might say something like "Up you come" or "You're on my knee."

• Speak slowly, with pauses between each phrase or sentence.

• Use a variety of different pitches, higher than those you use when you speak to adults.

• Utilize lots of repetition, for example, "Here are your fingers, one finger, another finger, another finger" and so on, or "Teddy's eyes, teddy's nose, teddy's mouth."

• Make sure that you are next to him, face to face, so you will not be able to resist touching him a lot.

• Use the kind of delicious nonsense that comes naturally at this time, things like "Who's gorgeous? You are! Yes, you are. You're just gorgeous!"

We all have a built-in way of talking to babies. This trait not only evolved because infants have been found to prefer these sounds from birth,[27, 28] but also because they are helpful to them in a number of very important ways. Babies are particularly sensitive to rhythm, loudness, and tunefulness, and the high-pitched voice adults tend to use at this time relates to the fact that the size and shape of the baby's outer ear canal makes it resonate at higher frequencies than that of adults. They actually hear these sounds better! It is also exactly the form of speech that best enables a baby to develop the amazing ability to distinguish between phonemes—those little sounds that change the meaning of words—by the time he is a month old!

High-pitched speech is most likely to gain the baby's attention. A baby's attention is also attracted by the smiling, moving, changing face that accompanies this kind of speech. Linked closely with attention is the baby's level of arousal. By varying the frequency of your head movements and eye gaze to accompany your voice, you will ensure that baby is neither bored nor overstimulated.

The conversation

At around six to eight weeks, you will start to notice that you and he are beginning to build "conversation." Now is the time to fit your vocal "turns" into his activities. For example, coo back to him when he coos, move your head from side to side immediately after he does, or return his smile with a beaming one of your own. Notice that he coos more at this stage when you talk to him animatedly, with exaggerated facial expressions and lots of tune in your voice. You should naturally respond to his sounds, his body language, and his facial expression. When he fusses you can answer, "Oh, you're hungry. Let's get you some milk." This will help him to understand that our vocalizations can have particular effects, communicating specific messages.

As he approaches three months, you will find yourselves engaged more and more in interactive "conversations," copying the sounds he makes and responding to his still unintentional communications.

Now that you've established a BabyTalk routine, it's time to expand your repertoire a bit. Make sure you spend time singing. Not only will he enjoy and be soothed by your voice, but he will begin developing his listening techniques. There is no better foreground sound to listen to during your half hour of program time. Which songs, tunes, or pop hits you choose to sing at this stage is not important—just sing what you remember and enjoy. Frequent repetition of the same tunes is helpful.

You may be wondering whether you will find yourself talking to him in this way outside the BabyTalk program. Probably. But at other times, of course you will be busy with other things, like cooking. When you can, try to provide a running commentary about what you are doing or what is happening. For example, explain to him what or why you're cooking: "I'm peeling the potatoes. Here goes one into the pan, and here goes another. I'd better hurry up—we need to have lunch early today." This kind of talking serves two purposes. First, it keeps you in contact with each other when you are not directly involved in an activity together. Second, it also enables him to hear the whole "shape" of the language, in terms of the rhythm, tune, and stress of continuous speech—very important information for him.

Questions

Questioning is a large part of adult conversational input to children and can be very helpful or very unhelpful according to how and why questions are used. In the first three months, you will find yourself asking lots of purely rhetorical questions, like "Who's a clever boy?" Such questions expect no reply, are in fact emotive statements, and are absolutely fine. In later chapters we'll discuss the questions that are not fine to ask older children during your time together.

A special note for bilingual families

I have received many queries about which language to use for babies born into families where more than one language is spoken. One of the most recent was from a father who told me that he was French, his wife was Greek, and the family lived in London. He wanted to know which language they should speak to their month-old daughter. My first reaction, as always upon hearing about situations like this, was to think, What a lucky little girl to have the chance of becoming fluent in three languages. I told the man that the one language they did not need to worry about at all was English, as their little daughter would absorb that from the environment in due course. I then advised him and his wife to always use their respective mother tongues with their baby when they were alone with her, and assured them that she would learn both languages without any difficulty, particularly if each of them participated in the BabyTalk program. By developing basic language skills in this manner, she would be able to acquire English as a third language extremely easily later on.

Many parents think that their children might be confused and held back by exposure to more than one language, but this only happens if parents mix up the two to a very high degree. For instance, a parent who uses a number of words from each language within one sentence or speaks a language that is not his own mother tongue can confuse his little children. It is particularly important to only speak in your native language. It is very difficult indeed to modify the way we speak in a language other than our mother tongue, and a very central theme of the BabyTalk program, as you will see, is to modify the way you speak to your little child in very specific ways. It is also helpful to use traditional rhymes and word games with your baby, which won't come naturally in a second language.

I recently saw an enchanting dark-eyed Greek three-year-old girl called Elysia suffering from delayed language development. She was using mainly single words, with only the occasional two-word phrase, and appeared to have great difficulty putting sentences together. Both her parents were Greek, and English was a second language. However, as they lived in England, they thought they should speak to her in English. Fortunately, the family was about to go to Greece for the summer, to stay with Elysia's grandparents. I recommended total immersion in Greek and the BabyTalk program daily. I saw the family again two months later, and Elysia's parents were amazed at how quickly she had acquired Greek. Though they continued to speak to her in Greek at home, they were soon astonished to see how quickly she learned English at her playgroup.

Pacifiers

Another anxious call I had recently was from the mother of a colicky three-week-old baby, asking if I thought it would be very damaging to give him a pacifier when he was distressed in the evening. My reply was unhesitating. "Of course not!" As new parents, we need all the help we can get, and I have not yet come across a baby or young child whose speech and language development I considered to have been seriously affected by the use of a pacifier. The only possible problem could arise if a baby had so little to interest him or to do, and such limited interaction with others, that he ended up sucking a pacifier or his thumb for hours every day. This will not be the case with your baby.

Three to Six Months

In the second trimester, we see baby making more huge strides. By the age of six months she will have begun to understand words, will comprehend many of the rules of conversation, and will show the very beginnings of intentional communication. By the end of this period, she will be vocalizing to the adults around her, a vital precursor to the development of expressive language.

The baby builds upon the skills developed in the first three months as her innate interest in people leads her toward true communication. She is still preverbal, but a number of enormously important developments now occur, leading her along the path toward the magical moment of her first word! At three months, her newly developed control over neck and eye muscles has enabled her to turn her head to locate speakers, and she now shows increasing interest in the speech she hears around her. She starts looking for speakers other than those she is most familiar with, and by five months can usually find anyone making noise in her vicinity.

She now knows something about the communicative intent of speech—for example, whether what she hears is a greeting or a warning. She is also very much aware of the emotional tone of what she hears, showing a marked reaction to different tones. She is frightened by angry voices and comforted by soothing ones. By the time she is five months old, she is more likely to look at a face associated with approving than disapproving sounds.

The baby is already beginning to associate "chunks" of language with particular activities or situations. She is likely, for example, to raise her arms when hearing a tuneful "Up you come." The magical moment when she first associates a word with meaning occurs within this time period. By five months she appears to recognize her own name. It's interesting how early this happens. Soon after this, she seems to understand what "no" means, although she does not often comply!

Her sound-making is also developing apace, and she begins to express her feelings verbally toward the end of this period. The number of both consonants and vowels increases considerably. She enjoys playing with sounds when she is alone, and by six months begins to babble repetitively, repeating strings of the same syllables, first with lip sounds "p," "b," and "m," and later with sounds made at the back of the mouth, like "g" and "k."

She also begins to "drift" toward the speech sounds of the language she hears around her. The sounds within her repertoire reflect those of the language around her, and those not in that language begin to fade out. (Interestingly, babies who are exposed to more than one language will actually retain the sounds of both languages.)

The other area of enormous importance in this trimester is the development of the "rules" of conversation. Baby begins to realize that people take turns making sounds to each other. She will stop babbling when she is spoken to, and whereas earlier her sound-making had no communicative intent, she will now engage in "conversations" synchronized jointly by her and her adult partner in terms of rhythm, movement, timing, and duration. At this stage she will also vocalize to attract attention or request an adult to play with her. She loves turn-taking in ritualized games like "clap hands." From around five months, she will begin to initiate dialogue, babbling to people and clearly addressing them vocally. She will also now synchronize gestures with sounds—for example, gurgling and waving her arms when she sees her mother.

By the time she's six months old, she will also begin to smile and vocalize to her peers.[1]

Language and General Development

THE FOURTH MONTH

The baby's developing interest in people and in socializing with them is shown by her frequent laughs and smiles, both spontaneous and in response to those of others. She even smiles at herself in the mirror. It is also shown in her frequent search for speakers, finding them even when they are out of sight. She is gaining more control over her body. She can now sit with help and can hold her head up continuously. She is also able to lift her head and chest when she is lying on her tummy.

She shows increasing control over her eye movements, so that she can start to explore her visual environment, looking longer at one object after another and tracking moving objects. Sound-making continues to develop. She now begins to babble, repeating little sounds, most often those made with her lips—"p," "b," and "m."

Alongside these developments, she begins to become aware of her hands and to play with her fingers. She makes reaching movements toward objects that interest her and can grasp a ring if it is given to her. She also resists when you try to take away something she is holding.

THE FIFTH MONTH

The baby has, at this point, a rapidly expanding awareness of her environment. Watch her excitement when hearing her food being prepared—she is showing anticipation of an event for the first time. It is also shown by the fact that she stops crying or fussing when she's talked to or when she hears music. A little magical moment happens at this time too. She appears to recognize her name, promptly looking for the speaker when she hears it called.

The baby can now sit up with only very slight support, can turn her head, and can lift her head when she is lying on her back. She may roll from side to side, giving her her first approach to mobility and some control over her environment. She can then begin to explore more widely and see objects and activities from different perspectives.

The baby is also trying to access and handle objects. She can reach and grasp things, although she sometimes overreaches. She carries objects to her mouth, which is her main means of discovering their properties. She's now even more aware of her hands as well as her feet and enjoys playing with both fingers and toes.

Visual perception is now mature, leading to more frequently shared attention focus between baby and adult. Understanding the meaning of what she sees is increasing too. She can now recognize her siblings and enjoys watching them play. She begins to understand how the world works.

She plays a lot with sounds, both when she is alone and when with others, utilizing a range of noises. She can now make sounds at the back of the mouth, like "g" and "k." You may hear a special sound to signal her displeasure. This is unique to each individual baby and therefore only recognizable to those who spend the most time with her.

While baby's communication is still not intentional, her wider range of actions, sounds, and facial expressions make it easier for the adults around her to understand what she is feeling and what she wants. Understanding her intentions leads toward shared intention between baby and adult, which will become important in the development of language.

THE SIXTH MONTH

This month the baby responds differently to different people, in particular becoming aware that strangers are just that, and showing shyness for the first time. She now shows awareness of her peers, smiling and vocalizing to them.

She understands general meanings of speech such as warning or anger and begins to sense a broad range of emotions, which will later come into her pretend play. She can comprehend certain words like "daddy" and "bye-bye," again very well ahead of the time she will come to use them. She is beginning to remember and respond to the routines of her day. She understands "no" a little more fully and now obeys about half the time.

At this time, the baby can almost sit unsupported and shows a crawling

 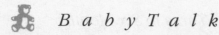

motion when placed on her tummy. Her ability to roll is widening her horizons. She loves being lifted and swung, and will put up her arms in invitation to adults to do this. Her reach is much more accurate, making it easier for those around her to know what she wants. She sometimes accompanies this reaching with vocalizing—an early precursor to naming.

Now that she can reach and grasp, she begins to explore objects. At this stage, she treats all objects the same way, banging and shaking them, and still trying to put everything in her mouth! The very beginnings of cause and effect are now emerging—for example, as she discovers that banging a toy makes a particular sound. This is helped by her growing manual dexterity and skills. Hands and eyes work together, enabling her to manipulate objects more purposefully. She can pick up small toys from a table and grasp something held in front of her. She cannot yet voluntarily release objects or handle more than one at a time. If given a second toy, she will drop the first. She is beginning to become aware of the function of certain things—for example, that a cup is for drinking.

The baby at this age is visually insatiable. She watches intently everything that goes on. She will try to copy what her mother does and will now have fun imitating facial expressions. Another new skill is that she will now look for a toy that has rolled out of her reach.

You will see big changes in her sound-making at this time, both in terms of the noises she makes and the ways in which she uses them. More consonants are appearing, and she begins to produce strings of babble in which she repeats the same syllable several times. These usually involve the sounds "mama," "dada," and "baba," which are sounds made at the front of the mouth and easy to produce. You may think these are your child's first words, but this little miracle does not happen just yet. It's obvious that the baby is having lots of fun playing with sounds. A very important stage in her communication development is that she now begins to address her babble to people, as if she has become aware that we all make lots of sounds to one another and she wants to join in the game! She will sometimes interrupt another person's vocalization, starting to make sounds without waiting for the other person to pause, and will now start to sing along with music. She will sometimes accompany a gesture with a vocalization and finds it very funny to imitate a cough.

In summary, by the time your baby is six months old, she is likely to

- recognize one or two words she has heard frequently, like "bye-bye" or "daddy";
- babble tunefully to herself and to other people, sometimes repeating the same sounds several times;
- imitate a cough;
- respond to little requests like "Up you come";
- acknowledge the emotional tone in your voice, making it clear by her body movements and facial expression that she can tell the difference between cross and friendly inflections;
- appear to know what "no" means and will stop what she is doing some of the time in response;
- start a "conversation" in sounds, by clearly addressing someone with a noise; and
- play at sound-making, both when she is alone and when she is with other people.

Listening Ability

THE FOURTH MONTH

Because of her greatly improved control over the muscles of her head and eye movements, the baby can now look around from side to side for sounds. This is an important first step toward locating and linking a sound with its source, building her knowledge of the auditory world. She shows a particular interest in voice, making strenuous attempts to find speakers who are outside her field of vision. So interested is she that she will often stop her activity to listen more closely.

She is now beginning for the first time to attribute meaning to the speech she hears, by responding to different tones of voice. She is aware that her mother's voice can express pleasure, warning, or even displeasure. She is noticeably frightened by angry voices.

The baby appears to be listening to her own sound-making too, experimenting with various tongue and lip movements.

THE FIFTH MONTH

The baby is becoming more adept at finding the source of sounds now, although she still needs to turn her whole head toward them rather than just her eyes. She can eventually locate a source that is below her and not just in line with her ears. She is likely to turn toward any voice in her vicinity, and not only those of familiar people. She is still most likely, however, to turn toward the voices of people in her family. She is also now beginning to associate more familiar sounds with their meanings, becoming very excited, for example, when she hears the noise of a key in the door. She is becoming interested in music and immensely enjoys being sung to.

There are some interesting research findings that show that the baby at this age is already sensitive to patterns of rate, stress, and tune that mark some of the boundaries between major parts of a sentence.[2] The language acquisition device is already coming into play!

THE SIXTH MONTH

Some very important developments in listening occur during your child's sixth month. The baby is beginning to turn more quickly to find sound sources. She can now find sounds that are coming from above her head as well as those coming from a spot in line with her ears or those just below her.

She shows enormous interest in listening, beginning to scan all the sounds in the environment and to build more meaningful links to what causes them. Her ability to listen is still, however, very limited. She cannot hear in a sustained way, as her auditory attention span is extremely short, but she can maintain focus for a little longer on sounds that have meaning for her. Even so, she is extremely distractible.

She is beginning to be able to discriminate between sounds that are near to her and those farther away.

For the first time, she may be able to occasionally look and listen at the same time—a huge landmark. However, it is still a fragile skill. She can only do this if the room is quiet, if what she is listening to and looking at is familiar and is something that she is interested in. She is totally unable to listen if she is busy investigating something else with her hands or mouth. You will see that when you give her a new toy, there is no point in talking about it until she has first finished exploring it. This will continue to be the case for some time to come.

There are significant differences in babies' listening abilities at this very early age. Our research into this area indicates that environmental circumstances have a notable impact on development in the second trimester.

Attention Span

THE FOURTH MONTH

Being aware of your baby's attention development at four months can influence her language skills at thirteen months.[3] According to one study, mothers who realized that their babies were unable to cope with information from more than one sense at a time had infants with larger vocabularies at thirteen months than did those who did not. It is important, therefore, to tailor speech to correspond with baby's limited attention focus.

At this stage the baby also starts to find ways of attracting her mother's attention, especially when it is directed elsewhere. She makes strenuous body movements, sometimes accompanied by little sounds, to get her to notice her.

THE FIFTH MONTH

There is relatively little change in this month from the last in terms of attention development. The baby's span of attention is still extremely short, and she is very easily distracted. To attract her mother's attention, she will now "call" her by making loud vocalizations.

THE SIXTH MONTH

The baby's attention span gradually becomes a little longer, but only to objects and activities that have become meaningful and are her choice of focus. You'll see her focusing on what is important and interesting, so vital to later learning. She is, however, still extremely vulnerable to distractions and can only attend to information from one sensory channel at a time. When she is totally absorbed in exploring with her hands or mouth, she will not be listening. You may even wonder fleetingly if she is deaf or autistic when she ignores you. She's not—she's just busy!

The most important skill she'll be developing at this time is shared focus—when she will look where you are looking, so that you both pay joint attention to the same object or activity. As we shall see, this opens up the way to a huge amount of learning.

Baby is also fascinated by watching an adult play with a toy. She attempts to copy what the adult does. Playtime can now include sharing a toy as a focus of attention.

Play

In this trimester it is important to engage in play that is based on one-on-one interaction between adult and baby—as you did in the first three months. However, now you'll want to add objects to your play to stimulate baby's growing control of her body, hand-eye coordination, and increasing perception of her environment.

THE FOURTH MONTH

Repetitive, interactive play will long continue to be enormous fun for both baby and adult and is a lively precursor to the conversational interchange of a lifetime. In this play, the actions of adult and baby are both synchronized and structured and form a setting in which the baby can begin to anticipate and predict what is coming next. Baby gains an inkling of understanding into a sequence of events and how and when she can join in.

At this stage, physical games involving the baby's body parts continue to be great fun. The baby is just beginning to become more aware of these and loves it when the adult brings them into repetitive and ritualized language games like counting her fingers and toes. She enjoys tickling and the frolics in response. Some early turn-taking should now begin, led by the adult. For example, you can slowly move your face toward your baby. Allow baby to anticipate the "Boo!" that comes next.

Rhymes and songs now become an important part of play, as they will be throughout babyhood and childhood. Again, babies are very expressive in their enjoyment of these activities, particularly when they are accompanied by rhythmic movements. This enjoyment coincides with the baby's emerging interest in the rhythms of speech.

External objects now begin to become the focus of play. For example, use a favorite teddy to make up a rhyming song involving body parts. As in all these types of play, repetition is hugely enjoyed.

Your baby will also begin to enjoy exploring objects by means of rather uncoordinated handling and mouthing. So let her investigate a variety of shapes and textures. She is learning a great deal about her environment from these investigations.

THE FIFTH MONTH

Your baby's enjoyment of simple interactive games is enormous, and now the anticipation of each partner's actions becomes an important part of the fun. Peekaboo has to be the all-time favorite at this age. The baby's body language and the sounds she makes clearly show that she is understanding each partner's role in the game. She also makes it clear when she wants the game to continue. She anticipates what is coming next and is beginning to take an active part in turn-taking. The foundation of social interaction is now being laid down, and her understanding of the communication process is being forged. She still very much enjoys the play involving her body parts. She has started playing with her fingers and toes, and language games like "This little piggy" really come into their own.

The baby's relatively well-controlled ability to reach and grasp objects increases her interest in them. She is still exploring them by means of mouthing and handling, but now starts to shake and bang them as well. The beginning of her understanding of cause and effect starts to emerge now, as she realizes, for example, that banging an object will cause a noise. She appreciates playing with toys with a wide range of colors, textures, and shapes to investigate.

Your baby will watch others play—both adults and children—and will begin to copy them. She will also now perpetuate the play, making it clear to the adult that she is to continue the activity!

THE SIXTH MONTH

The baby is now a full participant in the ritualized turn-taking games she has been enjoying for the past two months. She loves games in which movement is linked with vocalization, such as "Row, row, row your boat" and patacake. She also loves being bounced on an adult's knee as she makes funny noises, and being lifted and swung as part of the play.

Her hands and eyes are working together so that looking is now part of her exploration in addition to mouthing and handling, and her interest in toys and other objects, is intense. She will now explore each for a little longer, and will become totally absorbed in this exploration, so much so that she will be unable to look at an adult at the same time.

She now watches her mother and others more and more, learning about the function of objects and the sequences of events that she will later incorporate into her play.

She needs many objects to explore at this stage, as her attention span is very short, and she needs to be able to move rapidly from one thing to another.

The main need is still for a wide variety of textures, shapes, and colors to explore and investigate.

TELEVISION AND VIDEOS

The comments made in relation to the first three months still apply—there is still no place for TV in her life. Her need is still, above all, for a responsive interactive partner.

Cause for Concern

Below are circumstances in which it would be advisable to seek professional advice about your baby or little child's language development. (Please remember, though, that rapid progress in one area can result in a temporary delay in another.)

It is important to recognize, too, that no checklist can be a substitute for a professional opinion. If you are in any doubt, even if the reason for your concern is not mentioned here, do take your baby or little child to see a speech and language therapist as soon as possible.

It would be advisable to seek a professional opinion

- if your baby doesn't often look around for speakers;
- if she rarely follows a moving object with her eyes;

 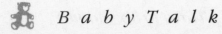

- if she seldom makes sounds back to you when you talk to her;
- if she doesn't make babbling sounds with a consonant and a vowel (for example, "pa" or "goo"); or
- if she makes very few sounds apart from crying.

The BabyTalk Program

In this second trimester, you need to follow some basic but extremely important guidelines. It is very likely that you'll be able to follow your baby's lead toward the kind of activities she needs for development, which as we have seen is extraordinarily rapid at this stage.

THE RIGHT TIME

Half an hour a day

If you are lucky, your child may now be in a routine of feeding, sleeping, and play, and you may be getting a better night's sleep as a pleasant consequence! If and when this is so, start your playtime when you and your baby can enjoy each other's company free from distractions. Rather than trying to fit in time around feeding and diaper changes, as you have up to now, schedule a specific time every day. If your baby has not established a routine, continue as you have before this point.

Stay focused

Your full attention is a great gift that you can give your baby, and she will relish it above all else. Being there for her as a consistent partner in her gradual discovery of the world is the most wonderful learning opportunity that you can give her.

Your playtime environment

As you know already, choose a room that is very, very quiet, with no radio, music, video, or television. You want to be focused and free from distractions—background noise in particular. The baby needs opportunities to hear her own sound-making clearly, in order to make the essential links between her tongue and lip movements and the resulting sounds.

Remove distractions

In terms of attention, she is very easily distracted. It is important, therefore, to have many interesting objects around for her to reach for or look at and that you can hand to her if she wants to bring objects into the play. Make a point of including some simple noisemakers, as she is likely to particularly enjoy these.

Arrange the play space so that you and your baby are close together, either with her in your arms or with you sitting on the floor with her in front of you in a bouncer chair. This way she'll be able to watch your facial expressions. Make sure too that the toys are within your easy reach.

Pay attention

It is essential that you never *try to keep your baby or little child's attention on an object or action for longer than she wants to.* Nothing impedes the development of attention more than forcing this. (Of course, there will be times later in the little child's life when it will be appropriate to draw her attention to something and encourage her to keep it there, but not now, and never while you are following this program.) Any attempt to keep the baby or young child's attention on a particular focus after she has shifted it spontaneously to another only serves to fragment that attention, by splitting it between

> *Keep the room quiet.*

the child's and the adult's chosen focus. If this happens to any significant extent, it delays the child's progression through the stages of development, as well as causing much frustration for both baby and parent. Sadly, this is a very common problem indeed.

A little boy named Imran came to see me with his mother and father a few months ago. They were in despair, as Imran would not do anything they told him to, hardly played at all, spending his time instead rushing around the house, breaking things in his wake. His parents were trying harder and harder to get him to listen and play with toys of their choice, and he was becoming more and more resistant not only to their play suggestions, but to any directions at all, including those connected with eating and sleeping. His mother in particular was very frustrated, saying, "Of course I love Imran, but I'm finding it very hard to like him or enjoy his company." Two weeks of daily playtimes in which it was made clear to Imran that he was free to change the focus of his attention as often as he wanted to brought about a change that astonished and delighted his parents. He played appropriately and for considerable spells with toys and finally began to listen to his parents. His mother was able to enjoy him once more.

HOW TO TALK WITH YOUR BABY

Let her voice be heard

Continue to talk—lots! It's important that she has time to "reply" now, so don't flood her with speech. During your special playtimes don't be tempted to chat away to her on your own agenda, as is fine to do outside these times. Instead, be very much aware of the "conversations" in sounds between the two of you. Pause after you have said something to give her time to reply, and watch for her pauses, which allow you to respond. You'll start to notice that there is less overlap between your vocalizations and hers. By giving your baby this undivided time, you will progressively increase your sensitivity to her communications, and she will lead you to respond to her in the most appropriate and helpful way.

A study found that the frequency with which mothers responded to their five-month-old infants' attempts to engage them in vocal turn-taking correlated strongly with the level of the babies' attention spans, ability at symbolic play, and understanding of words at thirteen months of age.[4]

The conversation

You will probably find that at the beginning of this trimester, your play and the language input that can so beautifully accompany it will focus on interactive play between the two of you. Later on, your baby's increasing interest in toys and other objects will enable you to bring them into the play. As long as you and the toys are available, your baby can and will dictate the terms of playtime. Follow the same general guidelines for conversation found on page 17 of the BabyTalk program.

Repetition

One routine she'll appreciate and respond to now is the repetition of the sounds she makes. Copy either the last sound in the string or a single sound. For example, she says "oo," and you say "oooooo"; she says "ayay," and you say "ayayayayay." (It can be fun sometimes to make your sounds longer than hers.) This is the earliest form of turn-taking and a vital precursor to conversation. It is also one of the easiest things for a baby to focus her attention on, and is therefore very helpful to this area of development. You will see how she loves your enthusiasm for her sound-making and will be encouraged to do more. You will find that the more you imitate, the more sounds she will make. Later, she will start to make the sounds back to you again, and the two of you will be having a wonderful "conversation."

Repetition also serves to enhance

• the perceptions of her own sound-making, as it gives her the opportunity to hear one or two syllables at a time, rather than the rapidly changing stream of sounds in normal speech;

- her perception of the effects of different lip and tongue movements on the resulting sounds; and
- the message that listening to voices is fun and rewarding.

Continue to make lots of noise throughout this three-month period. Contrary to the common view that adults should only speak in "real" words to babies, BabyTalk is just that—baby talk!

Remember, your objective here is to let your baby have an active role in a conversation in sounds. Never think of it as an attempt to get her to copy you. Two babies I saw recently, Susie and Charlotte, had similar backgrounds. They were firstborn babies, adored by the extended family, and fortunate in receiving almost full-time devoted attention. They were extremely attractive, bright, and alert. There was only one difference. Charlotte's mother responded joyfully to all her sounds, making them back to her and letting her know that this was an interactive conversation. Charlotte responded in turn by making more and more sounds and by clearly taking great pleasure in both her own and her mother's sound-making. Susie's mother, in contrast, saw her role in making sounds to Susie as doing so in order to get her baby to copy her. She made sounds and then waited anxiously for Susie to copy her. Interestingly, as we have seen, babies know a great deal about communication, and Susie's response to this regime was to gradually cease making sounds altogether. Her distraught mother brought her to see me when Susie was sixteen months old. We put her on the BabyTalk program, and within a few weeks, her sound-making had caught up with that of her peers. She and her mother now have regular conversations and a lot of fun together in the process.

Make lots of "play sounds" to go along with her interests at that moment. These fun sounds can be made in many different ways. They can be single sounds like "wheeeeeeee" as a ball rolls along. They can take the form of repeated sequences of words linked to interactive activities, such as "Up, up, up you come" as you lift her up, or delicious nonsense like "oochi coochi coochi coo" as you walk your fingers up her tummy. Rhythmical ritualized vocalizations such as "upsidaisy" fall into this category. These "play sounds" add to the fun, but also serve a number of important purposes, in the same way as does imitating the baby's own vocalizations. They help to maintain attention and arousal and serve to give the baby the message that a voice really is great fun to listen to. You may also find that she begins to practice speech gestures like lip rounding while she is watching your face. She's fascinated by speech sounds.

Keep it simple

Talk to your baby in short, simple sentences and speak slowly, with pauses between phrases. You'll attract and keep your child's interest, as it is still the kind of speech that babies prefer at this age and therefore focus on much more easily.[5, 6, 7, 8] "Here's Daddy! Here he is! Daddy's here!" is a great deal more fun for a baby than "I think I can hear Daddy's car coming down the road—he'll be here in a minute." Short tuneful sentences are also very important in terms of the bonding between the two of you, as they carry emotional tone. Later in this trimester, simple sentences will help your baby to link words with their meanings. It has been found that four-month-old babies listen to this kind of speech even when it is heard in the background of adult conversations, and that they even pay attention to videos in which adults are using this kind of speech.[9]

Taking turns

Games are of huge importance in laying the foundations of all conversation and social interaction, and they are also immensely enjoyable for both adult and baby. They will help her to start anticipating events, and in doing so, gain a measure of speech control. While you will be the sole initiator of the turn-taking early in this period, by the time she is approaching six months, you will find that she is becoming a full partner. You will notice that she starts to pause between vocalizations, as if waiting for you to take your turn. She may say, for example, "ah di baba" and then look expectantly at you for a reply.

> *Speak slowly and tunefully.*

Early in the trimester, initiate simple activities like counting her fingers and toes, later progressing to more complex action rhymes and games like "Ring around the rosie," and "This little piggy," which really come into their own at this stage. Later in the trimester, other objects such as soft toys can be involved in the play—for example, playing "Eyes, nose, cheeky cheeky chin" on teddy's face, or playing "bang bang bang" with spoons. Make sure that your facial expression is always lively, as it has been found that babies vocalize a lot more when looking at such faces. Play games so that she has the opportunity to anticipate your actions, which is turn-taking in its earliest form. At the beginning of this trimester, for example, advance your face toward her slowly, giving her time to anticipate the "Boo!" that will follow. By the time she's six months old, she will love games like "clap hands" and peekaboo.

Rhyme time

In the fifth and sixth months, sing and tell her lots of rhymes. Use those with a strong beat, and repeat the same ones often, so that they become familiar and there can be an element of anticipation for the baby. Toward the end of this period, she will particularly enjoy those in which the words are accompanied by actions, such as "Row, row, row your boat." As we have seen, by the fifth month she is becoming sensitive to the patterns of tune, rhythm, and stress that will later help her to decode sentences. She will also enjoy being bounced and tickled as you make funny noises.

Questions

If you find yourself asking your baby a question, don't forget to pause afterward. This allows your baby "response time." Examples such as "Shall we do that again, then?" or "Who's a very clever girl?" are fine. You are also likely to

> ## See what she is looking at, and talk about it.

find that you sometimes say "What's this?" This does not perform as a true question at this stage, but rather an alerting device, used when you are aware that there is something in her environment that she is likely to find interesting. Keep asking!

PLAY

Follow her focus of attention

Start to become very much aware of your baby's focus of attention. Get into the habit of looking to see what she is looking at and making that the subject of what you talk about, following from moment to moment as she changes her focus. If she looks at you, for example, start one of your interactive games, or if she looks at an object, give it to her, either telling her its name or making an appropriate play sound to go with it. Be alert to when she looks toward a toy, bringing it to her and including it in the game. Although she cannot look or listen during the early part of this trimester, she can occasionally focus in particular circumstances. She can do this when there is nothing else to distract her, when the focus of her attention is one of her own choice, and when what she is listening to and looking at is the same thing. For example, she can possibly follow a noisemaking toy or a person singing or talking to her about whatever her attention is focused on. At this stage, you are the initiator of most play activities, but remember to be careful to stop an activity the moment she seems to be losing interest. Following her focus of attention will help her at this crucial developmental stage.

Working with the child's focus of attention is the most essential part of the BabyTalk program!

OUTSIDE YOUR HALF HOUR

Continue to give a running commentary about what is happening, or what you are thinking about when you are busy and your baby is nearby. You might find yourself saying something like "Shall we go to the store now? No, I don't think so—it looks as if it's going to pour with rain. We'll go tomorrow instead." Of course your baby won't understand what you are saying, but you will be giving her an opportunity to hear the rhythm and tune of the language.

Six to Nine Months

The third trimester of the first year again sees the baby making great strides toward becoming a verbal conversationalist. During this period, there are additional bursts of cell connections within the speech centers of the infant's brain, and the network of nerves that allows for this to occur is believed to be very much affected by how much "exercise" it receives.[1]

The influence of the environment, therefore, now becomes a crucial factor in the baby's development. From the age of six months, babies start to show a greater variation in the pattern and range of some milestone attainments than they have previously, which is likely to be attributable to variations in their environments as well as to genetic factors. In a number of studies, children living in families have been found to make much better developmental progress than those brought up in orphanages.[2]

By the age of six months, babies in favorable circumstances are beginning to become aware that words are meaningful symbols, and they can already recognize one or two words like "Mommy" or "bye-bye." It's rather like visiting a foreign country and suddenly realizing after you have been there for some time that you know the meaning of a few words. By the end of the trimester, baby may understand the names of a number of familiar objects or people. Babies at this stage also come to recognize the meaning of little phrases as long as the situation they are in is a familiar one and the context gives them clues. Another seemingly small but very important attainment by the end of the trimester is that they begin to associate pictures of familiar objects with the objects themselves. This is the very beginning of the long pathway toward reading.

The baby develops a wide range of communicative behaviors at this time, such as gestures, tugs, pulls, pushes, and facial expressions. He is adept at communicating a wide range of messages, including drawing attention to himself and to other people and objects, greeting, refusing, requesting, commenting, and acknowledging. He is already a competent communicator and is extremely effective at controlling the people within his environment. As early as six months, he realizes that vocal sounds in particular can be used to make things happen around him. He finds that making noises will bring his mother to him and so begins to "call" her purposefully. By the end of this trimester, he has made a major realization—not only can vocal sounds magically bring about what he wants to happen, but that specific sounds can bring about very specific effects. He does not yet have any true words at his disposal, but he begins to develop some of his own, sequences of sounds that have a specific meaning and vary from infant to infant. The nine-month-old baby of a friend of mine, for example, firmly and consistently says "oof" when she wants a drink.

In this trimester, baby is also progressively seeing the connection between the movements he makes with his lips and tongue and the sounds that ensue. He becomes aware, for example, that smacking his lips together makes a "p-p-p" sound. This is extremely important in the development of his speech sound system, and its effect is evidenced in the continuation of the "babble drift"—the process by which more and more of the sounds in his repertoire are those of the language or languages he hears around him with the simultaneous fading out of those that are not. In parallel, there is a marked decrease in the baby's ability to distinguish contrasts between sounds that are not present in the language around him. By nine months, he is using jargon, strings of sounds that have the rhythm and tune of speech and can sound from a distance very like a true language. This jargon contains no true words yet, but it is a wonderful vehicle for expressing feelings and emotions.

Strategies are being developed at this stage for exploring and interacting with his environment and the objects and people within it. As the baby's awareness grows, his social interactions start to involve a much wider range of topics, allowing him and his mother to begin to develop shared views of objects and events,[3, 4, 5] for example, having common experiences of play with particular toys, and associating particular games with other people. He may know that his brother loves to become involved in games of peekaboo. The increase in the amount of shared focus of attention will lead to the crucial ability to attach meaning to words. This period sees the flourishing of vocal "conversations."

Toward the end of nine months, the baby develops the beginnings of another very important skill: that of integrating the interactions of both objects and people. He can now use a person to acquire an object or do something with it, for example, by pointing at a toy car and vocalizing as he looks at his mother, so that his mother winds it up and hands it to him. He can also use objects to gain attention, for instance, by banging loudly on his chair with a toy.

In this time period, the baby is also taking giant strides in other areas of development, such as the motor domain. Inevitably the different areas of development impinge upon one another, so that an early crawler may cease to be interested in communication for a time, so enchanted is he by his new-found mobility. Similarly, nobody who has just learned to stand up unaided has an ounce of energy left to do anything else. It is very important to recognize this, so that you do not worry unnecessarily if development in one area seems to slow down for a little while. It is possible, however, to prevent language and communication falling behind.

I recently saw a little girl named Alice who was six months old. Her mother was extremely concerned because she was neither showing any interest in voice or speech nor was she doing more in terms of sound-making than making a few rather vague vowel-like noises. Alice was clearly developing well in many ways, and in particular was very advanced physically—sitting firmly alone, rotating her trunk with ease, and manipulating and investigating everything she could get hold of. She was also mobile, rolling at speed and navigating with considerable skill. These two areas, manipulation and mobility, were clearly absorbing all her attention. We started the BabyTalk program, and within three months, her communication skills had completely caught up with her other areas of development, and she is now considerably advanced in all areas.

Language and General Development

THE SEVENTH MONTH

The enormous interest in speech that the baby has shown from the beginning of his life has now resulted in the fact that he is already recognizing the names of a number of familiar objects and people. He even starts to look around for members of his family who are not present when he hears their names mentioned.[6]

At this time, he also shows by his actions that he understands something about the meaning of little phrases that he has heard a lot, waving when he hears "bye-bye," for example. He can only do this when the phrases occur in a familiar context, such as when one of his parents is routinely leaving for work. He cannot yet generalize to another situation and may puzzle a parent who wonders why he doesn't wave bye-bye when leaving the house of a friend of hers he hasn't visited before.

His understanding of the emotional tone of speech is very much in advance of his understanding of words and is well developed at this early stage. He is clearly aware of his mother's pleasure or displeasure. He enjoys listening to music and singing now, and shows his delight with his whole body. He recognizes his own name and often vocalizes back when he hears it, as if answering a call.

He definitely uses vocalization intentionally to communicate, not only with adults, but also with his peers, beginning to babble purposefully to them, and is enthusiastic about joining in "conversations" in sounds. By seven months, much of his play is accompanied by sound-making, and he is beginning to control the people in his environment by his shouts and other vocalizations. He appears much more aware of the sounds he is making, and uses a smaller number with increasing frequency. He enjoys repeating them, producing more and longer replicated strings like "mamama" or "bababa." He also begins to use two syllables at times rather than one and may begin to repeat two or more different sounds, like, "bedebedebede." His babble sounds progressively more like speech in terms of rhythm and tune, and he is already making rudimentary attempts to "name" objects by referring to them with consistent sounds. These are idiosyncratic and specific to each baby and may have little or no resemblance to the real word. They mark, however, an extremely important stage in the baby's recognition that specific sound sequences can refer to specific objects or events.

These developments in the areas of social interaction and communication are occurring in parallel with big changes in the areas of motor and intellectual development. In terms of motor development, the baby can now take his weight on his feet if he is held upright and can sit with his head steady and his back straight. He can also roll from his back to his tummy. He can now adjust his position in order to see a particular object better, and his ability to grasp and manipulate things is getting more dexterous. He will attempt to grab an object that is just beyond his reach, and he can now transfer things from hand to hand. His fingers close with decision now, and he can lift one hand toward a toy, imitate beating on a table with his hand, and bang two objects together. These are no small achievements! Initiating a reaching movement involves more than thirteen muscles in the arm, and adjusting the hand to grasp an object more than twenty in the hand.[7]

Big steps in intellectual development are also occurring. By the age of seven months, babies can show that they understand some of the properties of partly occluded objects, knowing, for example, that a rotating screen can compress a soft object but not a hard one.[8]

THE EIGHTH MONTH

In this month, the baby not only looks for speakers who are out of sight, but begins to listen to whole conversations, turning to one speaker and then to the next, and then back to the first again, looking for all the world like a spectator at a tennis match. He demonstrates that he has made the link between some common objects and the words that stand for them by turning to look at an object when he hears it named. He usually recognizes the names of all immediate family members at this time and will usually listen intently when he hears his own name called.

By eight months, baby may respond to some familiar simple commands with an appropriate gesture, for example putting his arms up on hearing "Up you come" or waving a hand when hearing "Wave bye-bye." He still needs the support of a familiar situation for this understanding. He is extremely adept at this stage in understanding the state of the speaker's feelings and emotional tone from her gestures, facial expression, and intonation patterns.

The sounds within baby's vocalizations at eight months are continuing to come more and more into line with those of the language around him, and there is a marked decrease in his ability to detect small differences between sounds that are not in that language.

Babbling at this stage occasionally begins to sound more like little sentences in a foreign language, being full of rhythm, tune, and stress patterns. There is much controversy about the relationship between babble and later speech.[9] Research indicates that speech does not grow directly out of babble, but babbling does indicate that there is an underlying state of readiness of the nervous system in preparation for speech. A baby at this stage will occasionally sing along with music, but without any true words as yet.

He also still relies upon nonvocal means of communication, which are now becoming refined. He will make a request by opening and shutting his hand and indicate refusal by pushing the adult away or shaking his head. He begins to combine a gesture with a sound, waving his arms and gurgling at the sight of his mother, for example.

In terms of general development, a baby of this age can usually maintain a sitting position for a few minutes. He can rotate both head and trunk while doing so, allowing him to look around more easily and so explore the visual environment. When helped upright, he will now take steps, placing one foot in front of the other.

Reaching is becoming more skillful. He will reach persistently for a toy, adjusting his position in order to enable him to do so. He can now for the first time manipulate two objects at once, comparing two cubes by bringing them together, for example. He can also pull a string to retrieve a toy and will remove a cover from a hidden object or pull a cloth to retrieve an object resting on it.

THE NINTH MONTH

The baby's understanding increases considerably in this month. He may recognize as many as twenty names of objects and people by the end of this time. He now responds appropriately to a wider repertoire of little phrases like "Let's go" or "Come to Mommy." He still only understands them in a familiar context. He has a more substantial understanding of the meaning of "no" and will now usually stop what he is doing on hearing it. He will also perform an action related to a routine on request, for example rocking back and forth on hearing the rhyme "Row, row, row your boat." He still loves music and singing.

His own babbling contains an ever-increasing repertoire of sounds and is full of rhythm and tune. It can be hard at times to accept that it is not true language, as it sounds more and more like real "sentences." He will now use a word invented by himself to denote an object, rather than a sound pattern as in the previous month, being delighted when the object appears. He can now combine gestures with sounds and eye gaze, for example, looking intently at an object, pointing at it at the same time, and accompanying both with a loud "uh uh," making it extremely clear that he wants to be handed the object!

He loves to "talk" back when he is spoken to and enjoys speech games like patacake even more. He is also beginning to become a mimic and will often imitate the sounds, tune, and number of syllables used by others. He will also copy facial expressions.

He has a very wide range of communicative behaviors now. He can use some conventional gestures as well as pointing, such as shaking his head to indicate "no" and waving as a greeting. He still also uses tugs, pulls and pushes, and facial expression to communicate and is now overall an extremely able communicator, giving information as well as greeting, protesting, acknowledging, and drawing attention to himself and other objects and people. He is well in control of the people in his environment and is beginning to understand the connection between his behavior and adults' responses; as a consequence, he has learned to show off!

He can associate pictures of familiar objects with the objects themselves and will enjoy being shown books for a short time, thus taking a first step on the road to reading.

The most marked feature in terms of general development in this month for many babies is the ability to get around the room other than by rolling, which considerably widens his horizons. The baby's growing awareness of his environment is demonstrated by the facts that he will look for a dropped toy, showing that out of sight is no longer out of mind, and will imitate simple actions like ringing a bell, indicating that he is now watching closely and learning from the actions of others.[10]

Intellectually, an essential precursor to the use of true language is developing—the formation of concepts and categories. The baby's previous play activities will have enabled him to form concepts of what things are by now (for example, that cups are for drinking from) and also to begin to form categories (for example, that as well as cups, glasses and his bottle are all for drinking from). These categories are very broad at first and are subject later to finer and finer subgroupings.[11] Concepts and categories such as these need to be in place before meaningful language becomes possible—we can't, for example, talk about cats and dogs unless we understand that they are two different kinds of animal.

To summarize, by the age of nine months, your baby is likely to

- shout to attract your attention;
- imitate sounds that you make and the tune in your voice;

- understand "no" and "bye-bye";
- babble with long strings of repeated sounds;
- often stop what he is doing when you say "no"; and
- understand the names of some familiar objects and people.

Listening Ability

THE SEVENTH MONTH

This is the beginning of a critical time in the development of two skills vital to the successful acquisition of speech and language: discriminating and differentiating between all the different sounds in speech, and understanding what words mean. In terms of speech sound discrimination, it has been found that there is a considerable difference in the ability of seven-month-old babies, and it seems likely that the different auditory environments of the babies would largely account for these startling differences. There are indications that both too little and too much sound stimulus can affect the process. Children who have been deprived of sound for much of their early lives by hearing problems often later show considerable difficulties, not only in discriminating between sounds, but also in making sense out of sound and in listening in the presence of noise. Babies who have had to spend much time in incubators, in which the noise levels are very high, often later show similar difficulties. (It is important to recognize, however, that these problems can be overcome. We have had many children with severe listening difficulties in our clinics, and the parts of the BabyTalk program that relate to listening resolve the problems in a remarkably short time.)

In this month, the baby continues to build links between sounds and their meanings. He is still not able to localize sound directly—that is, to turn immediately to a sound source—but has to look around until he finds it. He is now looking a little more directly for sounds, and can find those coming from above his head.

THE EIGHTH MONTH

The eighth month, if all has gone well up to this point, sees some extremely important emergents in terms of listening. First, baby may be localizing sound directly for the first time. This coincides with the ability to sit up alone and is made possible by the completion of the covering of the nerve that connects the ear and the brain. The baby can now focus on sounds that are horizontal with his ears and within a few feet of him. The ability to localize depends upon being able to make judgments about the timing and loudness of the sounds and requires normal hearing in both ears.

Along with this new skill comes the start of that crucial ability to scan the auditory environment and focus upon a chosen sound. Scanning is slow at this stage, and the baby is very easily distracted, but it is immensely helpful to him in making links between sounds and their sources. These links are now being built up more rapidly and are vital not only to language, but also to his understanding about the world.

The baby is now listening more closely to his own sound-making and comparing the sounds he makes with those he hears around him. This will eventually enable him to bring his sounds completely in line with those of his mother tongue.

He is immensely interested in sound now and derives enormous pleasure from playing with noisemakers and listening to vocalizations like rhymes and songs.

THE NINTH MONTH

In this month, the baby's ability to scan the auditory environment, focus on what he wants to listen to, and inhibit responses to other sounds gradually increases if environmental circumstances allow. The time required for scanning becomes shorter and attention to the chosen sounds a little longer, although he is still easily distracted. He systematically continues to increase his understanding of the meaning of sounds—like those connected with mealtimes—by attending to and comparing the sounds he hears with those he has experienced previously.

Attention Span

THE SEVENTH MONTH

As we have seen, the beginnings of sensory integration—the ability to use more than one sense at a time—continues to emerge in this month. Attention is still single-channeled, and you will continue to find that if you hand your baby an interesting object, he won't be able to listen to or look at you until he has completed his initial exploration. The baby can now attend to objects or activities of his own choice, but he remains easily distracted. This increase in attention span is very important. Both short- and long-term memory and, in fact, all later learning depend on the ability to maintain attention focus.

THE EIGHTH MONTH

By the age of eight months, the baby can follow an adult's line of sight easily, but he still has to do this by turning his whole head; he cannot yet do it by moving only his eyes.[12] This skill enables an increased amount of shared focus of attention between baby and adult, helping him to understand his environment and to come to share adults' view of the world, which is so essential for his intellectual development. The adult knows what is interesting him at that moment and can give him information about it. This leads to his understanding of emotion, and so enhances his ability to relate to and interact with people. It also, and perhaps most important, helps him to attach meaning to words.

His attention span is still very short and single-channeled, so he can only attend to the information from one sense at a time, despite his emerging ability to look and listen at the same time in very limited circumstances.

THE NINTH MONTH

The baby can, in this month, embark upon a stage of making rapid links between words and their meanings. This establishment of shared attention is enhanced by a new emerging ability: that of following a pointing finger. By the age of nine months, he can follow one that is close to him and straight in front of him. He cannot yet follow a point that would necessitate turning his head.[13]

The range of his attention focus is also increasing. By the age of nine months, he watches people and moving objects ten feet away with sustained interest.

Because his attention is virtually always single-channeled, he cannot yet relate words to what he is doing (despite the fact that he is making links between words and meanings now). He can either do or listen, but not yet both.

Distractibility, although a normal stage, is still a big problem and will remain so for some considerable time to come.

Another important development is his ability to pay attention for up to a minute to pictures when they are named for him by an adult. This is a first step toward sharing books.[14]

Play

Play shows some important developments in this trimester and, as always, is a wonderful vehicle for language input. The most marked feature of this stage is that more and more different objects and situations now become part of the play, as his understanding of the world and his interest in finding out all about the objects and people in his environment grow.[15, 16] (It's always important to remember that babies and small children readily move between stages of play—a tired two-year-old can want to be played with just in the way he loved when he was six months old, sitting on his mother's knee while she tells him about "the itsy bitsy spider.") He continues to enjoy both interactive play and play with objects. The latter can be so absorbing that at times he really doesn't want anyone else involved.

THE SEVENTH MONTH

At this time, he loves interactive play that is highly predictable, both in terms of language and actions, so that he can begin to anticipate what will happen next. He can also understand the roles of the two partners, in terms of who does what and when it's his turn.[17] This means that he delights in having the same little rhymes and games repeated over and over again. Repetition makes the world safe and understandable, and he does not want any variation. Very simple games like peekaboo, "Itsy bitsy spider," and "clap hands" fill the bill beautifully. The vocalizations are completely ritualized, and there is a delicious aspect of anticipation. The roles of each partner are simple and clear, involving few words and actions, but they provide extremely enjoyable social interaction to both partners. The turn-taking element is a wonderful foundation for later social skills.

Chants, nursery rhymes, and nonsense speech linked to body movements, such as bouncing the baby on your knee as you make funny noises, are still wonderful too. Babies at this age love lots of physical contact in their play and relish vocalizations that are linked to physical activity. These activities are very helpful indeed in maintaining that all-important joint attention.

The baby also loves the adult to mirror his actions. He is becoming more aware of his own actions and the effects of them on other people, and imitation also helps him to enhance the links between the information he receives through his senses and the movements he makes.

He wants to investigate a multitude of objects and materials now and needs to have lots available, as his attention span is still very short and he likes to move from one to another rapidly. He continues to be interested in shapes, colors, textures, and the noises things make or that he can make with them. He will now begin to remember these noises and want to make them again.

There is evidence that when mothers make these kinds of play available, and enter into them, their babies show a greater variation and diversity in their play than do those who are left to their own devices for much of the time.[18]

THE EIGHTH MONTH

In this month, babies still relish interactive games such as peekaboo and still love them to be repeated many many times. The turn-taking aspect of these games is hugely enjoyed, and his delight in anticipation, now that he is so familiar with them, can be enhanced by little variations like a longer pause before the inevitable "Boo!" in peekaboo. He is receiving, through these games, the message that listening to voice is rewarding and fun, and he is also building up a repertoire of shared experiences with his mother. He will begin to initiate some of these little games himself, for example, "hiding" by putting a paper over his face. He loves surprises at this stage, such as those provided by pop-up toys.

Imitation, both by baby and mother, now becomes part of the play. Each will begin to copy the facial expressions and movements of the other, and

---

THE TOY BOX

For exploratory play, he needs a wide range of different objects to investigate, which do not need to be exclusively toys. Boxes, bags, and almost any objects that are safe to chew are good playthings at this stage. He is interested in different shapes and outlines, colors and textures. Examples of good toys are

- Push-over toy
- Pop-up toy
- Roller rattle
- Activity playmat
- Spinning toy
- Baby mirror
- Activity center
- Blocks and boxes
- Vinyl ball
- Paper (Babies at this stage love playing with paper. It can be crumpled and waved around and can be part of hiding games.)

For enjoyment in listening to "foreground" sound, noisemaking toys are perfect for solitary or BabyTalk play. These would include not only rattles and simple musical instruments, but common household objects such as saucepan lids, spoons, and containers of rice or dried beans.

---

this leads to cooperative games of give and take, such as when the baby offers food to others.

Objects come more frequently into the play now, as the baby shows increasing interest in them. A common sequence at this stage is when he looks at an object, his mother follows his line of sight, hands the object of interest to him, and then brings the object into their play. For example, his mother may roll a ball or push a car toward his open legs.

He explores and investigates with great enthusiasm any objects he can get hold of now—mouthing, shaking, hitting, looking at, throwing, feeling, and nibbling them.

THE NINTH MONTH

Babies now show the most enormous enjoyment in being played with. Simple turn-taking games like peekaboo and patacake are still very popular but are developing in a number of ways. Not only does he initiate them now, but he also initiates "conversations," vocalizing to an adult and making it plain by his facial expression and body movements that he expects a reply. He also begins to create novel games, for example teasing by holding out a toy and then withdrawing it, or making exaggerated protests. The biggest change is that he wants variation in the games. For example, in a game of rolling a ball to each other, his mother must first roll it to teddy instead! He is now beginning to associate the games with the words they encompass, recognizing, for example, which game is going to ensue when he hears "clap hands." His memory is beginning to operate, impacting play. He remembers

---

THE BOOKSHELF

Cardboard or fabric books can be included in the toy box now, but must be suitable for chewing and banging, which is what will happen to them at this stage. It's not too early, if he enjoys it, to sit him on your lap occasionally and look at pictures together.

aspects of play and will look for a toy he has seen hidden and search for lost toys. His understanding about out-of-sight objects is still at a very early stage though, and he thinks that he is hidden from view if he covers his eyes.

Imitation is becoming an increasingly important part of play, and whereas earlier it was often automatic, it is now more often deliberate, as if the baby is trying to understand the meaning of different expressions and actions more fully by copying them. He can play with a toy and an adult simultaneously for the first time, for example in turn-taking games involving balls, cars, or other objects.

His passion for investigating objects continues unabated, and at this stage his increasing motor skills enable him to extend the range of his explorations to holding objects with a pincer grip, putting them in and out of containers, and at last to releasing them voluntarily, which leads to lovely games in which the adult is repeatedly "asked" to return them to him to drop again. He can relate two objects, for example by putting a cup on a saucer or a spoon in a cup. He still loves noisemaking toys.

The baby can now play alone for up to twenty minutes if he has enough different toys to keep him entertained, but he usually insists that an adult stay near. These times of solitary play are very important—he needs uninterrupted time in which he can give his full attention to his explorations. Remember—his attention is still single-channeled.

He is now starting to move toward his infant peers and will attempt to interact with them, waving toys enthusiastically in their direction.

TELEVISION AND VIDEOS

Baby is still not ready for TV, so please do not be tempted to use it. Your baby has so much to learn at this important stage, watching TV and videos would only hinder him!

Cause for Concern

Below are circumstances in which it would be advisable to seek professional advice about your baby or little child's language development. (Please re-

BabyTalk

member, though, that rapid progress in one area can result in a temporary delay in another.)

It is important to recognize, too, that no checklist can be a substitute for a professional opinion. If you are in any doubt, even if the reason for your concern is not mentioned here, do take your baby or little child to see a speech and language therapist as soon as possible.

It would be advisable to seek advice

- if your baby doesn't seem to recognize his name or those of close family members;
- if he seldom makes sounds to people as if he wants to talk to them;
- if he doesn't produce strings of babble sounds like "mamamama" or "babababa";
- if he doesn't enjoy interactive games like peekaboo; or
- if he doesn't show any interest in noisemaking toys.

The BabyTalk Program

THE RIGHT TIME

Half an hour a day

It is now of the greatest importance to get into a routine whereby you and your baby spend half an hour together every day, when you can focus entirely on each other and when he can take those small but essential steps in the development of social interaction. In this trimester, your baby will begin to anticipate and look forward to this time and will derive inestimable benefit from it. The assurance that he will have your undivided attention will engender calm, trust, and reliance upon a safe and stable world. You will be able to develop routines and shared views that are vital to his later understanding and use of words.

Continue with some of the earlier activities such as the turn-taking games, rhymes, and action rhymes. You will be doing some of them now for different reasons, and your baby will respond in different ways. There are also some small but subtle changes, which are very important, that will come during this time period. You may be going back to work now. If so, there's no need to worry. This half an hour a day will ensure that your baby continues to gain all the benefits of the program. So keep it up.

THE RIGHT PLACE

Keep it quiet

We have seen that there are enormously important listening and attention skills emerging during this period. The baby is beginning to structure his auditory field, to be able to scan his environment, to focus on what he wants to listen to, and to maintain that focus for a little longer, thus building up his repertoire of the myriad links between sounds and their sources. He can only do this, however, in an environment free from background noise. Please remember that babies need a much quieter background to be able to listen to what is in the foreground!

Do have his hearing checked if he has many colds or ear infections, or if you have any suspicion that he is not hearing well. It is very important to do this as even a small hearing loss resulting from a cold can affect this area of development. We localize sounds by comparing the way they sound to our two ears, and clearly this will be affected if hearing is different in the two ears. Even more important, slight hearing losses resulting from colds often vary from day to day. This has relatively little effect on an older child who has made firm links between sounds and their sources and has learned to listen in the presence of background sound. For a baby at this stage, however, it can have a serious effect by making the sense of hearing confusing and unreliable. Most affected babies simply decide to focus on looking and handling, with disastrous results on the development of their listening skills. The links between the baby's tongue and lip movements and the sounds he makes, and also between his sounds and the sounds of the speech he hears around him, are essential to the establishment of his speech sound system. Again a quiet environment is necessary if this is to happen satisfactorily.

Make it interesting

Babies at this stage are extremely interested in exploring many different objects and materials and in bringing them into their play. As attention span is still short, they need lots of different objects so that they can move from one to another frequently. As we now know, an essential principle of the BabyTalk program is that we never ever try to keep a baby or small child's attention on something for a moment longer than he wishes to.

Make sure the room is quiet for your playtime.

Make sure that you and he can be close together, with your faces on the same level, and that there are many toys and interesting objects within his easy reach. Making links between sounds and their sources is helped if the baby can move around freely, so make sure that the room is babyproof! I know that some people think that babies should learn from the beginning that there are things they are not allowed to touch. I think that there are many more important things to learn at this time. It makes life so much easier at this stage, for both you and your baby, if you simply remove the dangerous or fragile objects before you begin.

HOW TO TALK WITH YOUR BABY

Let your voice be heard—often

"Conversation" in sounds is really flourishing now. It is important that you see this play as one in which the two of you have conversations, rather than one in which you are principally talking to him. Always give him plenty of time to take his turn, and he will clearly indicate to you when it is yours. His interest in exploring and investigating objects is now very great, and if you see that he is engrossed in this, give him a few minutes before you speak. Again, he will make it clear to you when the moment has arrived,

When having a "conversation," give him plenty of time to reply.

by looking up at you, inviting you to do so. You will also notice that there are times when he is extremely interested in listening to his own sound-making, which is another time when it's important for you to remain quiet for a few moments.

Continue to enjoy repetitive language games and rhymes

He will enjoy and benefit hugely from the repetitive simple interactive language games you've played so far. In the sixth month, play "clap hands" and peekaboo, using the same words and actions each time, and always with a lively expression. You will see from his face how much he relishes this, how both of you are now sharing an activity, and how much these activities hold his attention.

Do lots of little repetitive rhymes and chants, like "Itsy bitsy spider" and "This little piggy." Make up your own if you can! Short rhymes are best at this stage, as his attention span is so limited.

As you have been doing before, bounce him on your knee as you make funny noises, for example, "dupedydupedy dup" as you bounce him, or "oo oo oo" as you move him back and forth. Again you will see his evident joy in listening to your voice by how closely he listens to you!

Copy his movements and actions as part of the game. You could imitate his smiles and waves and give him a chance to copy yours. You will see him busily working out the meaning of these actions and making comparisons between his and yours.

As he moves into the seventh month, bring some little variations into your turn-taking games, like making a little pause before the inevitable "Boo!" in peekaboo or before a clap in "clap hands." You will see by his body language that he is beginning to anticipate what is going to happen next. Pop-up toys will give him the same delicious sense of anticipation.

Continue with your rhymes, action rhymes, and songs, and you will see his attention span gradually increasing and his enjoyment becoming even greater. It is known that understanding of rhyme is a very important predictor of the ability to read. Always link the same words with the actions, and you will notice that he is beginning to link the words with the action, showing excited anticipation when you name a game. For example, when you say, "Let's play 'Row, row, row your boat,' " he starts to rock backward and forward as soon as you say the first "row."

As he moves into the ninth month, you are likely to find that he is beginning these games. Of course, you will respond enthusiastically. You can now build in variations like clapping teddy's hands as well as his and yours, or hiding behind a blanket for peekaboo.

Sing and tell him rhymes all the time.

Repeat his sounds back to him

It is extremely helpful to continue to make his sounds back to him. When you do this now, you will notice how intently he looks at you, and with what evident pleasure. You will also find that he now makes the sound or another back to you, so engaging you in one of those delightful conversations that follow many of the rules of adult conversation—taking turns to vocalize, listening to the other speaker, timing the vocalizations, and clearly enjoying the interactions. (Make sure you give him plenty of time to reply.) You will find that the more you do this, the more he vocalizes, and the more responsive he becomes. He's certainly getting the message that listening to each other is fun!

Making the baby's sounds back to him also enables him to hear separate sounds, rather than the whole speech stream, which contains many hundreds of sounds. By doing so, you will be helping him to make those very important links between the movements of his lips and tongue and the sounds that he makes, and also between the sounds he makes and the sounds he hears in the speech around him. You may very well notice him "trying out" different sounds, moving his lips and tongue purposefully and apparently listening with interest to the result.

At the beginning of this trimester, when he produces strings of repeated sounds like "bababa" or

Make his sounds back to him.

"mamama," repeat them back to him; later on, when he produces mixed sounds like "badigoo," for example, copy those as closely as you can. Your imitation of squeals and exclamations will also be much enjoyed.

Say for him what he means

It is important that you not only repeat his sounds back to him, but that now, as he is rapidly approaching the development of understanding words, you also now give him the words for what he is trying to express by means of facial expression and body language. For example, when he cries and you are not sure why, you could say, "Oh dear, you're sad. Johnny's sad," or you could respond to his gesture with, "Want up? Want to come up? Up you come," or "It's gone" as he discovers the new skill of releasing objects. This kind of input will greatly help him toward understanding words, and you will notice by the end of this trimester that he is indeed making these links.

Continue to make lots of play sounds to go with what is happening

These sounds, like "shshshshsh" as water comes out of a tap or "gugugugug" as it runs down the drain, continue to serve a number of important purposes. As they did in the previous age period, they add to the important message that listening to voice is fun, and they help him to notice all the different speech sounds by enabling him to hear them separately. They also help him to link sounds with their sources and to attract and maintain his attention. I was talking about this the other day to the mother of an eight-month-old baby who had been showing very little interest in voice and speech. Yet every time I demonstrated a play sound to her mother, the baby turned around and gazed intently at me. Perhaps her mother was being a bit reserved in the play sound department. Examples of fun play sounds at this stage are "brm brm" as you push a car along, "eeeow" as a plane goes by, and "uh oh" as you drop something. You may even notice him trying to imitate you by the end of this period.

This brings us to another extremely important principle of the BabyTalk program. Never ever under any circumstances try to get your baby to say or copy sounds or words. If you do, you will inhibit him. This is because that innate drive toward interaction and language includes a great deal of knowledge about communication. It is not part of normal communication to ask each other to say or copy words

or sounds, and babies know it. I can think of many children I have seen over the years who have been virtually silenced by parents who were trying in the nicest and gentlest way possible to encourage them to speak. One such was Harry, a delightful and very bright three-year-old whose understanding of speech was excellent, but who communicated constantly and highly effectively by every possible means other than speech. He pointed, mimed, and used a complex series of gestures, but would not say a word. It transpired that his grandmother had come to live in the household when he was a year old and had decided that it was time to teach him to talk. She had bombarded him with "Say . . . say . . . say . . . ," which had the inevitable effect.

Use short, simple sentences

As we have seen, the baby at this stage is rapidly moving toward the magical time when, if the circumstances are right, he will attach meaning to words. If we were to use sentences like "We're going to the park, so we need to get our boots and coats on," how in the world would the baby know which of those many words refer to the things we put on our feet? On the other hand, if we say something like "Here's your shoe. Johnny's shoe. Shoe on. On it goes," he has a much better chance of doing so. Don't use single words. This is not natural use of language and is much more difficult to listen to than little phrases and sentences.

Your sentences need to be tuneful and slow, with pauses between each one. As it did earlier, this still attracts and maintains the baby's attention and gives him time to take in each one.

At times other than your special playtime, give a running commentary about what you are doing, in order to keep the two of you in contact and to give him experience of the "shape" of the language.

Questions

The same rules about questioning apply as in the last trimester. You may find that you are asking questions as a way of describing your baby's activities, such as "Oh, have you kicked off your blanket?" and others that are really comments, like "Want your bottle?" or are alerting devices like "What's this?" All these are fine, as they do not call for a reply.

PLAY

Use lots of names

It is now very helpful to bring in names, rather than pronouns, since the baby is rapidly moving toward linking names with the people and objects they refer to. Say, for example, "Let's put teddy on the chair" rather than "Let's put him on there." The names of the most frequently heard objects and people are those earliest and most easily understood, so make a point of using the names of family members and his favorite toys often.

Follow his focus of attention

As we have seen, the baby can only look and listen at the same time if what he is looking at and listening to is the same thing. If, therefore, we watch what he is looking at at that moment and name it, he can listen to us and can

---

OUTSIDE YOUR HALF HOUR

Continue to talk a lot about what he is interested in. The more you get in the habit of observing his attention focus and speaking about it, the better.

---

continue to listen if we follow that attention focus from moment to moment. When he looks at a toy in your playtime, name it for him in a little phrase—"It's a ball"—and if his interest continues, bring it into the game, rolling it gently for him to catch. If it does not hold his attention and he looks at something else instead, name that for him too—"There's teddy." Following his focus of attention is also the most powerful facilitator of the development of attention. At every stage, trying to make a baby or little child focus on something for longer than he wishes to only serves to fragment that attention and impedes his progress through the different stages.

You will notice in this time the great increase in the amount of shared attention between you, and how much of the time you are both focusing on the same thing.

Nine to Twelve Months

Months nine through twelve are a time of enormously rapid brain development, in which the environment the baby lives in and the amount and way that she is talked to and responded to have a truly profound effect on the rest of her life. The baby makes great strides in communication now, moving toward verbal language with enormous speed. Yet it is important to recognize that there are considerable differences between babies, even in those from similar backgrounds, not only because of genetic differences, but also because of the powerful interaction between the different areas of development. A baby who is adept at getting around, and is delighted with her new ability to do so, is likely for a time to be less interested in communication.

At the beginning of this trimester, she already has the ability not only to follow the direction of an adult's eye gaze, but also a finger point, first to near objects and then to those far away, and this ability coincides with the ability to understand object names.[1] The baby now discovers, for example, which objects and events her parent finds interesting, such as a new book, and which are upsetting, such as something being broken. In this way, she is not only becoming more adept at relating to other people, but is also beginning to become sensitive to their reactions to the world. This awareness—that another person has feelings just as she does—is of great importance in the development of all future social interaction. She also now begins to understand the connection between her behavior and the adult's response, beginning to predict, for example, that if she spills her food on the floor, her mother will not be pleased!

During this time, there is a complete change from a situation in which the adult interpreted her unintentional communication to one in which the baby controls the dialogue. She initiates much of the interaction and can now terminate it by moving away. She is an immensely competent communicator, able to convey virtually all the meanings that adults do, although not yet in quite the same ways. Not only can she draw an adult's attention to herself, to objects, and to other people; request objects, actions, and information; and greet, acknowledge, and inform; but she can now negotiate failed messages and generally make adults aware of whether her communication has had the desired outcome. She often uses her whole body to communicate, tugging, pulling, pushing, gesturing, and vocalizing, and of course, by the end of the trimester, using words.

In terms of understanding, she progresses in this period from comprehending the meaning of the speaker's tone of voice and recognizing in context the names of some very familiar people and objects to understanding the names of more common objects in her environment, like "ball," "teddy," or "cat." She will also, at this stage, respond to a number of little commands, like "Up you come" by sitting up and "Wave bye-bye" by moving her hand.

She can make all the necessary discriminations between the speech sounds of her mother tongue, and in fact can now discriminate between phonemes (speech sounds that signal changes in meaning, like "pat" and bat") in that language. This matured discrimination interestingly coincides with the production of the first true words.

This is the magical time when her vocalization moves from babble containing no recognizable words, toward the repertoire of single words, which are soon to become her main means of communication. At the beginning of this trimester, she chatters in long strings of nonsense with intonation patterns, stress, and syllable length similar to that of the language around her.

She has changed from babble in which she repeats one syllable, such as "dadadada," to babble in which she mixes lots of different sounds.

At this stage, her communicative vocalizations progress from a simple "uh uh" accompanying a point, to the use of different tunes in her vocalizations to enhance her communication—for example, a rising inflection indicating that she is making a request. She will also make a few consistent sounds in particular situations—making a car noise "brm" when playing with a car, or "bang bang" as she slams her spoon on her tray. She also starts to imitate adults' vocalizations and even tries to copy a tune.

You'll see your child using some idiosyncratic "words" of her own, which may not be anywhere near the adult word, and which only her family may recognize. (One of my children called his cup "bi," for example, and this "word" persisted in our household for many months.) This represents an enormous step forward. The baby has now realized that a particular set of sounds produces a specific result every time she makes them, in that the object she's "named" is handed to her.

She is still using plenty of babble, talking away to people, toys, and herself. The first true words may appear right at the end of this trimester, although many babies take a little longer. These first words are usually the names of very familiar people and objects, and the baby only uses them in the situations in which she has heard her parent do so. They are often similar to sounds she has long been using in her babble, for example "mama" and "dada." This is almost certainly why those words for parents are similar in many languages.

By the time she is a year old, in addition to using up to three true words, she may be trying to imitate other words she hears. She has entered the world of verbal communication.

She will now initiate speech gesture games like patacake and will respond to rhymes by singing along rhythmically. The "babble drift," the process in which the baby's sounds become progressively more akin to those of the language around her, is nearing completion at the end of this trimester, when she begins to use true words. She has greatly increased control over her tongue and lip movements now, having in her repertoire of sounds those made at the back of the mouth (such as "k" and "g"), the middle (such as "t" and "d"), and the front (such as "b" and "p"). She can round her lips and close them with both a loose seal (needed to produce the sound "p") and a tight one (needed to produce the sound "b").

Language and General Development

THE TENTH MONTH

Babies at this age are becoming very sociable, more aware of other people, and showing considerable sensitivity to their feelings and moods. They are also very interested in words, and will listen intently to new ones. If all has gone well, they can now listen to speech without being so easily distracted.

A step forward in intellectual ability enables baby at this age to understand more clearly that both gestures and words can stand for objects. She begins to follow a point, first to near objects and then to those far away, and this ability coincides with the ability to understand object names.

Baby's increasing social awareness is exemplified by the facts that she will now consistently look toward speakers who call her name, will give an object to another person on request, and will perform other routine activities on request, like waving "bye-bye."

The baby's communication is fully intentional now, but despite her growing interest in other people, she doesn't yet have very much awareness of the effects of her communicative acts, being fully occupied with making them. She begins to communicate a range of different intentions, mainly by means of gesture linked with vocalization (usually a point accompanied by "uh uh," meaning that she wants a particular object). She demands attention, requests objects, actions, and information, protests, and greets. She loves to participate in routine speech games like "clap hands" and will now initiate them. She also loves to copy ritualized adult vocalizations like "uh oh" when something drops.

Her babble is very tuneful now, with all the rhythm and stress patterns of language, and indeed sounds increasingly like speech in a foreign language.

In terms of general development, there is much progress in this trimester. The baby can now sit alone for several minutes and finds it much easier to obtain objects to investigate. She can now lean forward to pick them up and turn sideways to stretch out for them. She is becoming more skillful in handling toys and can consequently play with them in a wider range of ways. She is now able to drop objects relatively easily. She can put cubes in and out of a box when she has seen this done and can ring a bell by holding the handle. She will watch a ball rolling and now anticipates the direction of its movement. She can also throw toys and unwrap them and will uncover a toy she has seen covered by a cloth. This increased ability to manipulate objects and explore them continues to be immensely helpful in building up concepts such as hard and soft, heavy and light.

Mobility greatly increases at this time and can bring about a temporary reduction in language and communication development, as it takes all her attention. She can now get around not only by rolling, but also begins to crawl or shuffle. She may pull herself up by the furniture into a standing position and stand for a while holding on, or even walk along holding tightly. She cannot yet sit down without support from this position. She will actively help with dressing now, putting arm and legs into her clothes, and is adept at pulling off her hat!

THE ELEVENTH MONTH

The baby's understanding of words is coming on quickly. She will look around for more familiar objects and people when they are named in conversation and will occasionally show that she is able to follow more simple questions or commands in context like "Where's Daddy?" or "Come to Mommy." The object of the request, however, must be visible. Her use of gesture is becoming more sophisticated. She will extend her arm to point out an object and will indicate "Where?" and "Gone" by her hand movements.

She enjoys imitating both speech sounds like "shshs" or "bababa" and nonspeech sounds like raspberries and, very occasionally, words. She responds with much enjoyment to rhythmic music, moving her arms or her whole body. She has a great appetite for speech games like peekaboo and "clap hands" and often begins them.

She "talks" a great deal now, both when she's alone and when she's with others, babbling away with lots of different sounds. She certainly knows what a conversation is and how to participate in it, gleefully taking her turns and anticipating her conversational partners taking theirs.

Her understanding of her environment and her control over her body are both developing, enabling her to undertake more detailed exploration of objects. She can now pivot, twisting around in a sitting position to retrieve objects and stretching to retrieve those out of reach. She will find a toy she has seen hidden in a box. She can begin to isolate her fingers and to pick up small objects with finger and thumb. She stands more confidently holding on to the furniture and may even stand briefly alone. She cruises around the furniture and may be able to crawl rapidly.

There are significant intellectual developments at this time. As her experience grows, she comes to understand the ways in which objects relate to each other (for example, putting a cup on a saucer) and can link objects with events (like using a brush to brush her hair). This is a very important foundation for the later linking of verbal concepts—"Bobby's brush" or "Drink's gone." She also begins to be interested in looking at pictures and begins to associate them with the objects they represent.

She becomes altogether more purposeful, beginning to use her ability to get around to solve problems such as how to reach a particular object, rather than just taking off for general exploration.

THE TWELFTH MONTH

Babies now show intense interest in speech over a prolonged period. Interestingly, there is a huge variation in how much different babies understand at this time, which depends upon their environmental circumstances, but the use of words is much more consistent.

Most babies at this stage understand a growing repertoire of names and little verbal requests in context, like "Want some more?" They demonstrate this understanding by means of a gesture, such as a head shake, but may also now on occasion try to comply vocally, for example saying "bye-bye" when asked to. Babies can start to integrate interactions, such as using people to acquire objects by pulling at an adult's sleeve or pointing at an object. They may also gain attention by banging vigorously on a tray with a spoon.

The baby very frequently vocalizes with intent now, calling to people to get their attention and expressing her desire for a change of activity. She also very often "answers" when she is spoken to. Tone of voice becomes an important part of her vocalization, and she uses much variation in melody and rhythm. Her parents find it much easier to understand exactly what she is trying to communicate. She loves clowning and showing off and enjoys an element of teasing during familiar games.[2] She joins in songs by singing along and will try to say "Boo" in games of "peekaboo." She chats away in long speech-like patterns throughout the day, both to toys and to people.

The "babble drift" (see page 44) is almost complete, and she uses the sounds of the language around her. Her repertoire now includes sounds made at the front of her mouth (for example, "p" and "b"), the middle (for example, "t" and "d"), and the back (for example, "k" and "g"). She begins to use sounds as if they are words, like "brm brm" for car, and also evolves some words of her own, individual syllables with a fixed melody that have come to be used consistently for a particular event or object. These are highly idiosyncratic and only recognized by her immediate family. The sounds are clear, but the meaning as yet is not. She also starts trying to copy words, again usually the names of familiar objects.

The magic moment of the first real word often arrives at this time, and some infants have as many as three by the age of twelve months.[3] They are most usually the names of familiar people or objects and tend to contain sounds that she has long used in her babble, often "p," "b," "d," and "m."

Parents are often very puzzled as to why there is such an enormous gap between the amount their baby understands at this time and the very few (if any) words that she uses. She may understand as many as sixty and yet use only two or three. Perhaps a useful analogy is to think of ourselves hearing a complex name of a foreign politician when it comes into the media. We recognize it the second time we hear it, if we have been interested and paying attention, but we cannot accurately recall the sequence of sounds in it well enough to say it until we have heard it many times more. We only need to do this with the occasional word—the baby has to do it for hundreds and thousands of them. Like us, she can often recognize a word at the second hearing, and link it with its meaning, but she needs to hear each one dozens of times before it can be recalled.

Progress is also rapid in other areas of the baby's development. She can pick up objects and give them to an adult, imitate tapping with a pencil, and hold a pencil as if to make marks on paper. She can push a car, imitate actions like stirring with a spoon, and play peekaboo by covering her face. She gets around with increasing ease, crawling rapidly and with great facility. She can stand alone momentarily and may take her first steps at the end of this period. This upright posture now frees her hands for action!

To summarize, by the age of twelve months, your baby is likely to

- try to "sing along" with music;
- understand her own name;
- understand the names of people and objects as long as she hears them in their usual setting;
- shake her head for "no"; and
- use one to three words.

Listening Ability

If all goes well, by the end of this trimester, the baby will listen selectively—the vital ability to scan all the sounds in the environment, choose what to listen to, and maintain that focus, "tuning out" unwanted sound. By the time she is twelve months old, she will be able to listen to speech without being easily distracted and will have made many links between sounds and their sources. As a result, the information she receives about the world through her ears will have become increasingly meaningful. These developments will be greatly helped by her ability to move around and explore, now that she can go to find out about the sources of sounds, rather than just looking around for them.

We have found that increasing numbers of children are failing to make these developments, and unfortunately the ability to listen selectively is not

B a b y T a l k

one that just comes with maturation, even many years later. It is the view of many teachers that difficulties in this area are the basis of learning difficulties. The problem has been growing over the last fifteen years or so, as our society has become increasingly noisy.

I made a study of listening skills in nine-month-olds fifteen years ago and found that an alarming 20 percent of them had significant listening difficulties. These infants had made very few links between sounds and their sources and were in fact listening less and less. Many responded so little to sound that they were suspected of being deaf. Others showed highly erratic and inconsistent responses. They were unable to scan the sounds in the environment and select what they wanted to listen to and could not listen at all if they were more than minimally occupied with looking at or touching objects. Needless to say, they were not making that astonishing progress in linking words with their meanings that is possible at this stage, and in fact tended to ignore voice more than anything else, almost as if they realized they were unable to crack the verbal code.[4] So please don't underestimate the importance of your baby's listening skills at this time.

THE TENTH MONTH

The baby is beginning to scan the sound environment a little more and to focus on a particular noise. Scanning is relatively slow, and attention to the chosen sound relatively short. This ability, however, greatly helps her to build up her knowledge of the meaning of sounds, listening to and comparing incoming sounds with those she has previously recognized. She is beginning to listen to a sound made by something she is looking at or touching a little more easily now. It is very noticeable that these emergent skills can only operate in a quiet environment, where there is a big difference between the level of background and foreground sound.

THE ELEVENTH MONTH

If all has gone well, the baby is now becoming more interested in listening to sound, particularly to speech. She is less easily distracted now. Scanning is faster, and attention to particular sounds longer. She is beginning to be able to inhibit response to other sounds, which is extremely important, and the number of links she has made between sounds and their sources is growing. She is better able to listen while she is looking at or handling an object.

THE TWELFTH MONTH

If all has gone well, the baby has now achieved that vital ability to attend selectively, which will stand her in good stead in all her future educational situations. The world of sound is meaningful! These abilities, however, are still totally dependent upon her being in an appropriate environment.

Attention Span

THE TENTH MONTH

The baby at this stage is able to attend to an object or activity of her own choice for a short time, but is easily distracted by noise or movement. Her attention is still almost totally single-channeled, but she can just begin to be able to look at an object and listen to a speaker at the same time if the level of distraction is extremely low. She and her mother are becoming much more efficient at establishing a shared focus of attention not only by pointing, but also by following the direction of each other's gaze.[5]

THE ELEVENTH MONTH

There is little change at this time, just a more frequent shared attention and slightly longer attention to a particular focus.

THE TWELFTH MONTH

By the age of one year, there is greater ability to listen to and look at objects at the same time, and the baby is not quite so distractible. At the end of this month, she is beginning to move into the next stage of attention development. She shows spells of intensely focused concentration on something she has chosen to be interested in. So intense is this concentration that adults will find themselves totally ignored.[6] This alternates for many months with the fleeting attention of the first year.

Play

Play develops during these three months. Exploration of objects continues, now in a somewhat more sophisticated way due to the baby's increased hand-eye coordination and control of her body, in particular of her hands. We have seen how she has acquired the skills that enable her to play in much more purposeful ways, for example emptying and filling containers, opening containers, unwrapping toys, stacking objects, pushing cars, rolling balls, matching objects to pictures, and fitting toys together. She very much enjoys all of these activities.

She'll also begin to look at books and grasp a pencil and make a mark on paper, thus taking the first step toward reading and writing.

She still loves the interactive play begun in the earlier months and now becomes much more proactive in initiating and maintaining the games.

Another new development is that of interaction with her peers.[7] She will offer or show a toy to another baby and point out things of interest to her. She can also grab toys from another child, and thus the beginnings of both cooperation and conflict emerge.[8]

THE TENTH MONTH

The baby now uses her index finger to poke objects, rather than just grabbing them with her whole hand, giving her further scope for her investigations and enabling her to gain more knowledge about textures and shapes. She still often conveys things to her mouth, but her mouth is giving way to her eyes and hands now as her main means of exploration. She is becoming interested in details now and will look intently at the pattern on a doll's dress, for example. She relishes being able to move around and explore and handle many different objects and materials, gradually building up her understanding of the world around her. This mobility is of great importance in the continued development of selective attention, allowing her to find out about the sources of sounds by going to investigate them.

She will also now start to copy an adult's actions with toys, such as making teddy jump up and down when her mother has shown her how.

All this exploratory play is immensely important in helping her to form concepts and categories, without which meaningful language is not possible. She will begin to understand thick and thin, and that there are some things that can roll or be thrown.

At this stage, she treats all objects similarly, and her ideas of cause and effect are still rudimentary, limited for example to the fact that banging a block on a table makes noise.

Rhymes are extremely important throughout this trimester. The great linguist Steven Pinker describes research that shows that human ears gravitate to rhymes as eyes do to stripes.[9] The language acquisition device is in operation once more. The baby loves to sit on an adult's lap to enjoy rhymes. She prefers those with simple, familiar tunes that relate to the world she knows and the activities and people she is familiar with. Good examples of these are "Rock-a-bye baby" and other lullabies relating to going to sleep, and "Humpty Dumpty," relating to falling down—a frequent experience at this age! Rhymes about clothes and dressing are fun too, for example, "One, two, buckle my shoe," and "Three little kittens have lost their mittens." Rhymes relating to body parts still appeal very strongly. Good examples of these are "I'm a little teapot," "This little piggy," and "Ring around the rosie." She will also love rhymes linked with actions, like "Row, row, row your boat."

The baby's participation in play becomes more active now, and she and the adult come to take equal parts in establishing games over this time.[10] She still enjoys a great deal of repetition from familiar games over many weeks. She clearly expresses, by means of gestures and vocalizations, her joy in knowing that the language and activities of the game are predictable, and that she knows therefore what is coming next. These games develop their own unique patterns of rhythm, tune, and stress as they are repeated.

Turn-taking games are the most popular at this stage, interestingly just at the time when she is taking the first steps on the ladder toward becoming a verbal conversationalist. She relishes reciprocal games, such as rolling a ball or pushing a car to a parent. She also loves games such as hide-and-seek or catch, in which she and the adult take turns in the different roles.

THE ELEVENTH MONTH

The baby now starts to treat objects in a more differentiated way. She becomes interested in putting them in and out of containers—for example, blocks in and out of a box—and opening containers. She can now competently roll a ball and push a car, often accompanied by those early sounds used almost like words, like "brm brm" for a car. She much enjoys imitating an adult's initiation of these activities. She is beginning to show understanding of how objects relate to each other, that a cup and saucer go together, for example. This understanding is another vital precursor to the use of linked concepts in language.

She loves bright pictures of familiar objects and really starts to look at them rather than being more interested in chewing or handling a book. She even starts to turn the pages now.

By eleven months, she has begun to anticipate the body movements that go with rhymes.

THE TWELFTH MONTH

She now very much enjoys play with soft toys, and simple pretend play is developing. She may hug teddy, or push a doll in a stroller. She also likes playing with real objects like a cup or hairbrush. She has seen her mother use them and now wants to know for herself how they work and what place they have in her life.

Her play with objects shows that she now understands their function: she will push a car along, and make teddy walk, but not vice versa. She also knows all about adults' objects—for example, that a telephone is for talking into.

Her increasing coordination and skill in controlling her hands enable

THE TOY BOX

Pretend Play

These toys will help her to understand what objects are for and what we can do with them:

- Soft animals
- Doll's buggy
- Tea set
- Simple wooden vehicles
- Doll's brush and comb

Investigative and Manipulative Play

These toys will give her plenty of opportunities to use her newfound manipulative skills:

- Cloth blocks
- Stacking rings
- Wooden blocks
- Large soft ball
- Thick crayon and paper
- Cardboard boxes of different sizes, including one big enough for her to climb into
- Large pegboard

Real Objects to Investigate

- Cup
- Spoon
- Hairbrush

Noisemaking Toys

These will help to show her that making and listening to sound is a lot of fun:

- Bells
- Drum
- Xylophone
- Maracas
- Castanets

- Containers with different substances inside, for example, rice, beans, lentils
- Pan lids and spoons
- Crumpled paper

her to put pegs into simple pegboards and stack toys such as blocks. She enjoys playing with paper and cardboard boxes, and loves a box big enough to get into!

She also enjoys adults bringing variations into games that are well

THE BOOKSHELF

Now that your baby has reached the stage when she can relate pictures to the objects they represent, she will start looking at books, and even trying to turn the pages, rather than chewing them. She will enjoy bright, colorful board or cloth books, with realistic pictures of objects familiar to her. A book of photos of the actual people and objects in her life would also be extremely popular.

Looking at books together can be a lovely part of your playtime. The most important thing by far, and extremely important it is, is that you make this a lovely interactive time, thereby giving books an extremely pleasant association from the very beginning. Sit her on your lap, and give her plenty of hugs as you look at the pictures together and show her how you turn the pages. Be close together, and share the same angle of view. It can be fun to sometimes show her the actual objects that the pictures relate to. You can also make sounds to go with the pictures, like quacking noises to go with a picture of a duck. Give her lots of time to explore the book as well as looking at the pictures. Remember: She is still at the manipulative and exploratory stage even while she's moving into others!

established.[11] The adult may, for example, make little pauses before the expected next action in the game, like delaying the "Boo!" in peekaboo, or in a game of catch, waiting for her to cue you to catch her. In other games, she relishes changes to the routine like the adult gesturing that she is about to roll the ball to teddy, when she is expecting it to come to her!

PLAY MATERIALS

It is now becoming more important to provide your baby with toys that are appropriate for the various kinds of play that are developing in this trimester. Her attention span is still very short in the main, so she needs a number of toys available, so that she can move from one to another with ease.

When your baby is playing with these materials, she will appreciate your being there and sometimes showing her what she can do with the toys. You can at times enhance her play, for example by returning an object to her repeatedly when she has discovered her new ability to release objects. It has been found that babies will play more innovatively if a supportive adult is nearby. Resist the temptation to take over. It is better at this stage to start off a new way of using a toy and then to withdraw. She needs to have time in which she can explore and work things out for herself.

TELEVISION AND VIDEOS

The comments made about this in previous chapters still hold. Language is learned by interaction, not media.

Cause for Concern

Below are circumstances in which it would be advisable to seek professional advice about your baby or little child's language development. (Please remember, though, that rapid progress in one area can result in a temporary delay in another.)

It is important to recognize, too, that no checklist can be a substitute for a professional opinion. If you are in any doubt, even if the reason for your concern is not mentioned here, do take your baby or little child to see a speech and language therapist as soon as possible.

Your baby may need some help

- if she never looks around for familiar objects like her hat when she hears you talk about them;
- if she doesn't turn toward a speaker when her name is called;
- if she doesn't produce lots of tuneful babble;
- if she never tries to start little games like patacake; or
- if she doesn't follow a point, looking in the direction you are indicating.

The BabyTalk Program

THE RIGHT TIME

Making a difference

Your baby will now relish her time alone with you above all else. Little children are inevitably directed by adults for a great part of their day, and to have some time when she is the boss is wonderful, and tends to make her much more compliant at other times. It has an enormous effect on emotional and behavioral development to be sure of a communicative partner for part of each day. Please do not let your daily playtime lapse, however difficult it may be to fit it into your schedule.

A note about twins

If you have twins, it is really worth pulling out all the stops to do the program with each of them separately. Twins often lag behind single children in terms of speech and language development, and although many catch up by school age, some do not. The reason for this is that, as we have seen, one of the most helpful and important ways of enhancing a child's language development is to talk about her immediate focus of attention. This is extremely difficult to do for more than one child at a time and is exactly the reason why

> *Keep up your
> one-on-one
> playtimes.*

second and later-born children tend to be slower to develop speech than firstborns. If you can possibly have even twenty minutes a day with each twin you can prevent the problem.

I remember Kevin and Nelly, a delightful pair of red-headed twins. It was clear, when I first saw them at ten months old, that they were extremely alert, crawling busily in different directions and investigating everything in sight. Kevin and Nelly only had the language development of six-month-olds, however. They only understood "no" and their own names and were making few sounds. Their mother was keen to help them and managed to find a neighbor who was happy to look after one twin for half an hour each day, and she waited until their father returned from work to spend time alone with the other. The biggest problem at first was that the twins themselves were extremely reluctant to be separated. They soon discovered, however, the delights of having an adult's exclusive attention and the fun of being able to dictate the play. Their mother, too, found it immensely enjoyable having the company of her babies one at a time. Both twins made excellent progress, and at the age of seven were reading and doing number work like ten-year-olds.

THE RIGHT PLACE

Eliminate noisy distractions

The setting for your playtime must still be very quiet. This is an extremely crucial stage for the development of selective listening, which can only occur if the environment is appropriate. In terms of speech, your baby now has to notice which speech sounds go in which words, and so it is vital that she is able to hear them clearly. It helps for you to be close to her in your playtime for this same reason.

Make sure she hears your voice

In terms of the amount your baby is spoken to at this stage, all the research evidence shows that quantity correlates highly with future language development.[12] So keep talking a great deal.

This is the stage at which your baby is beginning to link words with their meanings, and she can do so with amazing rapidity if conditions are favorable.[13] The importance of what you do to help at this time cannot be overestimated. Let's examine for a moment the process of linking words with their meanings. Think of the kind of sentence we commonly use, for example, "Oh look, the weather's clearing

Keep having sound "conversations."

up—let's go and get our coats and our boots and go for a walk." How in the world do we come to know that out of all those words, the one that stands for the things we put on our feet is "boots"? Baby clearly needs a lot of help with this, and the main focus of the BabyTalk program is to give her that help. Other crucial areas of development occur at this time. Selective attention, the discrimination of all the speech sounds in the language, and the beginning of the use of words can be seen. She is also making great strides in understanding the world around her. You will notice once again that some of the program items are continuations of those you have done before, but they now come to serve different purposes.

HOW TO TALK WITH YOUR BABY

Continue to make her sounds back to her

Making her sounds back to her helps greatly to reinforce the links between the movements she makes with her lips and tongue and the resulting sounds and lets her compare her own sounds with those she hears others make around her. You will still be having those delightful conversations in sounds.

Continue to make play sounds

These fun sounds, like "brm brm" as a car is pushed along, or "swishshshsh" as you sweep, are not only great fun at this stage, but also continue to be enormously useful in the same ways in which they were earlier. They help to encourage listening by giving the baby the important message that voices are fun to hear. They also help in that essential process of making all the necessary discriminations between the speech sounds of the language, which can also be completed by the end of this trimester. They do so by enabling the baby to hear and focus on one or two sounds rather than the whole rapidly changing speech stream. Be increasingly inventive! It's amazing how many play sounds you can attach to a dropped toy—"bang," "boom," "crash," "uh oh," and so on. Continue to use funny phrases like "upsidaisy," "whoopsie," and "uh oh."

I remember a little boy named Sean, for whom making play sounds made an enormous difference. He was brought to see me when he was eight months old, as he was virtually silent. He appeared to be an exceptionally placid and contented baby, making very few demands on his mother or his environment. He was initiating minimal vocal interaction and not showing a great deal of interest in communicating. His sound-making was at a level usually attained at around five months—just vowel sounds with few recognizable syllables. We put him on the program, with emphasis on his mother being highly proactive in terms of sound-making and response to his sound-making. Within two months his development was age-appropriate in all areas.

Follow her focus of attention

The importance of following her attention at this stage cannot be over-emphasized. By establishing joint attention to an object or event, you are creating the ideal conditions for language learning, as language is learned entirely in the context of shared information. Not surprisingly, there is much research evidence that the extent to which adults' speech relates to objects that are the focus of the infant's attention, and the longer the episodes of shared attention, the wider the child's vocabulary and more extensive her understanding of grammatical structures later on.[14, 15, 16, 17, 18]

Have lots of interesting objects nearby, and be face to face with your baby. Watch to see what she looks at or grabs hold of. Name it for her ("That's teddy"), or if the focus of interest seems to be what has happened, describe the action ("Dropped it"). The closer you can get, not only to the object of your shared attention, but to what is actually in the baby's mind, the more you will be helping her understanding. With a book, for example, her interest may actually range from chewing it, where you might say, "You're chewing it"; turning the pages, where you might say, "Turn over. Another page, turn it over"; or looking at the actual picture, where you could appropriately say, "It's a car."

In the same way, when she looks at you, wait to see what happens. If she seems to be expecting you to do something, point to an object and name it, or pick up a toy and start playing with it, saying what you are doing and making your meaning very clear. The moment she shifts the focus of her attention, you do too—never try to keep it on something for a moment longer than she wishes.

Help her to enjoy listening

By the end of this trimester, if all has gone well and the environment is appropriate, she will be able to focus her listening and tune out what she doesn't want to hear. Conversely, if this is not the case, babies can be in serious difficulties in terms of listening by this time. I have seen many children in my preschool audiology clinics who were suspected of being deaf turn out to be children who had not been able to build up those crucial links between sounds and their sources. The whole world of sound had become so meaningless to them that they had simply ceased to listen. Without help, they would go on to experience very serious problems in school.

A good example was Harry, who was brought to the clinic at nearly a year old. He looked around vaguely, ignoring anyone speaking to him, even his mother. He took no notice of noisemaking toys offered to him, even very loud ones, and totally failed to respond when a child in the next room started screaming loudly. I really thought that we had a profoundly deaf baby here, which was his parents' great anxiety. I asked what Harry's favorite snack food was, and his mother reported that it was potato chips. I also asked if any of the toys Harry had brought with him were particular favorites, and she told us that a little teddy was. We sent out for a packet of potato chips, and I set to work. I sat in front of Harry and gave him one chip at a time, crumpling the packet as I did so. I then started a game with his little teddy, approaching him and saying "Coming, coming, coming—boo!" as I did so. Harry enjoyed both of these activities hugely. I then had someone distract him in the front, while I went behind and crumpled the potato chip bag and spoke very quietly behind him and randomly to each side of him. He located every sound accurately. After four weeks on the BabyTalk program, Harry was responding perfectly normally. He just needed the opportunity to find a meaningful sound in a quiet environment.

Another little child who comes to mind is Alexandra. She was eleven months old when I first saw her. She was just beginning to repeat little syllables in her babble as a normal six-month-old does. She was not listening at all, ignoring voice and most of the sounds around her, although a recent hearing test had confirmed that her hearing was normal. Her mother reported that she often appeared to be in a world of her own. Alexandra was the less dominant of a pair of twins and had a very extroverted older brother. Not surprisingly, she had never experienced time alone with one adult, still less a quiet time. She had also had a number of ear infections since the age of three months, which may have affected her hearing at times.

We set up the BabyTalk program for her with emphasis on the listening sections. Her mother wrote to me a month later, telling me that there had been a marked improvement, which had started almost immediately. She had become responsive, her babble had developed enormously in both length and complexity, and she was listening beautifully during her quiet times. I saw her again a month later, and her listening, sound-making, and understanding of speech were all well within normal limits for her age.

In your playtime at this stage, give your baby lots of opportunities to get the message that listening is easy and fun. You can do this by providing her with fun foreground sounds that she can listen to with no competition from other noises in the background. Have plenty of noisemaking toys available, and occasionally show her how she can use them to make sounds. Be sure to give her time to listen, and do not talk at the same time. It can be fun to show her how you can use toys differently, for example, to make loud and quiet sounds.

> *Keep playing games that make listening fun.*

One note of caution! Some commercially produced noisemaking toys, particularly those that are computer operated, make sounds at very high levels, which can be damaging to a baby's ears. Follow this rule of thumb: If you find the noise at all unpleasant, it's too loud for your baby.

Bring into your playtime some nursery or action rhymes, or bounce her on your knee as you make funny noises. Your baby will love this, and she'll get the message that voice is good to listen to. The fun rituals like "upsidaisy" as you swing teddy into the air can also be a great playtime routine.

It is helpful, at other times, to help her to make the links between sounds and their sources; showing her, for example, that when you switch on the vacuum cleaner, or ring a doorbell, a particular sound results.

Keep your sentences short and simple

The ways in which you speak to your baby, some of which you have already been using for helping her attention, arousal, and communication of feelings, are now crucial for helping her to understand words.

It is extremely important that you keep your sentences short at this stage for a number of reasons.

First, in terms of understanding, it is much easier to figure out what a word refers to if it comes in a short phrase or sentence. It's clear, for example, what the sentence is about if we hear "There's doggy," but a lot less clear if we hear "I think that a dog and a cat just crossed the road."

Second, by the end of this period babies can make all the necessary discriminations between the speech sounds in the language around them. They now have the huge job of figuring out which sounds go with which words. It is much easier to notice sequences of sounds in a short phrase or sentence.

> *Use simple sentences, not single words. Pause between sentences.*

It is an important principle of the BabyTalk program that the adult's input is matched to the baby's level of understanding. At this stage, she is understanding at the single-word level, so the appropriate input for her is little phrases containing one important word, such as "There's the cat" or "It's the ball." Never use single words, as this is not normal communication and will not facilitate and stimulate the operation of the language acquisition device.

Short sentences are also appropriate for your baby's limited attention span. Keep your little sentences simple, but always well formed and grammatical. For example, it's fine to say "There's doggy . . . on the table," but "Doggy table" would not be grammatically correct. Studies have shown that there is a significant correlation between mothers using less complex speech at this stage and a more rapid increase in the child's sentence length.[19]

Pause at the end of each little sentence boundary to give her time to take in each one. We know that infants first attend to the whole "chunk" of speech between pauses and then to smaller and smaller units—that is, to individual words and sounds.[20] Make a slightly longer pause when you change the topic. Studies of infants at this age show that they prefer to listen to speech with such pauses.

Continue to speak slowly and loudly, with lots of tune in your voice. Babies of this age still attend best to this kind of speech, and the tunefulness and stress patterns also help them to understand the grammar of sentences. "Here's Daddy," with a rising intonation and slight stress on the "da," for example, will help her to identify that Daddy is the subject of the sentence. Similarly, a slight stress on the word "hedgehog" in the sentence "Hedgehog is coming" will help her to identify that here is a new word. (Be careful never to distort your speech—it should always sound natural.) Make sure too that you make yourself clear when naming objects, saying, "Let's put the cup on the table" rather than "Put it on there."

Speech of this kind is also by far the most effective for gaining and keeping her attention and maintaining her level of arousal.

Repeat, repeat, repeat

Repetition is very important. We all need to hear a word many, many times in a variety of different contexts both to fully understand it and also to be able to recall it. Think of yourself learning a foreign language: You need to hear words and phrases over and over again to master them. It's just the same for your baby.

Repetitive games and rhymes are wonderful, and you can also make a point of bringing names into a sequence of little sentences relating to the same object or event, for example, "There's doggy. Nice doggy. Here doggy. Doggy's here." Of course, washing, dressing, and feeding times are excellent for this, too. Repetition is great fun for your baby; children of this age love hearing words they already know!

Use lots of gesture

We have talked about the amazing process by which babies at this stage can rapidly form links between words and what they refer to if they are given appropriate help.

The use of gesture is an important way of helping—in particular, by pointing at objects that you name and, more importantly, by naming what she is pointing at. Notice how, at nine months, your baby can follow a point straight ahead, but not across her line of vision. By doing this, you are confirming the object of your joint attention, which is crucial in helping her to make the correct links between the word and what it refers to. I have seen a number of children who have made the wrong connections between words and meanings. One little curly-headed three-year-old girl named Molly called a car a door, and a shirt a shoe. She was a tenth child and had had no opportunity to have an adult follow her attention focus; and as a result, through looking at an object and hearing another named, she had made many wrong connections.

> *Playing games together helps your baby to link words with their meanings.*

Use gesture also to show her what you mean, for example saying, "Pouring the milk" as you do so.

It's fun sometimes to copy her gestures. This will make her laugh and will encourage her to communicate more.

Questions

You will probably find that you are still asking questions as an attention-getting device, and asking questions that are actually comments. This is fine, but make sure that you never ask any to try to get her to say words.

PLAY

Continue your interactive games

The play you have mutually enjoyed in the earlier part of the program should continue in this trimester. Those familiar, repeated, and enjoyable experiences will now greatly help your baby to link words with their meanings, whereas at earlier stages she just noticed the general shape and tune of your speech.[21] You and she have now developed a shared understanding of the world, which has enabled her to know the *meaning* of significant objects and events, and she is ready to understand the *words* that attach to them. She will at this stage, for example, link the actual words in a little phrase like "Up you come" directly with the action of being picked up.

These interactive games are also a wonderful way of establishing shared attention. Repetitive routines with your shared intentions and shared anticipation are perfect for this. As we have seen, your baby progressively becomes more of an equal partner during this period. Notice how she pauses between vocalizations as if to give you the opportunity to take your turn. You will also see that she often stops vocalizing when you speak and starts again when you stop. You have helped her to learn the basic rules of conversation.

Keep a routine in your games, but start to bring in the kind of variations we have discussed in the section on play. Pretend, for example, to get things wrong, or change the rules, or pause before an anticipated event. These kinds of activities will greatly encourage her to participate as a full partner in the game. They also help her to learn the sequence of steps involved.

Games in which there are repeated naming rituals, like "Eyes, nose, cheeky cheeky chin" are wonderful in helping her to link words with meaning.

Twelve to Sixteen Months

By the age of a year, babies for whom all has gone well can understand a number of words and may already be saying two or three. The next four months are exciting ones when babies greatly increase the range of their understanding of speech. There is yet another burst of brain development at this time, during which many more connections are made, and research shows that this is greatly affected by the amount of stimulation the baby receives. Babies who are not talked to and played with at this time are unlikely to fulfill their potential in the future.[1]

There are many important developments in social interaction at this time. At the beginning of this period, the baby starts to know that he is a separate person from others, and he has already become an equal partner in the interaction process. He often initiates "conversations" in sounds and speech gesture games like "clap hands." He is more aware of the likely effects of his different communications, for example anticipating being laughed at when he clowns, or expecting to be given an object he points to after looking at an adult.

The baby's turn-taking becomes more fully established—he waits for his conversational partner to finish her turn and pauses at the end of his own, clearly indicating that he is expecting his partner to speak. Toward the middle of this period, he will become more persevering if he does not obtain the response he wants, using more complex gestures and pantomime to make a point. This urge to repair a breakdown in communication is very important as it encourages him to find more effective ways of expressing himself.

At the beginning of this period, there may be two or three words he uses regularly, and also some sounds with consistent meaning, like "brm brm" for a car. However, he still relies mainly on a combination of a sound and a gesture to obtain his wants, pointing and stating firmly "uh uh" as he does so. He uses lots of babble, long strings of sounds that have all the rhythms of speech and indeed sound almost like talking, but contain no true words. He babbles for much of the time, both while playing by himself and when he's with other people. He listens intently to speech now and sometimes carefully imitates words. Words gradually begin to appear within his babble.

By the age of fourteen months, he usually has four or five true words, used consistently and communicatively. As with all first words, interestingly, there is little variability in the age and stage of use of these words between babies in different environments, although there will be huge differences later. This indicates that this aspect of development is governed largely by a biologically determined milestone.

The first words are usually the names of familiar objects like food, clothing, body parts, or toys, followed by those associated with actions such as "up." The baby only says them in the context in which he has heard them. For example, he is likely only to say "spoon" in his own home at a mealtime.[2]

The ways in which these early words are utilized is also interesting. They are often used not only as labels, but can also stand for whole sentences, representing questions, requests for objects or attention, greetings, information, protests, or commands. The word "cup" for example, could mean "I want a drink," "That's my cup," or "Where's my cup?" The baby becomes very skillful at making his meaning clear, expressing himself by the use of intonation patterns and gestures. A rising tune, for example, can clearly mark a single word as a question. Even at this one-word stage, the baby tends to talk about aspects of his environment that are the most useful to him for giving information and communicating, largely his toys and the people who are most important to him. As his world expands, so he gradually acquires new words.

When the baby doesn't know a word, he will use one that seems to refer to something similar. He may know, for example, that the nice furry purring animal who lives in his house is called "cat," and will then apply this label to any furry creature that walks on four legs. Whole phrases may also run together into one word, like "allfalldown."

These first words are used sporadically over a period of time. They may be implemented for a few days or weeks and then discarded. Interestingly, the first words often disappear for a considerable time. Nobody is quite sure why this is, but there is no need to worry—they eventually reappear. For this reason, parents can find it difficult to answer the question "How many words does he say?"

The baby's early words are often only understood by people familiar with him, although by the age of sixteen months, his babble contains virtually all the sounds of his mother tongue. The "babble drift"—the process in which the sounds in his babble become only those present in the language around him—is nearing completion. These words are usually a simplified version of the adult form of the word. (My daughter, for example, referred to her comfort blanket as "banna.") Most families enjoy and retain a few of these early words. In my family, for example, rabbits were long known as "bunnits" and guinea pigs as "wiggy wigs"!

By sixteen months, most babies use about six or seven words, and these now begin to appear within his babble. It's as if he knows full well that we don't speak in single words, but in long strings of them, and he is doing his best to do the same. His words work hard: even at this stage, much of his communication is accomplished by speech, although he often needs to supplement this by gesture. His messages are becoming altogether much clearer.

Right at the end of this age period, some babies begin to show a more rapid acquisition of single words, although others may not do so until a later stage. Many at this time also enjoy trying out adult exclamations like "uh oh" when something is dropped.

In terms of understanding, at the beginning of this period he is just beginning to crack the language code. There are huge differences between babies in how much they understand, indicating that unlike the use of words, understanding is highly dependent upon their experiences up to this time. There is also an apparently huge gap between what a baby understands and the relatively slow increase in the number of spoken words. This once again reflects the enormous difference between the number of times we all need to hear a word to recognize it when we hear it again and the number of times we need to hear it in order to be able to recall it accurately. While a baby may refer to all animals as "cat," he can often point correctly to pictures of a cat, a horse, and a sheep.

Toward the end of this period, babies learn to understand the names of smaller parts of a whole, for example "door" and "window" as parts of a house, or "sleeve" and "button" as parts of a coat. They now begin to comprehend a few familiar phrases like "Daddy's coming" out of their usual context, and with limited or no visual cues.

Some babies may be able to take language one step further with the ability to decode sentences as opposed to only single words. They can now follow little instructions containing two important words, for example, "Go to the kitchen and fetch your shoes."[3]

Language and General Development

TWELVE TO FOURTEEN MONTHS

The baby's understanding of words is increasing rapidly, and parents often notice that he understands several new ones every week by the fact that he looks around for people or objects who are mentioned. He is more adept at recognizing the feeling behind what the speaker says, knowing, for example, whether his mother is happy or angry about something he has done.

An important new departure is that he likes to look at books with pictures of familiar objects and to have the pictures named for him. He will understand little commands now, particularly if they are part of a game, like "Give it to Mommy" or "All fall down."

By fourteen months, he is likely to use four or five words fairly consistently, and there is often a favorite one he uses very frequently. One of my children said "up," not only meaning that he wanted to be picked up, but in general that he wanted attention. The baby still communicates most of his needs, however, by a point accompanied by "uh uh." He uses long strings of very tuneful babble, inserting real words. He becomes quite a little mimic and will try to copy both words he hears adults use as well as sounds like animals and vehicles make. He also imitates the sounds made by other babies.[4] He is very responsive to the vocalizations of other children and often initiates turn-taking speech games like "Ring around the rosie" with them.

These developments in communication are paralleled by those in other areas. At the beginning of this period, he is busy exploring by crawling or shuffling around and is now able to get up off the floor unaided to a standing position and to climb onto a low step. He may take his first steps at this time.

His has increased knowledge about himself and his environment. He looks in the correct place for a ball that has rolled out of sight and will repeat a performance that has made people laugh. He is generally helpful and cooperative at this stage, actively helping in dressing by putting out an arm or a leg. He is now capable of many emotions, including a sense of humor.

The baby's manual skills are developing quickly, and he has many new abilities that help him in his enormous task of exploring the world. He can put one cube on top of another at twelve months, but can't let go of it for another month. He may begin to show a preference for one hand at this stage, although many babies do not do so until later. His ability to take hold of objects is approaching that of adults, and he can now grasp two cubes in one hand. He still loves to put toys and other objects in and out of containers, and to scribble. He very much enjoys looking out the window and pointing at what he sees.

FOURTEEN TO SIXTEEN MONTHS

The baby's understanding of words continues to increase rapidly. He now understands the names of many everyday objects like clothing and furniture and can identify some body parts, such as ears or hair, not only his own, but also those of a doll. He is beginning to learn some words other than the names of objects or actions, for example words like "in" and "on." He also begins to understand adults' gestural points, first only when they are close to him, and later when they are farther away. He will show that he has understood a question by responding with a vocalization accompanied by a gesture. For example, when asked, "Where's your drink?" he will point to it, saying "uh uh" as he does so.

Perhaps the greatest achievement of this period is that by the end of it, he can understand little sentences containing two important words, such as "Go to the kitchen and fetch your shoes."

Babies can usually say up to seven or eight words consistently by sixteen months, and can use them communicatively along with gestures.

Words are becoming a little clearer now. A wide range of speech sounds can be heard, including those made at the front of the mouth (such as "p" and "b"), those made in the middle (such as "t" and "d"), and those made at the back (such as "g" and "k"). He can round his lips with both a tight seal, as needed for the sound "b," and a loose one, as needed for the sound "p."

The baby loves to take turns vocalizing with both adults and children, but most interactions are still quite short, being limited to one or two turns per partner. He is beginning to develop symbolic gestures, like shaking his head for "no," and now enjoys singing independently.

Most babies usually attain an independent upright posture within this time period, which frees their hands for yet more investigation and exploration. He may take a few steps now if he has not already done so, but cannot stop suddenly or go around corners. He walks with a "wide base," feet planted well apart for stability, and can climb stairs on his hands and knees. He tries to throw a ball, but cannot do so without falling over.

He begins to do more for himself, and now feeds himself with a spoon, although very messily, and can take off his hat, shoes, and socks. He is also becoming able to control his own behavior, for example saying "no" and withdrawing his hand when encountering an object he is not allowed to touch.

Manual dexterity continues to develop. He can now build a tower of two blocks, releasing the second. Throwing happens less often, but he still enjoys tossing and then picking up an object. He will offer a toy to an adult and release it on request. He can roll a ball easily and put several cubes into a container. He still enjoys playing alone at times as well as with an adult.

The baby's interest in books is increasing—he now helps to turn the pages and looks at the pictures with interest, sometimes even patting them.

There is a constant interplay between intellectual and language development, each enabling progress in the other. At this stage, he is steadily acquiring concepts that are essential for the development of meaningful language. He comes to understand, for example, that not only is there a cup and a coat that relate to himself in particular ways, but there is also a category of cups and coats containing many different ones. Such concepts begin as very broad global ones like "things you eat with," and there are then progressively finer sub-groupings like "cutlery" and "dishes" and finally "knife," "fork," and "spoon."[5] He also begins to comprehend size and number, like "one" and "many," "bigger" and "smaller." Without these concepts, the words referring to them would be meaningless.

In summary, by the time he is sixteen months old, your baby is likely to

- use from six to eight recognizable words;
- look with interest at picture books;
- use gestures to make his needs known; and
- look at familiar objects or people when he hears them named.

Listening Ability

If all has gone well, by the beginning of this stage, the infant will be able to focus on foreground sound and tune out background. He can only do this in conditions where there is little background sound and a low level of distraction. I saw Mary when she was fourteen months old. She had normal hearing in one ear and none at all in the other, as the result of a genetic condition, and her parents had been told that it would not cause any problems for her. This was not the case! We can only locate sound sources by comparing the differences in the sounds through both ears. Mary, of course, had been unable to do this. She had not been able to find the sources of sounds and learn what was causing them, so she could not attach meaning to the sounds she heard. Sound therefore was becoming more and more meaningless to her, and so she had totally focused on looking and handling and had almost stopped listening. She showed almost no interest in speech. She lived in a family where there were three older children and constant noise, which made things even more difficult for her. We put her on the BabyTalk program, with emphasis on the listening sections. She started to make progress almost immediately, and in only four months had caught up with her age level in both areas of development.

The baby's knowledge of sounds is still building steadily, helping him to understand his world. Through sound, he gets to know the rhythm and sequence of his day, as he recognizes, for example, all the sounds connected with mealtimes, bathtimes, visitors, and going out.

You may notice that in noisy situations your baby becomes quiet, perhaps just when you are hoping he will be sociable. This is not because he is contrary, but because he's too busy listening and trying to sort out all the different sounds around him to vocalize at the same time.

The baby shows intense interest in listening to speakers over quite prolonged periods. He makes it evident by facial expressions and body language that he enjoys hearing new words, and he is now less easily distracted when he is listening to someone talking to him.

His speech sound system is rapidly coming into line with that of the language around him, so he becomes absorbed by listening to his own sounds.

His ability to look and listen at the same time can still only operate if the focus of his attention is his chosen one, if there is very little distraction, and if what he is looking at and listening to are the same thing. When he is busy, he is unable to listen to anything unless it is related to what he is interested in at that exact moment. Even then, he may not be able to follow directions. This can be a source of considerable frustration to parents. They may suggest some wonderful new ideas to him and be confused when the child ignores them.

Attention Span

Although the baby's attention span is still short, he continues his progression into the next stage, that of long spells of intense concentration on activities or objects of his own choice. The phrase "of his own choice" is extremely important. Although at the beginning of this period he can reliably look where an adult is looking (you may notice that he can now follow a point to a far object and across his line of vision, whereas earlier he could only do so to a nearby object), he is still far from being able to give sustained attention to his parent's chosen focus. When he is concentrating in this way, he finds it virtually impossible to shift the focus of his attention when he is asked to. He is not being uncooperative; he just cannot do it.[6] It is of great importance that he has opportunities to engage in periods of concentration when he chooses to do so.

He can now maintain attention to pictures and link a name to a picture. To hone this skill, it is essential that adult and infant share the same focus of attention, so that the adult can make it clear to the infant exactly what the words refer to.

This coordination of attention is achieved by the adult following the direction of the baby's gaze and talking about the focus of his attention. The more that this is done, the more effectively he will arrive at a situation in which an adult will be able to direct his attention, vital for all future learning in school. It has been found in studies that infants at this stage show more focused attention during interactive play with an adult than in solitary play.[7] (Of course don't forget to point out interesting objects and events to him outside your special playtimes!)

At the beginning of this period, baby will point to an object and then look at the adult, indicating his interest. By the age of fourteen months, he will point to the object and look at the adult at the same time, and by the end of this time will look at the adult before pointing to ensure that he has his parent's attention.

Play

Babies at this stage are busily continuing their quest to find out how the world works. They are doing this in a number of different ways—through investigative play, interactive play, and now also with symbolic and pretend play, often involving interactions with other people. The development of the latter is of great importance as a precursor to creative imagination and all that stems from it.

Your baby's new skills in manipulation and increasing control of his body help in his investigations, and he can now literally learn from any situation and any material. All his experiences help him to continue his understanding of his environment and to form more concepts—for example, of what is rough or smooth, big or small—which are all important if language is to be used meaningfully.

Your baby needs to have some time to play on his own and opportunities to work things out for himself. Adult involvement, however, is enormously important, and he is most helped by a sensitive partner who knows when to join in and when to leave him alone. The development of pretend play can be greatly helped by an adult showing him the kinds of things he could do and using appropriate language input.

INVESTIGATIVE PLAY

Your baby's increased dexterity enables him to investigate toys with more sophistication. At an earlier time, his investigations took the form of shaking, banging, and tasting in an attempt to find out the basic properties of objects, such as size, shape, and texture. Now, while there is still much looking and touching, greater control of hands and body enables him to engage in more complex and wider investigations. He begins to become interested in fitting and matching, as well as stacking objects on top of each other, and will work hard, for example, at using a simple shape sorter. He is beginning to find out how objects relate to each other, still enjoying putting objects in and out of containers, pulling toys apart and putting them back together. All these activities are enormously helpful in forming concepts of size and position, like "bigger" and "smaller," "in" and "under."

Baby will be able to use tools like a toy hammer, understanding rudimentary concepts of cause and effect when, for example, banging a peg with a hammer causes the peg to go down. The baby starts to be able to handle pull toys. Water play is also a source of great enjoyment, wonderful for language input, as so many marvelous words like "splash," "splosh," "drip drop," and "pitter patter" go with it. Many concepts can also be acquired through water activity, such as "light" and "heavy," "float" and "sink," "full" and "empty."

The baby now begins to look at books much more appropriately, opening them and really looking at the pictures instead of chewing and tearing them as he did earlier.

Investigation of sound is vital. The baby still loves to play with noisemakers like music boxes, cymbals, and squeaky toys.

Baby now wants to learn all about the mysterious ways of adults. At this stage, he wants to "help" with chores like sweeping and dusting, in order to find out what these activities mean, why the adults around him want to "play" with brooms and dishrags. He loves toys such as telephones, using them to demonstrate his skills at mimicry!

INTERACTIVE PLAY

Rhymes and songs, particularly those with simple tunes and words that relate to people, objects, and actions the baby is familiar with, are lots of fun. Any song is fine, but the traditional nursery rhymes in most languages tend to have qualities of strong beat, rhythm, and repetition that appeal hugely to this age group.

Interactive games involving turn-taking continue to be important and are more frequently initiated by the baby. Through his body language you'll see when he wishes them to continue. These games quite often involve toys and other objects. Blocks and a bucket, throwing games, mailboxes, and rings on a stick all lend themselves to turn-taking. These basic activities soon expand into games involving pretend, like waving bye-bye to each other. Such games often begin by the mother imitating the baby. The baby now clearly alternates turns with his partner, completing his before waiting for the adult to take hers. When the adult brings a variation into the game, such as patting the doll's back, he can now successfully imitate such new actions.

All such play, accompanied by talk, enables the infant to discover the ways in which language can be used to get things done, to understand the meaning of actions and events, and to enhance his interaction skills.

PRETEND PLAY

After one year, pretend play begins to take shape. This play, in which pretend objects are used to represent other objects, and thus are used as symbols, is critical to children's intellectual development. It is the precursor to the ability to think through problems in the abstract and to find creative solutions. The ability to use imagination freely and creatively helps in every aspect of life. Einstein once said, "Imagination is more important than knowledge." Pretend play and language reflect the same underlying intellectual capacity—the ability to represent things symbolically.

The little child starts to act out simple familiar daily routines and soon brings in toys, like pretending to drink from a toy cup, followed by giving dolly or teddy a drink from the same one. At this early stage of pretend play, the baby is active and teddy or dolly passive recipients of his actions, but they gradually begin to "act" on their own. Teddy, for example, will later hand back the cup. The baby loves to involve an adult partner in his pretend play—for example, offering his mother a soft toy to hug, or pretending to feed her in a simple tea-party game.

THE TOY BOX

The following toys and play materials will enable the baby to meet his needs for investigative, interactive, and pretend play. Many will be used in different ways as he establishes his own games with them, and will also be used in new ways in the future.

When you are thinking about toys for pretend play, such as dolls and toys that help him to copy your activities, please make sure that they represent reality. Talking trains and flying cars are enormous fun later on, but at this stage, when the baby is just learning about the world and how it works, bizarre objects can be confusing.

The toys suggested here are divided into those that encourage investigative and pretend play, but this is subjective. You will probably find that your little child will play with them in ways you would never have thought of.

Many excellent toys for this age group can be made at home for very little cost. A box and washcloth or hand towel can be a doll's bed. A container with a slot in the lid can be a makeshift mailbox. Paper and boxes in themselves are great fun.

Investigative Play

A baby walker or truck, or other toy he can push

Pull toys, such as a duck on a string

Thick wax crayons

Simple shape sorter

Chunky peg men in a boat

New noisemakers, such as drum, xylophone, maracas, or squeaky toys if he does not already have these in his toy box

A simple mailbox

A hammer and peg toy

Pretend Play

Toy telephone

Large doll and teddy, with bedding and doll's clothing

A simple train

Planes

Cooking utensils

Toy household objects like dustpan and brush or broom

By the age of fifteen months, he will use objects that are less similar to real ones, for example using a box as a doll's bed, or blocks for sandwiches. He will also start to relate several objects and actions together, like putting a doll in a bed or a tablecloth on a table.

Infants benefit greatly from adult involvement in pretend play. They try out different activities and incorporate into their play actions the adult has shown them.[8]

COMPUTERS

Please don't be tempted to introduce him to computer games yet. The under-fives are being pursued by software manufacturers as a potential market and programs are being produced that target infants as young as nine months. The big worry about very young children using computers is that the machines have the same attractive qualities as do television and videos, and there is a real danger of little children spending hours on their own playing with them. Interaction and exploration is what children of this age are all about. Starting computer use later won't give him any disadvantage over those who started as babies. A recent study has shown that children introduced after seven years did not take any longer to learn to use computers than those who started as babies.

Another study showed that the *creativity* scores of preschool children who were using computers actually dropped. So, at this age, focus on the nontechnical toys for your child.

THE BOOKSHELF

Sharing books offers a cozy interactive experience for baby. You can now establish a foundation of pleasure in books that will stand him in good stead for a lifetime. Sit him on your lap so that you are close together while you look at the pictures.

Look for books with brightly colored pictures of objects familiar to him. Photos of real people and objects in his life are wonderful now. (It can be fun to make homemade books by cutting pictures out of magazines.) He will enjoy looking at small details in pictures, so his new books can be more complicated or contain more complicated backgrounds than those in his very first books. He will also love some of the wonderful books now available for little children that have different textures. He'll react by stroking with his finger or pressing a button to make a noise to go with the picture. He will be enchanted to find, for example, that the duck actually quacks.

Follow his lead. He will help you turn the pages and will make it very clear which pictures he likes by patting and talking to them. Never try to keep his interest in a picture or book longer than he wishes to. Wonderful books for this age include

PAT THE BUNNY
Dorothy Kunhardt

DEAR ZOO
Rod Campbell

TOUCH AND FEEL FARM

GOODNIGHT MOON
Margaret Wise Brown

WHERE'S SPOT?
Eric Hill

THE VERY HUNGRY CATERPILLAR
Eric Carle

EVERYONE HIDE FROM WIBBLY PIG
Mick Inkpen

DR. SEUSS'S ABC

There are many television programs and videos being produced for young children, and these can be fun for your baby from this age, but it is extremely important that they be used in the right way.

Do limit video watching to half an hour a day at the most. Your baby needs to be spending lots of time interacting with people and learning through play. This is a wonderful time in which this learning can be amazingly rapid. Opportunities lost now are lost forever. The medium of television is so attractive because of its intense colors and rapid movements. I have seen a number of children who watched for more than six hours a day! Not only were their language skills considerably delayed but, more important, so were their interactive skills, their play, and their understanding of the world. They were very sad and confused little children.

Watch videos with your child, so that the experience becomes an interactive one, and you can then make what he sees meaningful for him. A nursery rhyme video, for example, can be great fun if you join in with the actions together.

The content should relate to the world as he understands it. Fantasies of talking vehicles, for example, would be very confusing for him at this stage—after all, he is only just finding out what people, animals, and inanimate objects actually do.

Please do not fall into the trap of thinking that the television can help him to understand words. Babies and young children are totally fascinated by the sight of the bright moving lights and colors of the television and learn nothing from the sound. In an experiment, Dutch children who watched German television for extensive periods of time were found to have learned no German at all.[9]

Cause for Concern

Below are circumstances in which it would be advisable to seek professional advice about your baby or little child's language development. (Please remember, though, that rapid progress in one area can result in a temporary delay in another.)

It is important to recognize, too, that no checklist can be a substitute for a professional opinion. If you are in any doubt, even if the reason for your concern is not mentioned here, do take your baby or little child to see a speech and language therapist as soon as possible.

Your baby may need some help

- if he never takes turns with you in making sounds;
- if he doesn't respond by looking in the right direction to little questions like "Where's your hat?";
- if he does not babble with lots of different sounds, sounding almost as if he is talking;
- if he is not interested in starting games with you like patacake; or
- if he never concentrates on anything for more than a few seconds.

The BabyTalk Program

THE RIGHT TIME

Half an hour a day

Daily one-on-one playtime is still the very best possible situation for language learning and emotional development. Nothing gives a little child more confidence than the certainty that he will receive undivided attention from a beloved adult every day. He'll especially desire this attention if he has brothers and sisters.

In a busy household, parents are only too happy when their little child seems content to occupy himself for long spells, rarely seeking interaction. Sadly, the effects of this are often noted when the baby reaches the age of two years and is not yet talking. In one case, a little girl named Natasha was brought to me at two and a half because she was only using three words. Her parents were also concerned because she preferred solitary play, showing great reluctance to let them play with her. She was clearly bright and immediately began to play with the toys I put out for her in a very constructive way, setting out teddy's lunch on a small table. Her mother then joined in and began to give Natasha a stream of suggestions and directions about how the play might go. Natasha not only ignored these, but turned her back on her mother, clearly feeling that she was interfering in her activity.

So we set up daily playtimes for Natasha in which her mother began to operate under the principles of the BabyTalk program, particularly in terms of following the focus of Natasha's attention and avoiding directing her play in any way. Natasha soon began to see her mother's presence as enhancing her play, and they began to interact with each other. Natasha's language skills quickly caught up with, and exceeded, her age level.

Recently, Natasha and her mother brought Natasha's baby brother for a visit. He was six months old, and as soon as we met, he made it clear by his facial expression and body language that he was absolutely determined to relate and communicate with me! I found it impossible not to respond and had to postpone conversation with Natasha and her mother for some time. Their mother was amazed, as we all can be, at the difference in personality between siblings.

THE RIGHT PLACE

Make sure the background is quiet

We have heard how babies of this age have now acquired the vital skill of being able to focus on a foreground sound and tune out others in the background. This skill, however, is still new and not yet well established and needs careful nurturing, or it can be lost. This listening can only operate in distraction-free conditions, so a quiet background in your playtime continues to be vital for the program.

Your baby's play at this time ideally involves many more play materials. These give him the opportunity to develop investigative, interactive, and pretend play alongside each other. It's good to have a number of different objects available in the play space, as his attention span is still very short for most of the time. Make sure that the objects include those that encourage various kinds of play.

As you did before, sit on the floor with your face at his level, and the toys within easy reach of both of you.

He may move around the room a lot now. If so, follow him! You need to stay close to him so that he hears everything you say and all the sounds you make clearly.

HOW TO TALK
WITH YOUR BABY

We have seen how babies can hugely increase their understanding of words in this time period. There is a great deal we can do to facilitate this process.

Follow his focus of attention

There is a great deal of research evidence that connects the degree to which adult and baby share the same focus of attention and the complexity of the child's sentences later on.[10]

Comparisons have been made between situations in which the adult directs the child's attention and those when the adult follows the child's focus. It has been found that children understand the language much more acutely when they dictate the direction of the play.[11]

A less academic reason for following the child's focus of attention is that children just love it! Don't we all, even as adults, enjoy it when people we love show real interest in what we like? The same principle applies to your little one.

As before, always comment on what is interesting him, and avoid questions and directions. Both interfere with his listening, whereas comments just add to the fun of what he is doing and do not cause him any communicative confusion or stress.

The more closely you can work out what is in his mind at that moment, the more helpful you can be. Watch carefully to see what he's looking at. It may be an object he's interested in and would like named, in which case you might say, "It's a chick" as he looks at a picture. A play sound to go with his focus might amuse him, like "cheep cheep." His interest might be in an action, and you might say, "All fall down" as blocks collapse or "Crashshsh!" as

> *Questions and directions interfere with his listening.*

cars collide. It usually isn't difficult to know what is appropriate. You are interacting with a pretty accomplished communicator now!

I have seen many little children who had received a great deal of verbal direction literally turn their backs on me as I approached them to play. Almost invariably, though, within half an hour, they come to realize that I am following their focus of attention and adding to their interest by naming an object or making a play sound to go with it, like "brm brm" when they picked up a car.

Help him to continue to enjoy listening

Do make a point of including noisemakers in his toys so that he can have fun listening to them in this quiet environment.

Take every opportunity to show him where sounds come from, using, for example, a "noise" book. Opportunities can also be taken to show what sounds things make as he moves around the room. It could be fun to tap with your nail on the window, or run your finger across the slats of blinds if he shows interest in these items.

Rhymes are still wonderful for encouraging him to listen to your voice in this quiet, interactive setting. These can be recited when he looks at you expectantly, indicating that it's your turn to initiate an activity.

Continue your turn-taking games, such as hiding and clapping hands. He will love them, and they are still an important precursor to true conversational skills.

Help him to crack the language code

At this time, you'll want to pay particular attention to your own speech and tailor it using the following modifications. Think of yourself as a foreign language teacher!

USE SHORT SIMPLE SENTENCES. It's important always to adjust our input to the level of the baby's understanding. Use little phrases and sentences that contain just one important word, but add a modifier. Examples are "It's teddy," "Your duck," "Another car," or "Here's dolly." Be sure to bring in the names of objects at this stage, rather than referring to an object vaguely, such as "There it is." Your child wants to learn and understand right now. To make what is happening the focus of interest, it's okay to say, "It crashed" or "They fell down." Put a slight stress on

Sentences must always be grammatical.

the important word, to help him to identify it, but as before, be very careful that you don't distort your speech—it must always sound natural.

Your little sentences must also always be grammatical. We wouldn't say, for example, "It car," but rather "It's a car." Pause between each little sentence to give him time to take it in.

Research studies have shown that the simpler a mother's speech is at this time, the more rapidly the little child's length of sentence increases later. I have seen lots of mothers and babies who were enjoying a very close and loving relationship, in which the mother talked a great deal to the baby, but in enormously long sentences. I recall a little girl called Isla, whose mother talked to her constantly, using sentences like "It's time we went to the shops; I wonder if we should buy the bread now or wait until later." Not surprisingly, at this stage Isla had only managed to understand her own name and the words "Daddy" and "no." As soon as her mother realized the importance of short sentences and began to use them, Isla learned the meaning of words incredibly quickly.

SPEAK A LITTLE SLOWER AND LOUDER, WITH TUNE IN YOUR VOICE. You will notice that your baby listens to you intently when you talk to him slowly with lots of expression. Speaking like this gives him the best chance of noticing which sounds go in which words.

You may be wondering how to talk to him outside your special playtimes. It's fine to continue your running commentary at times when you are busy and want to keep in touch with your baby. The more that you can modify your speech now, however, the better for his language learning. It would be

> *He needs to hear words many times in order to learn them.*

a good idea to teach the baby's extended family how to modify their speech when talking to him.

USE LOTS OF REPETITION. Baby has most of the speech sounds of the language within his repertoire now, and so the reason they do not yet appear in the right places in the right words is largely that he can't recall what goes where. The only way he will do this is by hearing the same words many, many times.

It is important for his concept formation to hear words in different contexts, discovering, for example, that his hat is always called "hat" whether it be on his head, on the floor, or squashed up in his mother's handbag.

The best way of bringing repetition in at this stage is by putting the name of an object into a sequence of little sentences for as long as his interest can focus. For example, as he picks up and plays with a ball, you could say, "It's the ball. Your ball. Ball's rolling." Little naming rituals like "Sock off, shoe off, gloves off" as you undress him are also fun, as are games like "Johnny jump, Mommy jump, Daddy jump." Put a slight stress on the key name as you say it the first time so that he identifies it clearly.

REPEAT HIS SOUNDS BACK TO HIM. We know that at this stage, all the sounds of his mother tongue are now coming into the baby's sound-making, and this enables him to compare his own sounds with yours. Saying his sounds back to him can be a little more complex at this stage, as his sound-making is so much more complex. If he produces a long string of sounds, try imitating the last couple of syllables. He will love it, and he is likely to make more sounds back to you.

Some don'ts for this age
This is the time in which your baby is likely to become mobile and will want to explore and investigate anything and everything—including outlets, light

fixtures, and your precious knickknacks. It is all too easy to find yourself saying "No," "Don't touch," "Stop it," and "Put that down." Try to avoid "negative" speech. You have been, and still are, spending lots of time and effort giving him the message that voice is fun to listen to, and nobody likes to hear yelling or negativity. Furthermore, it is always necessary at this stage to intercept and distract him physically. (Please do not think that I am advocating letting him do anything he wants to. My concern is *how* you stop him.)

> *Never comment about what he has said or how he has said it—and never ask him to say or copy words or sounds.*

Another don't

Your baby is very likely to produce those magical first words at this time. Please resist the temptation to ask him to "Say it for Daddy," "for Grandma," "for Aunty," or for anybody else! It just serves to make him inhibited and self-conscious. Share your jubilation with other people on the phone when he can't hear you, but never comment to him directly about what he has said or how he said it. Instead, always respond to the meaning of his communication.

I and many of my colleagues have seen many children who began to say words and then ceased to do so for six months or more because of over-enthusiasm on the part of their families.

Remember: Never ever ask your baby to say or copy words or sounds! Our job is to respond to him in the most appropriate, normal way. If we do this, he will look after the talking!

Questions

Adults frequently ask questions to children of this age. They are asked for two purposes—first, to gain information ("Do you want an apple?") and second, to get the child to answer ("What's this?"). The first is fine, and the second is not! Asking just to get an answer that is already known has nothing to do with communication, and is in fact a test. The little child also knows this. The question adds nothing to his knowledge and can seriously inhibit a child's communication.

I saw a little boy in my clinic once who said virtually nothing but "What's this?" It's not difficult to work out what he had been hearing over and over again! I'd go so far as to ban "What's this?" from communication at any stage unless there were an odd occasion when you really did not know what something was and your child might!

(When he is much older, questioning skillfully can help a child to think and work things out and can be a way of passing the conversational turn to the child. But he is very far from that stage now.)

PLAY

Make play sounds to go with things that happen
Keep his attention with sounds like "brm brm" and "eeeeow" to go with cars and planes, "swishshshshshsh" as you sweep the floor, and so on. Continue to show him that a voice is fun to listen to, and give him a chance to hear speech sounds separately. Little phrases like "upsidaisy" as you lift him up and "dompedy dompedy domp" as you go upstairs are much appreciated at this stage. You will see from his facial expression how much he enjoys them and how closely he listens even if he is tired or a little cranky.

Always respond to what he means
Now that he is able to use some words, please don't try to encourage him to do so. He will use them when he is ready, and he will be ready much sooner if he never feels under pressure to speak. The important thing is always to respond to what he means in whatever way he tries to tell you. He is adept at using body language, facial expression, gesture, and even elaborate pantomime to express himself, so it is seldom difficult to know what he means. It has been found that the degree to which parents do this—paying attention to their baby's intention in whatever way this is expressed—accounts for much of the differences in language development between children.

Show him what you mean

It is important that you continue to use hand gestures to refer to what you mean. It is hugely helpful
for your baby if you point to things as you name
them. For example, if he looks at the ducks, say, "It's
a duck," accompanying this with a point in its direction. There is very little chance of him being under

> *Point to objects when you say their name.*

any misapprehension about what that word "duck" represents. Perhaps unsur-
prisingly, it is easy for children to attach the wrong meaning to words if they
are not given this help.

Speech and language therapists all see children who have attached the
wrong names to objects. I saw a little boy called Jerry a few years ago. His
speech was in a state of great confusion. He called a button a coat and a fork a
plate. He was one of a large family, and his mother suffered from long-term de-
pression. As a result, he had not been talked to very much, and certainly had not
had any one-on-one time. What had happened was that he had heard a word
while he was looking at a different object and so had made the wrong connection between them. Can you imagine what a confusing world he lived in? Just a
few basic misconceptions are enough to cause a major language problem.

OUTSIDE YOUR HALF HOUR

Remember to keep your sentences short for much of the time when you talk
to him. The more that you can modify your speech now, the better for his language learning. It can be beneficial to enlist the help of the whole extended
family at this stage.

Sixteen to Twenty Months

The little child's language skills develop considerably now. Taking turns in conversation with others becomes well established in a one-on-one setting, and a conversation can now extend to four "turns," two from each partner.

Her understanding and her use of words can increase enormously in this time, if she is given lots of adult support and help. As we have seen, language develops in a social context and at this time the little well-established social routines involving her and an adult partner now evolve into more complex ones. A simple activity like waving "bye-bye" to teddy, for example, might extend to waving not only to teddy, but also to the doggie in the corner, the dolly behind the door, and so on. Action rhymes and games also tend to develop in complexity, more actions coming into rhymes like "The wheels on the bus" and more and more people or toys taking part.

In terms of understanding, at the beginning of this period the little child is likely to recognize the names of most everyday objects like furniture and clothing and may have taken the momentous step of being able to begin to follow little sentences containing two important words—for example, "Your *cup* is in the *kitchen*" or "Let's find *teddy* and give him to *Daddy*."

Understanding continues to develop. There is now a more rapid increase in the number of words recognized and understood, often new ones every day. At this stage, these usually include more names of body parts, clothing, and animals. An important development toward the end of this period is that the little child also begins to understand some basic verbs like "eat" and "sleep" and some pronouns like "him" and "her." Understanding words other than names is of great help to her in following two-word phrases and sentences such as "Baby's drinking" or "My cup."

An important realization occurs within this time period. She'll come to understand that many words and phrases can mean an object or person not actually present. The child will now respond to more familiar phrases like "Where's Daddy?" in an unfamiliar context. She also becomes adept at using nonverbal cues like gesture, gaze direction, and context to help her to understand what a word refers to, and she can make quite sophisticated deductions about what appears to be the object of the adult's interest and intentions. Her knowledge of the sequences of events—like those connected with going to the store or bathtime—are acquired through repeated experience. It is easy, for example, to deduce the meaning of the word "towel" in the sentence "Here comes the towel to dry you with" if you hear it as you are about to come out of the bath.

The little child will still be using long strings of highly tuneful babble, and around six or seven true words at the beginning of this time period, and is still heavily reliant on gesture. The gap between what she understands and what she uses appears enormous!

At the end of this period, there is a huge and sudden increase in the number of words used. Once spoken vocabulary reaches around fifty words—which for a few happens by the end of this time—another little magic event occurs: that of linking words together in true language.

These new words are usually the names of the people and objects that become important to the little child as her world expands—for example, those of family members, pets, and toys. They also often include some action words like "bye-bye." The little child also begins to imitate environmental sounds like "choo choo" when she hears a train and to respond to speech by using speech—for example, saying "bye-bye" when asked to, whereas at the beginning of this time period she responded with a nonword vocalization or gesture. Gesture now starts to fade out as words take over as her main means of communication.

At around eighteen months, she acquires more concepts about objects, events, and people. As a consequence, her use of words can move away from the specific. For example, "dog" first meant only her pet, and now "dog" extends to all dogs. This development may to some degree account for the sudden increase in spoken vocabulary, as words are now truly becoming used as symbols.[1]

Once she has reached the stage of putting two words together, her communicative ability is greatly extended, and she uses these first "sentences" in many ways. She makes requests—for example, "More drink," "Want apple"—and responds to questions with replies like "There cat." She also now describes objects, like "big car," makes statements like "Drink gone," and uses language as a conversational device, as in "Mommy see."

Language and General Development

THE SEVENTEENTH AND EIGHTEENTH MONTHS

The baby's understanding of the world around her and the people in it continues to develop rapidly at this time. This is accompanied by a rapid increase in her understanding of words. She shows this understanding by responding appropriately to an action. For instance, she'll go to fetch her shoes when you are preparing to go out, or go to her chair when you are making food. She now associates words with their categories, recognizing, for example, that an undershirt is an item of clothing, in the same category as shirt and socks.

She can answer simple questions like "Where's teddy?" Some words, however, are still only recognized in a familiar context. She may, for example, only look around for "bowl" when her own bowl is likely to be within sight.

The little child understands the way in which you are using language now and will respond appropriately to a question ("Want an apple?"), a comment ("There's kitty"), or a direction ("Get your shoes"). She understands words other than names. By the end of this time period, she will understand some simple verb phrases like "sit down" and "come here." Her increasing awareness of herself as a separate person is evidenced by her newfound understanding of pronouns like "you," "me," and "mine."

She shows increasing ability to understand sentences and phrases containing two important words, rather than single words only. You may notice this in a number of ways. You might find that she can follow little instructions like "Go to your room and fetch your coat" or "Get your ball and give it to Johnny." She may even bring you two things you ask for, as in "Give me the brush and the spoon."

Many babies at this stage understand familiar adults much better than people they don't know well. This can lead to much frustration in a proud parent when his baby fails to demonstrate what she knows to others.

The little child is still using lots of babble containing many different sounds and a wide range of pitch and intonation patterns. The increase in her spoken vocabulary is steady but still gradual. Most babies have not quite arrived at the stage of rapid vocabulary expansion just yet, and their use of words can appear frustratingly far away. An important development at this stage, however, is that words now begin to take over from gesture as the main means of expressing her wants and needs. These are now indicated mainly by pointing, accompanied by a word.

Most of the early words are the names of people and objects of great interest to the little child. They often also include social words like "hiya" and "bye-bye." Other early words are those that accompany familiar actions, such as "up." Most are only used at this stage in specific and familiar contexts. For example, "teddy" may only refer to the baby's own teddy. The length of a word is not a key factor. My daughter added "hippopotamus" to her limited expressive vocabulary at sixteen months. (She had at the time a toy hippo to which she was greatly attached.)

As was the case with the very first words, many of these new words have to work extremely hard for a time because of their limited number. The little child will use one word that seems to her to be connected to what she wants to refer to when she doesn't know the right word. She might, for example, use "ball" to refer to many round objects including the moon and a wheel, and even a teabag. (The gap between understanding and production of words is again clearly shown at this stage in that the baby is very likely to be able to identify all these objects correctly when hearing them named.)

These early words also have to express a wide range of communicative intentions. "Car," for example, could mean "I want the car," or "That's my car," or even "I don't like the car." The baby's accompanying facial expression and body language makes it clear which is meant.

Conversational skills are improving steadily too, and may now consist of two turns from each partner. For example, the baby might say, "Car," and her mother reply, "Here's your car." The baby might follow with, "Brm brm" as she pushes the car along, and wait for her mother to say, "Crash!" as she crashes it.

The development of the little child's intellect, ability to move around, and manual dexterity enables her to increase the understanding of the world around her so essential for her language development. Perhaps the most important intellectual development at this time is the rapid increase in the number of concepts. For example, what starts as a class of four-legged animals gradually becomes refined into different kinds of animals, and finally to individual animals.

Developments in the areas of manipulation, motor skills, and social awareness are all enormously important to concept formation, as they enable the little child to explore and investigate her world and acquire a number and variety of experiences. We could not, for example have any concept of "heavy" unless we had handled many varied objects of different weights.

In this age period, increased hand-eye coordination and manipulative skills now enable the little child to handle materials in ways that are very helpful in forming concepts—for example, filling a container right to the top with blocks and then emptying it. She now scribbles and dots purposefully with pencil or crayon and looks at the results with great interest. She likes to push and pull large toys and vehicles around, and so acquires better judgment about the size and position of objects. She is now more interested in the completion of events—for example, putting all her dolls in one place, or putting all her blocks into a truck.

The little child's motor development also helps in her explorations of the world. She can kneel upright without support and seat herself in a small chair. She walks confidently with a wide base and enjoys pushing a cart. She carries a chair to climb on in order to reach a toy and can walk upstairs two feet to a step if her hand is held. She has an idea that she would like to kick a ball, but she just walks into it right now.

There is much investigation on the social front too. The baby engages in lots of imitation and mimicry, partly to find out how it feels to do the things she sees those around her do, and also in order to find out how other people are different from her. This interestingly often links with the first use of the word "mine," as the baby distinguishes herself as a separate person. She makes it clear that she welcomes other people in her play and often invites them to do so by offering them a toy.

THE NINETEENTH AND TWENTIETH MONTHS

By the end of this period, she begins to understand words and phrases outside the context in which she usually hears them. She will respond, for example, to "Lunch is ready" in a neighbor's house, and not only in her own. This means that she is now truly beginning to understand spoken language, recognizing the meaning of a word without the support of a familiar context.[2] Her understanding of words as symbols is also reflected in the fact that she begins to recognize the names of play objects such as toy cars or dollhouse furniture, as well as of real objects. She recognizes too the names of items in pictures. She will look at these for up to two minutes now and will point to several parts of the body and clothing when they are named.

Most babies at this stage continue to vocalize for much of the time with a wide range of sounds and pitch and intonation patterns, but there is an enormous range in the number of words used. Some use only nine or ten, and others show an enormously rapid increase in spoken vocabulary and may use up to fifty words meaningfully by the end of this period. The majority of these words are still names, but by twenty months those babies whose spoken vocabulary has increased dramatically are now using a wide range of types of words including verbs like "drink" and adjectives like "big" and "little." Words at this stage are still used to express a wide variety of meanings and purposes. "Dada," for example, may be used to mean "Pick me up, Daddy," "Come here, Daddy," "Daddy's car," or "Daddy's turn."

The generic use of words gradually decreases as she acquires more of them. A word used for all four-legged animals, for example, will be replaced by the names of different kinds of animals. She gains her full understanding of words as symbols so that words are now used in a variety of contexts. She will no longer, for example, only say "cup" when referring to her own cup, but will now say it in a neighbor's house while playing with a tea set.

Babies who reach a spoken vocabulary of around fifty words at this stage now begin to combine two words, although many single words will be used for some time. This is an exciting and momentous stage—her first sentences! The earliest two-word combinations are usually two separate words put together, like "Me car," meaning "I want the car." (My daughter at this stage announced firmly "Mommy see" when she wanted to see me.) The first words that are truly linked to another are often "gone" and "more," as in "Daddy gone" and "More drink." These early two-word sentences often have several meanings, as do the early single words. "My hat," for example, could mean "I want my hat," "Give me my hat," or even "I don't like my hat."

Babies' interest in mimicry at this stage extends to speech. Most will imitate two-word sentences, and they also enjoy aping environmental sounds, for example, calling out "woof woof" when hearing a dog bark.

Pronunciation of words is far from mature at this age, and proud parents quite often find that only they understand their little child's language. This results largely from the fact that she still has a long way to go in terms of being able to remember which sounds go where in which words, but also some speech sounds such as "ch" and some clusters of sounds like "scr" require extremely fine adjustments of tongue and lips. (Try them to see how much more complex the movements are compared with those needed to say "b" or "p".) Only by having many opportunities for comparing the sounds that she makes herself with those she hears around her is she eventually able to bring her speech sound system into line. These are the common mispronunciations of early childhood:

• Difficult sounds are replaced by those that sound similar but are much easier to say, for example, "wabbit" for "rabbit" or "tat" for "cat."

• The same consonant may be used twice in a word where there are two similar ones, for example, "goggie" for "doggie."

• The fact that the child has not yet noticed all the sounds in words, particularly at the end, means they won't vocalize some of a word—for example, saying "bo" for "boat" or "bana" for "banana."

• Similar sounds may be substituted, such as "s" for "sh."

• Changing sounds in complex words so that the syllables become similar. My younger son charmingly called a "bunny rabbit" a "bunny bunnit."

The little child's ability to manipulate and investigate objects shows further sophistication now. She can unscrew a lid and open a door, can turn the pages of a book a few at a time, and build a tower or train of three blocks. She can pound six pegs in a pegboard and fit a square and a circle into a formboard. She shows interest in matching two similar objects—for example, putting together two cars that are the same. She can now throw a ball, but it may well go in the wrong direction!

She now has increasing control over her body. She walks with a heel and toe gait and can start and stop safely. She can squat to pick up a toy and climb onto a large chair and turn around to sit. She has much more understanding of her own body size in relation to spaces—for example, knowing whether or not she can fit into a particular box.

On the social front, she becomes very interested indeed in imitating adults' actions, and loves to pretend to read a book, make coffee, and do all the other things she observes happening around her.

In summary, by the age of twenty months, your baby is likely to

- imitate sounds like those made by fire engines or planes;
- copy little phrases like "Here we go";
- point to a doll's hair, ears, and shoes if asked;
- have a spoken vocabulary of somewhere between ten and fifty words;
- sometimes imitate two- or three-word sentences and some of the sounds she hears around her, like "woof woof" when she hears a dog;
- understand the meaning of some words that are not names, such as "eat" and "sleep"; and
- know what the words "you" and "me" refer to.

Listening Ability

The little child can now localize sound from most directions, which is of great help to her in making the links between noises and their sources. If all has gone well, she will now have the ability to scan the sounds in the environment, choose what she wants to listen to, and focus on that for a little longer, tuning out background noise. This ability is still not well established, however, and needs favorable environmental circumstances if it is to be maintained.

Sensory integration—the ability to look and listen at the same time—also develops, but is still only present in particular circumstances. The environment must be free from distractions; what she is looking at and listening to must be the same thing and be her chosen focus of attention.

The little child's interest in listening to speech is shown by the fact that she will sometimes repeat the last word of a sentence she has heard. She is now much less easily distracted when she is listening to speech.

Attention Span

It's still difficult for your child to control her concentration, so you'll continue to see the rapid shifts of attention focus that she's been demonstrating for the last sixteen months, but they will now become interspersed with spells of intense concentration on something she becomes passionately interested in, and she absolutely doesn't want to be interrupted.[3]

When she is not so deeply engrossed, she will show an increased interest in following your focus of attention, but when she is concentrating hard on something, she cannot even listen to anything you say to her—unless it is directly related to her chosen focus. For example, she would be able to listen to the words of a game such as "Where's your hand?" when she is trying to figure out how to put her arm in her sleeve, but would not at that time be able to listen to you pointing out a cat in the garden.

Play

This period sees continued big developments in each of the areas of play—investigative, interactive, and pretend—all of which serve to help the baby in her quest to discover how the world works. She enjoys investigative and pretend play both on her own and interacting with a partner, and it is very important that the adult is sensitive to which she wants at a particular time. Your little child usually makes it clear when she is inviting you into her play.

It's important that she has a wide range of experiences both of play materials and of different situations in order to continue to build up and extend those concepts about the world that are such a vital underpinning to language.

INVESTIGATIVE PLAY

The baby's increased control over her body, manual dexterity, and hand-eye coordination enable her to make many discoveries. She can relate objects more accurately to each other now, like carefully placing a cover straight on a doll's bed, and she can also link different parts of an object together in more complex ways, such as fitting pieces into simple jigsaw puzzles. She finds out a great deal in the course of these activities, like how to place blocks so they balance, and which pieces of a puzzle are too big or too small, and how turning them around may help.

She now uses objects as they are intended to be used. For example, she'll bang those that are intended to be banged, such as drums and xylophones, and push those meant to be pushed, such as vehicles. She has come a long way from the stage in which all objects were treated the same. Her interest continues in fitting and sorting, and she becomes more skillful in successfully placing pegs of different heights in a pegboard. She still loves filling and emptying containers. It is interesting that many of these activities involve relating two objects and appear just at the time she is also linking two words together.

She begins to enjoy Play-Doh now. She won't yet try to make anything, but will enjoy patting, pulling, and twisting it. She also likes to sit in a sandbox, particularly if there are other children to watch, but she won't yet play or build with the sand.

Interest in coloring with pencil or crayon continues. She can now imitate vertical strokes as well as scribble.

Water play is still great fun. She loves to pour water back and forth from different containers and to investigate objects that float and sink.

Interest and enjoyment in noisemakers continues. The little child loves to find out all the different sounds she can make with them, and this is an activity she often relishes with another person.

The little child now loves an adult to show her what she can do with all the toys and other objects she plays with.

INTERACTIVE PLAY

The interactive rhymes and language games of earlier times continue to entertain. Whereas once repetition made the world seem safe and predictable, the little child now loves variation and even chaos brought into the games. The adult purposefully getting things wrong, like hiding in a way in which she can easily be seen, is a source of great hilarity. The child is very much an equal partner in these games, indeed often taking the lead. The child delights in games in which she and the adult take turns imitating each other, copying

THE TOY BOX

The following are a few ideas for play materials you could add to her toy box. Remember, though, babies are adept at finding their own ways of playing with different materials. Don't become frustrated when a wonderful toy you have bought is used in a different way from what was intended.

Investigative Play

She's now ready for a few more complex toys, including:

> Objects and toys that float and sink and more containers for water play
> Very simple puzzles
> A screw toy
> Pegboard with pegs of different heights
> Play-Doh

Pretend Play

Although she can use objects symbolically—for example, pushing a box along and pretending it's a car—realistic toys will encourage her a great deal. Here are a few suggestions:

> Dishes and pretend food
> A toy vacuum cleaner
> Small dolls
> Doll carriage, bedding, bath, and towel
> Toy vehicles

THE BOOKSHELF

Your baby will enjoy opening and closing books and helping you turn the pages, looking at the pictures as she does so. As before, looking at books needs to be a lovely interactive time where you both enjoy physical closeness. Let her lead, turning the pages as she wishes, and give her whatever time she wants to look at each of the pictures. (Please remember to tell her what the pictures are, rather than asking her to tell you.)

She will still very much enjoy the books she had at an earlier time, particularly those with interesting textures, those that made sounds, or those that had flaps that could be lifted.

The content of the book should, as at earlier times, relate to her everyday experiences. She will love simple bright pictures containing quite a lot of detail. The pictures can now be of children doing familiar things, rather than simple pictures of objects. She will enjoy those involving little sequences of familiar events, like going shopping or to the park. Those that lend themselves to lots of sentences containing two important words, such as "Doggy's barking. He wants dinner. Here's his dinner," are perfect for her level of understanding.

Repetition of words and sounds are quite popular in books at this stage.

There are many wonderful books that meet these criteria. The following are examples of those that do so beautifully:

WHERE'S THE CAT?
Stella Blackstone and Debbie Harter

CATS SLEEP ANYWHERE
Eleanor Farjeon

SPOT SLEEPS OVER (AND OTHER SPOT BOOKS)
Eric Hill

COME ALONG, DAISY!
Jane Simmons

I TOUCH
Rachel Isadora

> *JUMP LIKE A FROG!*
> Kate Burns
>
> *MIFFY*
> Dick Bruna
>
> *BABY FARM FRIENDS*
> Phoebe Dunn

each other's facial expressions or actions with a teddy or other soft toy. She will keep this going for some time and will make it clear how and for how long she wants these games played. She understands the sequence of actions and events in games and loves for her and her play partner to change roles in games such as hide and seek or run and chase.

PRETEND PLAY

Pretend play now comes to dominate interactive play. The little child pretends to do things herself, such as eating or sleeping. As this stage progresses, she more and more loves to imitate what she sees adults do. These are usually short single actions, like pushing a sweeper along or briefly pretending to use a dustpan and brush. She will also like to play with small dolls, feeding and bathing them and taking them for walks in a stroller.

TELEVISION AND VIDEOS

The same three important rules apply:

• Don't let her watch for more than half an hour a day. There is so much she needs to be doing at this important age, in terms of play, having real experiences, and, above all, interaction with other people. She will get none of this from the television.

• If you are keen for her to enjoy a program or video, never leave her to watch it alone. Always watch it with her so that it can become an interactive experience.

• Remember that she is just learning about the world and what objects are for and why people do what they do. She doesn't know, for example, that trains don't talk, and could well believe that they do, creating confusion with her concepts. (Such themes can of course be great fun later, when the little child has learned what people, animals, and inanimate objects actually do!)

I know a three-year-old boy called Billy who was causing great concern to his parents and playgroup leader. He interacted very little, even with his mother, his language development was extremely delayed, and his play was bizarre. He had no idea of what to do with the toys and just lined them up or twirled them around. I found that he had been watching videos for over six hours every day, from the age of a year. He had, of course, missed out on all those wonderful developments in play and interaction that would usually have occurred by now. We made big changes to his life, mainly in terms of banning television altogether and establishing the BabyTalk program, ensuring that he had lots of appropriate life experiences. He made steady progress and went to school at four and a half with the skills expected for his age. I still don't feel that he will ever reach his full potential, and am concerned that he might have some social difficulties in the future.

Cause for Concern

Below are circumstances in which it would be advisable to seek professional advice about your baby or little child's language development. (Please remember, though, that rapid progress in one area can result in a temporary delay in another.)

It is important to recognize, too, that no checklist can be a substitute for a professional opinion. If you are in any doubt, even if the reason for your concern is not mentioned here, do take your baby or little child to see a speech and language therapist as soon as possible.

Take your little child to see a speech and language therapist

- if she is not yet using any words;
- if she seems to have difficulty following a sentence like "Your shoes are in the kitchen";
- if she doesn't want lots of attention from you;
- if she doesn't want you to play with her; or
- if she doesn't often look around to see where sounds are coming from.

The BabyTalk Program

THE RIGHT TIME

I hope that you and your baby have now been enjoying your daily playtimes together. Not only are you providing her with the best possible opportunities for language learning, but you are also doing great things for her emotional development.

THE RIGHT PLACE

Your baby's ability to listen to what she wants to and tune out other noise is still not well established and could be lost without these quiet times. Check that television, music, and radio are all off, and remind anyone in the house that you are only to be interrupted in the case of a dire emergency.

> *Turn off the phone in your quiet room.*

I was puzzled a while ago when the mother of a little girl called Zara reported that the extremely rapid progress she had been making on the BabyTalk program had slowed down. Zara's mother assured me that she was following the program to the letter. I decided that the best thing would be to go to see them at home. I found that the next-door neighbor had music playing so loudly that it was clearly audible in the room Zara and her mother played in. Zara's mother hadn't noticed it, as it was not at a level that would cause difficulties for an adult. As soon as Zara and her mother moved their playtime to another part of the house, rapid progress resumed.

> *Space out your toys so she can see what's there.*

Remove distractions

Attention development is greatly helped by providing your baby with an environment in which there are not too many distractions.

There is now a balance to be struck between having enough toys around so that she can change from one to another rapidly at times, and so many that the room is too distracting. I tend to have plenty of stuff, but I make sure that there is lots of floor space for the baby to play on, and that the toys are arranged so that she can easily see what is there without the need to tip them onto the floor. Make sure that there are materials that give her opportunities for both investigative and pretend play—for example, shape sorters, blocks, puzzles, and dolls and doll accessories. Don't forget to include some noise-makers, and put in some books as well.

HOW TO TALK WITH YOUR BABY

You will find that the program for this age period has many similarities with that of the last, but there are some subtle and important differences. She needs lots of play experiences, so that she can come to understand what objects and events are all about and help to understand relevant words.

There is a huge amount that you can do to help at this stage. Be assured that this work will stand your child in good stead for the whole of her life. It is important now to be sensitive to your child's level of attention development, which as we have seen now fluctuates between rapid shifts of attention focus and prolonged and rigid attention to objects or activities of her own choice. It isn't difficult to see what is happening once you are aware of these stages.

> *Never try to
> direct her
> attention.*

Never try to direct her attention. If you try to shift her focus, particularly when she is concentrating intently, you will both become frustrated—she simply cannot comply with your demands. I remember an occasion on which my elder son at this age was busy pushing blocks down a cardboard tube for what seemed like ages while I was dying to show him a wonderful new toy. How frustrating that was!

Give your running commentary, but don't be surprised at these times if you feel that no one's listening. As before, the more exactly you can relate your speech to what is in her mind at that moment, the more likely it is that she will be able to listen.

Follow the focus of her attention

The amount of time in which you and your baby share the same focus of attention is still of paramount importance for her language learning, and this focus still needs to be led by your baby. Of course you can now sometimes draw her attention to something interesting, particularly outside your playtime, but during your BabyTalk routine, let her be the leader still. One study in the United States in 1983 found that there is a strong relationship between the amount of time that the mothers of twelve- to eighteen-month-old infants shared their children's focus of attention and the size of the infants' vocabularies later on.[4] Another study of eighteen-month-olds in England, carried out in 1993, found a similar correlation. The infants' rate of word learning increased significantly when adults followed the infants' attention focus.[5]

As you have done before, try to work out what is actually in her mind by carefully watching what she's looking at, and make a comment on that. Does she want the object named—"It's a hippo"? Does she want you to do something with the object—"Let's make teddy jump"? Or is she interested in what is happening—"It broke"? It's not usually difficult to know her meaning; babies are very skilled at communicating by gesture and facial expression. As before, go with the flow, allowing her to move her attention focus from one thing to another as often as she wishes. This won't go on forever, and she will reach the stage when she is ready and able to accept adult direction much sooner if she is allowed to go through these stages at her own pace.

Remember: Always *comment* on what she is interested in here and now. It is still vital to avoid questions and directions in these playtimes. If you ask her a question, part of her mind must shift its focus to figuring out the answer, or indeed to whether or not to answer at all. Similarly, if you give her a direction, part of her mind must shift its focus to deciding whether or not to follow it. Comments cause her no stress and are very much the easiest and most attractive kind of speech for her to listen to.

Watch her face to work out what she's thinking—and then make an appropriate comment.

I recently saw a little boy called Naseem, whose family were in acute distress at his failure to use any words by the age of nearly two years. When I observed him playing with his father, I saw that the man was delivering a series of nonstop questions and directions, such as "Come and look at this, Naseem. What color is it? How does it go? Right, let's look at this one then. How many bricks has it got in it? What shape is it? Say 'triangle'." Naseem was busy ignoring all of this, frequently turning his back on his father, and his father was becoming more and more frustrated! He was convinced that Naseem would only learn to speak by being asked to do so, and to play by being told what to do. He took a great deal of convincing that the reason Naseem didn't speak yet was that he did not understand more than a few words. Once I showed him how to help Naseem to increase that understanding, he worked very hard at changing his interaction style. It took him about a month, but as soon as he managed it, Naseem's progress quickly convinced him that he was doing the right thing. I was delighted when he told me how much he and Naseem were enjoying their playtimes together. Four months later, Naseem's language development was considerably advanced for his age.

Avoid questions and directions.

Help her to continue to enjoy listening

It's good to make sure that your baby likes to listen. There is noise almost everywhere we go now, in stores, restaurants, and even in the streets, and your playtimes are possibly the only ones in which she can have time to listen. Continue with the activities you learned the last time period:

• Make sure that you have noisemakers such as musical instruments or containers full of substances that make different sounds when shaken.

• Continue to tell or sing her rhymes. Not only do they give much pleasure in listening to voice, but it has been found that children who have been exposed to lots of nursery rhymes become better readers later on. The strong, powerful rhythm and high level of repetition enable little children to understand a great deal about how syllables and words are constructed, which they can easily translate to the written form later on.

• As you did before, show her where sounds come from when opportunities arise. As you open a box at her request, you could show her where the clicking sound originated—if she is interested.

Help her to continue to crack the language code

It is vital that you continue to use short, simple sentences at this time, as this is enormously helpful for enabling your little child to link words with their meanings. It is so much easier, for example, to recognize the key words in sentences like "Car's on the table" than in those like "Let's put all your cars on the truck and then pretend that the table is the seaside and that's where we're taking them."

You can use lots and lots of new words; she can learn to understand as many as nine new ones a day as long as you put them into short sentences! Doing so makes it clear to her what the key word is and exactly what it refers to. It also gives her the opportunity to contrast it with words she knows already. When you think you may be using a word she does not know, put it into a little sentence that has only one important word in it, such as "Here's hedgehog" or "It's huge."

As before, always make sure your sentences are grammatical. For example, "Daddy's gone to work" is, while "Daddy work" is not.

Your sentences should now, however, differ in a very important way from those you used in the last age period. Your baby is likely to be understanding little sentences with more than one concept. Consequently, you should now use *two* important words, rather than just one as in the previous time period. Baby will understand sentences such as: "Shoes are in the kitchen," "Teddy wants his dinner," "Your fingers are sticky," "Johnny's in the park."

Keeping to this length of sentence is important. It is easy at this stage to overestimate the amount your child understands. If you said, for example, "Please will you go upstairs and fetch your shoes and your socks and bring them down here to me," she would actually only comprehend "shoes" and "socks"—if she recognized them. Don't be tempted to gallop away into long sentences yet.

I've seen many children in the clinic where exactly this had happened, and whose language development, having started well, slowed right down. I can think of one in particular. Rachel was an enchanting little blond girl who came with her family to see me when she was nearly two. She looked the picture of health, but her mother had convinced herself that Rachel must have some terrible degenerative illness, because she had been acquiring new words very fast indeed up to two months earlier, but this progress seemed to have stopped rather suddenly. When I observed Rachel's mother talking to her daughter, I realized what had happened. She was using enormously long sentences like, "Oh look—there's a sweet little tiny shopping basket which would be just right for a picnic if we made this clay into lots of little sandwiches and cakes and fruit." Rachel alternated between looking bemused and tuning out entirely. Her understanding of speech had developed rapidly in the preceding weeks, and her mother was convinced that she "understood everything" and could now be spoken to like an adult. As soon as she began to speak to Rachel in short sentences that were within her level of understanding, Rachel's rapid rate of language acquisition returned. When I saw her at two and a half, she was understanding and using speech like a three-year-old!

Speak a little slower and louder, with lots of tune in your voice

This is still the kind of speech your baby will find the easiest and most attractive to listen to. It helps her to maintain focus on your voice and is also enormously helpful to her in her task of sorting out which sounds go where in which words.

This makes me think of Marcus, who was brought to the clinic at nearly four because only his mother could understand what he said, and school was on the horizon. He was clearly intelligent and immensely keen to communicate. His understanding of speech was fine, and so was the size of his spoken vocabulary and sentence construction. The problem was his speech sounds, which were in a state of total confusion. They were nearly all there, but Marcus was totally unsure of which went where in which words. His mother was just about the fastest speaker I have ever heard. It took me a while at times to figure out what she had said if it was out of context. Having his mother slow her speech down so that Marcus could begin to notice which sound went where was the most important part of the BabyTalk program for him. When I modeled the appropriate speed for his mother, within an hour he began to use sounds in the right places.

Use lots of repetition

Your baby needs frequent repetition of the same words in different sentences and also in different situations. This continues to be essential both in helping her to understand their meanings fully, and also to enable her to hear the sounds many times so that she can recall them accurately.

Bring words into lots of different little phrases

and sentences, for example, "There's the elephant. Elephant's huge. A huge elephant."

Labeling games are still useful and fun, too. Babies at this age love repetitious ones like "Teddy's nose, teddy's ears, teddy's eyes, Jane's nose, Jane's ears, Jane's eyes" and so on.

Some daily activities also lend themselves well to repetition—for example, "Pants off, shoe off, sock off" at bedtime, and "Wash your hands, wash your face, wash your feet" at bathtime.

Tell her the names of things.

Use names often

Your baby is still building up her vocabulary and needs to hear the names of objects many, many times. As you have already been doing, make a point of using names rather than pronouns. It would be better, for example, to say, "Let's put the book on the table" than "Let's put it on there."

I'm often asked if it's a good idea to use baby words like "tummy" and "horsey." The answer is a resounding "yes!" These words have become consistently used variations in nursery speech and indeed in nursery rhymes, and the reason is that they make it so easy for the baby to notice and say the sounds. Compare, for example, the word "tummy" with "stomach." Don't worry—these terms won't stick forever. Your baby will soon use the adult forms.

Repeat clearly what she has said

As we know, little children often don't pronounce words in the adult way, largely because they cannot remember which sounds go where. They are also not entirely sure exactly what they all sound like. Babies need to hear words over and over again, until eventually they can recall them correctly. Saying words back to her correctly will help her enormously at this stage. A word of caution, however: Never sound as if you are correcting her. The golden

Repeat what she says back to her—but don't *sound as if you're correcting.*

rule is always to start with a "yes." For example, she says, "Nana," and you say, "Yes, it's a banana. Would you like the banana?"

Her little two-word sentences can also be confused; again, the most helpful thing you can do is to say them back to her correctly, as part of the natural conversation. She might say, "Car Daddy," and you could say, "Yes, that's Daddy's car." This is very different from repeating what she has said without a preceding "yes" and without making it part of the conversation, which would give a very different message.

My colleagues and I have seen many children whose communicative attempts have been stymied because they're confused. One was a three-year-old little girl named Anna, whose mother was extremely keen for her to "speak nicely." She responded to most of Anna's early words by looking her firmly in the eye and slowly and deliberately repeating each syllable she had said. I remember Anna being delighted at coming upon a little elephant in the toy box. She wanted to share her joy with her mother, holding it out and saying "efant." Her mother, rather than affirming the communication Anna had made, looked at her with an expressionless face and very slowly said, "E-le-phan-t." Anna's disappointment was almost palpable. She dropped the toy and made no further attempts to share her discoveries with her mother. The change in the whole relationship between Anna and her parent was a joy to see once her mother altered her response to Anna's communications.

Say back to her what she means

It is still very important to reflect back to your baby the meaning of her communications, even if only part of it is verbal. She needs you to show her that you understand what she is trying to tell you. As before, always focus on her message and not on how she is communicating it. She might point at the sky, saying "Eeeooow" and showing by her facial expression and body language that the plane she can see is of huge interest to her. She wants you to share this

> ## Fit the words to the action.

excitement, showing her by your facial expression and enthusiastic tone that you too find this a very interesting event. The more responsive you are to her as a communicative partner—whatever form her communication takes—the better her future language development will be.

Show her what you mean

It is still important that you help her to know exactly what you mean, by gesturing and adding language at the exact moment you are doing something. For example, say, "I'm pouring the coffee, and in goes the milk" as you are doing so.

Questions

The golden rule for this stage is "Never ask her a question unless you need to know the answer." There really is no point in "What's that?" or "What does the cow say?" and so on. If she knows the answer already, you have added nothing to her knowledge, and if she does not, you just make her feel inadequate.

Please try to make sure that nobody asks your little child questions of this kind. One of the central principles of the BabyTalk program is that it is based entirely on input, with no demands at any time for output. If we talk to children in the right way, they will look after their own talking.

I remember a bright little boy called Christopher, whose frantic parents brought him to see me when he was two and a half. It emerged that he had started speaking early, to the delight of all the family. He had then had a series of ear infections in his second year, which are likely to have affected his hearing. He did what many children who have this problem do: He began to concentrate on looking and handling and to engage less in conversation. It was stressful for him to try to hear in the noisy environment he shared with his older brother and sister.

> *Don't ask questions unless you need to know the answer.*

> **Don't talk about her speech in front of her.**

As soon as his parents noticed that he was speaking less, they did what most concerned parents do and began to try to get Christopher to speak by asking him endless questions like "What color is this?" "What does the cow say?" and so on. Christopher knew perfectly well that they knew the answers to the questions and began to feel increasingly pressured. As a result, he spoke less and less, and the whole situation became a vicious circle. Once this circle was broken, it was amazing how rapidly Christopher's language development flourished. I saw him recently at the age of five and was pleased to hear that he is doing exceptionally well in school. If you are a father doing the program, it is likely that you will find not asking questions difficult. In my experience, this is always the hardest thing for fathers to do. I have known many who were doing all the rest of the program beautifully, but could not resist the temptation to ask questions. Believe me: Your little child will come along more quickly if you can bring yourself to stop asking questions.

DON'TS FOR THIS AGE GROUP

As in the last time period, during BabyTalk time, never comment on how she has said something or even that she has said it.

I recently saw a little boy called Umar in my clinic. I don't know who was more frustrated, Umar or his parents. He was a long-awaited first child, living in an extended family, and the apple of everyone's eye. Almost every time he spoke, an adult joyfully reported this to some of the others, in front of

> **Continue to avoid negative speech.**

Umar. He had become very inhibited, and his powerful desire to communicate was clearly in conflict with a strong feeling of self-consciousness. As soon as his family realized what the problem was—and only shared their excitement about his prowess out of his earshot—Umar began to talk happily and constantly.

Continue to avoid negative speech

Your baby's explorations are still likely to involve dangerous activities such as trying to climb the bookshelf, and investigations of your prized knick-knacks. As before, you will have to move her away bodily, and it's important *not* to accompany this with saying, "Stop it," "Don't touch," or "Put that down at once!" You want her to feel that your voice is something she wants to listen to, not fear.

You can learn a lot from "splish splosh," "beep beep," and "moo."

PLAY

Make play sounds for her

These sounds continue to serve important purposes. They help her to focus her attention, to enjoy listening to voices, and to have opportunities to hear speech sounds separately rather than in a rapidly changing stream of speech. Her play lends itself well to such play sounds now: the lovely sounds like "splish splosh" or "drip drip" that can accompany water play; those accompanying vehicle play, like "crashshshsh" and "beep beep"; and animal sounds such as "baa baa" and "moo."

OUTSIDE YOUR HALF HOUR

Talk to her a lot! Tell her about whatever is going on.

Involve her in many different activities, like visiting friends, going to the park or the store. Make a game of naming her body parts as you wash her, and naming her clothes as you dress her. Talk to her as much of the time as you can in the same way as you do in your half-hour playtime.

Twenty to Twenty-four Months

Many little children are now really taking off both in terms of understanding and use of language, although there is a wide variation in language abilities in this age group. Conversation skills are well established, and interacting with this age group becomes an absolute delight! Adults often feel that the child is an equal partner, in that he takes as big a role as the adult in maintaining the conversation. He also takes an equal part now in terms of repairing any breakdowns in communication, seeking or giving further information to clarify a topic. His mother might say, for example, "We'll see Mary later," and he replies, "Mary house?" He becomes extremely persevering in engaging others in conversation and is virtually impossible to resist.

From the age of around twenty months, his communications become more frequent and diverse. He begins to use language to express his feelings, rather than doing so by crying or fussing. For example, he might say firmly, "Johnny mad!" He also starts to initiate conversation by using a name, catching his mother's attention by calling out, "Mommy!" Even more important, he tries to tell others of his experiences by an eloquent mixture of babble, words, gesture, and pantomime. Questions also begin to appear in his conversation for the first time, such as, "Where Daddy?"

Understanding of language continues to flourish. At the beginning of this period, he comprehends the names of virtually all the everyday objects around him, is increasingly able to follow little sentences containing two important words, and is starting to recognize words other than names, including verbs like "eat" and "sleep" and pronouns like "him" and "her." He now knows, for example, that "drink" means a drink wherever he is, and that the people in his world may appear in many different places. He realizes that words can be used to refer to whole categories such as "animals" or "toys." This is a considerable intellectual step.

As was the case in the last age period, the little child's understanding is enormously helped by his ever-increasing knowledge of the sequences of events that make up his daily life. He now anticipates these in more detail, for example becoming aware of the transaction of money after going around the supermarket and the events of packing and unpacking the groceries. This knowledge, as before, helps him to attach meaning to words very easily. For example, he soon learns what "pennies" mean after hearing the word in the context of paying for groceries.

Linked to this ability to anticipate longer and more detailed sequences of events is his growing understanding of longer and more complex sentences, including those about items and events that are not present. He also comes to understand the meaning behind them more fully. By the end of this age period, he will not only be able to follow a sentence like "When we get to Mary's house, we'll see her doggy," but will also link this statement to all his previous knowledge of Mary, her house, and her dog.

Progress is also great in terms of using speech, although at the end of the age band, the gap between understanding and use is still very large indeed. At the beginning of this time, spoken vocabulary is usually somewhere between ten and fifty words. Children with vocabularies at the top end of this range may already be linking words and imitating two-word sentences. Most other children now begin the rapid expansion in spoken vocabulary, producing more new words every week. By the age of two years, many little children have a spoken vocabulary of two hundred words, or even more. The types of word also broaden, and vocabulary at the end of this age period may include verbs, like "swimming" or "playing," and adjectives, like "quick" and "slow." This helps him greatly to put together more and more little two-word phrases and sentences like "Joey slide," "Going quickly," or "Daddy jumping." He also uses more pronouns, but may make errors with these, saying, for example, "Her gone!" He usually refers to himself by name, to ensure that there is no confusion, as in "Johnny cookie!" He begins to use negatives like "Not want" and for the first time responds verbally to questions with a "yes" or "no."

He can copy three-word sentences at times, and by the age of two, may even put some together himself, such as "Johnny want drink." He has now truly begun to use not only words, but also grammar.

Language and General Development

TWENTY TO TWENTY-TWO MONTHS

Understanding of speech continues to develop rapidly. This is greatly helped, as we have seen, by the little child's increasing knowledge and understanding of the sequences of events within his daily routines. He now knows and anticipates, for example, not only the point in the day when he will be dressed, but also the sequence in which his clothes will be put on him. This knowledge helps him to attach meaning to new words extremely easily. The name of a new garment would readily be understood in the context of those he knew already. Similarly, he would understand the word "soap dish" without difficulty once he was aware of the purpose of soap, its slippery qualities, and tendency to disappear into the bathwater.

He is beginning to understand much about the ways in which language is used. He knows, for example, the situations in which it is appropriate to use greetings, and when he is being asked for clarification.

He has some understanding of what other people know, which is vital information for the initiation and maintenance of conversation. He realizes, for example, that when he refers to his brother by name, everyone in his family knows exactly whom he is talking about, but that the doctor or somebody he has just met does not, and needs to be told.

The number of words the little child recognizes now grows at an ever-expanding rate, and several may be added every day. By the time he is twenty-two months old, he is likely to recognize the names of all the objects in his home that have relevance to him.[1] He also shows increasingly good understanding of sentences containing two important words. You may notice him responding with alacrity to instructions like, "Get your hat from the closet." He may even be able to follow a little series of three simple instructions. For example, "Fetch your ball from the basket and give it to Daddy" might be managed at this time. The little child displays a new ability to identify objects that are not referred to directly, being referred to by place as in "the one by the stove" or by a pronoun as in "Give it to him."

This is also a time of rapid expansion of spoken vocabulary, although as before, there is still a huge gap between understanding and use of words. As we have heard, understanding can increase by several new words every day, and production simply cannot keep up. At the beginning of this time period he is likely to be understanding as many as two hundred or even more words, and only using somewhere between ten and fifty of them.

The little child's increased spoken vocabulary now enables him to increase the ways in which he uses language, although again there are wide variations. He begins for the first time to try to tell other people about interesting events he has seen or experienced. He doesn't have quite enough language to do this entirely verbally and often has to supplement words with gestures and pantomime, filling in the gaps with babble. It can be quite a problem working out what he means, particularly if he is excited. In this new situation of talking about events that are not present, he may begin to use some past tenses, although often not entirely accurately. You may, for example, hear something like "He goed."

Question forms show up, such as "Where dat?" or as a friend of mine reported the first question her granddaughter asked, "Where sink?"

He also begins to use negatives, usually at the start of the sentence. For example, "No drink" means "I don't want a drink."

He recognizes that words can be used to stand for whole categories, such as animals or clothing, and he begins to use them in this way.

Although he has so many more words now, babble has not entirely disappeared and is used at times as "padding" between true words when he can't quite produce the whole string he would like to.

The child's increasing control over his body means that he can now concentrate more fully on what he is doing and learning, rather than on how he is going to reach a particular object and how he will handle it when he does so.

In terms of mobility, he can now run smoothly and even walk backward. He can squat on his haunches and lean forward to pick up a toy without tipping over. He can throw a ball without falling. He walks upstairs holding the handrail and can propel a riding toy, using his feet to push himself along the floor.

Manual dexterity and hand-eye coordination are developing fast as well, enabling him to explore objects to his heart's content. He thoroughly enjoys these newfound abilities. He can hold a pencil with thumb and two fingers to scribble, and he can now turn the pages of a book one at a time. His eyesight is now as good as that of adults, and he can thread a shoelace through a large hole. He can fit shapes into a three-hole formboard after a demonstration and build a tower of four blocks.[2] The first idea of number sometimes begins to develop now, as he acquires a vague idea of the difference between "one" and "many."

The little child enjoys being shown what to do with toys and will pull an adult to show him a toy. He will imitate the adult's actions with the toy—for example, pulling a train after being shown how to do so.

He has as yet no concept of playing with other children, but will happily play alongside them. He certainly has no idea at all about sharing and will protest vigorously if another child grabs his toy!

A little role-play starts at this time, and he may, for example, pretend to be his mother going shopping or his father writing a letter.

TWENTY-TWO TO TWENTY-FOUR MONTHS
The little child begins to attach meaning to words more and more rapidly, and there are a number of factors that enable him to do this.

As in the previous time period, his increasing conception of how the world works in terms of the meaning and sequence of his daily activities helps him to understand more and more of the language he hears around him. When out shopping with his mother, for example, he is now likely to anticipate the whole sequence of events from the items of food going into the shopping cart to their appearance on the table. As a result, it wouldn't be difficult for him to deduce the meaning of the word "tomato" in the sentence "These tomatoes will go with the egg you are having for lunch."

Another factor that helps him to link words very easily with their meanings is that he begins to be able to fit them into categories. At this stage, he understands where to put new words such as those naming body parts or clothing.

He understands the ways in which language is used, such as when it is appropriate to use a greeting or when to give information. Coupled with his knowledge of the "rules" of conversation, these skills are of great help to him in working out the meaning of new words. Hearing the words "See you" in a context in which he usually hears "Bye-bye," for example, makes it easy for him to know that the new phrase is a variant of "bye-bye."

By the time he reaches the age of two years, he can usually understand quite long and complicated sentences, and the meaning and reason behind them. He would understand, for example, sentences like "When Daddy comes home, we'll play hide and seek" (and remember it when the time comes!) and also the meaning behind his mother saying, "I'll close the window to keep the rain out." Yet another little milestone is that he can now give both his first and second name if he has been taught to do so.

His use of negatives now extends into denial. He might, for example, tell you, "No drop," meaning "I didn't drop the plate." He also uses questions, inquiring, "Where Daddy go?" These little phrases and sentences are still usually a bit telegrammatic at this stage, but usually convey his meaning pretty clearly.

The "babble drift"—the process in which the sounds not in his mother tongue cease to appear in the little child's speech—is now complete, but his pronunciation is still quite a bit different than that of adults. He continues to replace difficult sounds with easier ones, for example, "tat" for "cat" and "tair" for "chair." Clusters of sounds are still reduced, as in "tep" for "step," and sounds and syllables that do not have a stress on them are omitted, as in "bella" for "umbrella." Interestingly, he can clearly detect these substitutions in the speech of others. You will find that if you mispronounce a word in the way in which your little child does, you will get a very funny look indeed, and he may even try to correct you, continuing to use his version of the word.

This considerable increase in the ability to use language results in a huge enthusiasm for conversation. The little child now expects to engage adults in conversation and perseveres determinedly if he doesn't get a response. A busy adult may find herself subject to pulls, pushes, and persistent and repetitive vocalizations. The little child is also extremely keen to repair any breakdown in communication and will go to great lengths to be understood by means of alternative words, if necessary supplemented by gesture and pantomime.

Once again, intellectual and language processes are developing at the same time. He can climb on a chair to look out of the window and walk upstairs two feet to a step. Other motor skills developed at this time are those of walking backward while pulling a toy, and picking up a toy from the floor without falling over. He can now throw a ball overhead and sit on a small tricycle and propel it with his feet. The great pediatrician Arnold Gesell coined a wonderful phrase about the two-year-old: "He thinks with his muscles!" Gesell comments on the total interdependence of motor and mental activity at this stage, describing how the two-year-old "talks while he acts and acts what he talks."[3]

Manipulative skills are also developing fast. The little child can pick up tiny objects like pins and thread with a very fine grip, can make a train of three blocks, and can turn the pages of a book easily one at a time. His hand-eye coordination now enables him to insert shapes into a simple formboard not only when it is facing him, but also when it is turned at an angle.

He is becoming a little more independent now in terms of daily living skills, and by two years he can remove most of his clothing, wash his hands with little help, and feed himself well with a spoon.

By the time he is two years old, as Gesell observes, he has an emotional life of considerable depth and complexity and can show a good deal of sensitivity to the feelings of others. He likes things to remain the same; after all, it is not long since he learned to anticipate the pattern of his days. Change needs to be gradual and gentle.

In summary, by the time he is two, your little child is likely to

- understand quite long and complicated sentences;
- use around fifty words;
- link two words together, and occasionally three; and
- use words like "he" and "she," "him" and "her," but with some mistakes.

Listening Ability

If you have been following the program, your little child will be able to choose what he wants to listen to and continue to do so for as long as he wishes. He still needs, however, a much bigger difference between the background and foreground sound than does an adult, as he is still relatively easy to distract.

He will now have built up his comprehension of the meaning of most everyday sounds, such as those connected with mealtimes, traffic, visitors to the household, and the voices of many people in his life.

Attention Span

You will probably see him more often giving that very concentrated attention to objects and activities of his own choice. Don't worry; it won't be long now before he moves into the next stage, in which he will be able to shift the focus of his attention with your help and follow your directions. Resist the temptation to try to bring this about before he is ready. Allow him to progress through the stages at his own rate.

His attention is still entirely single-channeled, in that what he is doing totally absorbs him. You will find, though, that he can now almost always listen to meaningful language added in a fun way to what is happening. When dressing him, "Arm in" and a "Where's your hand?" game, for example, will receive attention, whereas "Put your arm in your sleeve" will not.

Play

INVESTIGATIVE PLAY

The child loves to explore different materials now, and in doing so he learns a great deal about their properties. Water play delights him still and will continue to do so for some considerable time to come. He loves to pour water from one container to another and to find out what floats and what sinks slowly and not so slowly. As we have said before, this play is wonderful for building concepts like quick and slow, closer and farther, first and last. Children who do not have these experiences or have them to a limited extent are at a great disadvantage. A little girl of four named Melissa was brought to my clinic recently because she had failed to be accepted into the school of her parents' choice. I found that her mother was extremely house-proud and as a result had very much limited the kind of play she allowed Melissa to engage in. She had never been allowed to play with water, sand, clay, or Play-Doh, and certainly not with crayons or paints. Scissors were also forbidden, and Melissa had not been able to spread play materials like blocks around the floor or to move the furniture about in any way. As a result of all these restrictions, Melissa, who was a much-loved and beautifully cared for child, had lacked experience to the degree where her concepts and consequently her understanding and use of language were well below those to be expected at her age. Melissa caught up with her age level in terms of language skills within six months of starting the BabyTalk program, but I felt very sad, as I was sure that had she been able to have a wider range of experiences earlier, her attainments could have been considerably higher than normal.

Clay and Play-Doh are lots of fun at this stage, and the two-year-old now begins a little basic manipulation, banging clay with a cutter or roller. He enjoys scribbling with a fat crayon or pencil and will do so for longer spells than earlier, marking the paper more heavily now.

Sand is popular, and rather than just sitting in it as he did at earlier times, the little child now likes to tip it into a truck or wheelbarrow.

Throwing games are fun too, and lend themselves well to turn-taking, now often with several people.

The little child's increased manipulative ability and longer concentration span enable him to enjoy toys that need more effort and finer control of his hands. He likes to try to put giant beads onto a lace rather than a rod, and to do simple puzzles rather than just simple inset formboards. He loves toys that fit together, particularly those that are graded, like boxes, rings, and barrels.

Matching and sorting continue to be of great interest too, and he much enjoys games like large picture dominoes, color matching games, and sorting large beads.

The little child shows interest in construction toys, as long as these are large and easy to fit together, for example large interlocking bricks or giant Legos. He doesn't try to build anything yet, but his enjoyment in manipulating the materials and finding out how they fit together will stand him in very good stead a little later on when he does.

He has a much more sophisticated idea of cause and effect now and relishes toys like a jack-in-the-box or other pop-up toy.

INTERACTIVE AND PRETEND PLAY

The favorite play of children of this age is "helping" adults in their daily activities and reenacting them in play. You will find that your little child watches you intently and later shows in his play that he remembers what you were doing when he imitates the activity. This is still usually single actions like putting potatoes into a pan. The little child will also reenact many of these activities with his teddies or dolls, and he very much enjoys adults joining in this play.

His knowledge of how the world works is also shown in his appropriate use of objects and materials. He now, for example, correctly places both the doll's pillow and cover and puts knife, fork, and plate on the table. He loves toys that represent implements used by adults, such as an iron and ironing board.

He also loves to play with model people, objects, and animals, such as a farm or a zoo with animals, or a garage and vehicles. A simple dollhouse can also be fun.

Adults have an important role in all his play now. In terms of manipulative and investigative play, he loves an adult to show him ways in which his toys can be used, but then he likes her to withdraw while he tries out for himself what he has been shown. Little children at this stage can benefit from adult intervention when they have mastered the basic skills, with the adult showing them a variation. For example, once he has learned to thread beads, you can show him how to make a pattern with alternate colors.

Turn-taking with an adult is still great fun and can become a lovely part of pretend play—for example, in games involving feeding teddies and dolls, or taking turns being the shopkeeper and the shopper. In both this and imaginative play, the adult can make helpful suggestions like showing him where the furniture goes in a dollhouse or helping to set up the materials for a shopping game.

Rhymes and songs will continue to be popular for a long time to come. The little child at this stage loves those involving actions, like "Row, row, row your boat" or "The wheels on the bus." He particularly relishes rhymes in which the words relate to people or objects he knows, made up to go with traditional songs with familiar tunes.

As in the previous time period, the little child likes to play on his own at times, although he usually wants to be near his parent, and is likely to cry if she leaves. Once again, considerable sensitivity is needed to recognize when he wants the adult to join in and for how long, and when he wants to get on with his explorations and activities by himself.

There is still not yet any real play with other children. Two toddlers may be engaged in pretend play next to each other, but the only interaction is likely to be the occasional grab at the other's toys.

THE TOY BOX

The following toys and play materials would make good additions to your little child's toy box at this stage. They are again divided into those likely to be used for investigative and for interactive and pretend play, but as at earlier times, he may think of ways of playing with them that you never would have thought of!

Investigative Play

   More containers for water play, such as squeeze bottles and different
      shaped containers
   Simple rolling pin or cutter for Play-Doh
   Truck or wheelbarrow that can go in the sandbox
   Interlocking barrels or boxes that fit into one another
   Large picture dominoes
   Color matching game
   Large interlocking blocks
   New noisemakers, musical instruments, or filled containers that make
      interesting noises
   A jack-in-the-box or other pop-up toy

Interactive and Pretend Play

   Shopping bag
   Iron and ironing board
   Wash-up bowl and brush
   Zoo with animals
   Farm with animals
   Garage and more vehicles
   Dollhouse and furniture

THE BOOKSHELF

It's now very important indeed to establish a routine in which you share a book with your little child every day. This could be part of your daily playtime, at bedtime, or whenever it conveniently fits into your schedule.

I can't overstate the importance of reading together. The extent to which books are shared between adults and children in the preschool years is the best predictor of reading success later. It isn't the early teaching of reading that achieves this, and in fact too early teaching can have a strongly adverse effect. It is the sheer enjoyment of books that matters, as they become part of a lovely interactive situation.

When we looked at the results of our follow-up study, we found that some of the children who had extremely high spoken language skills had only average reading ability. We thought this was likely to be because they had rarely shared books with an adult before they went to school. Sadly, many children now arrive at school in this situation, some of them not even aware of how to open a book, that the text runs from left to right, and that the story continues from one page to the next.

Regarding content, your little child will certainly continue to love books to which you can attach lots of play sounds, such as those about animals and vehicles; these are wonderful for helping him to acquire an early appreciation of the fact that sounds can have their representation in books. This will lead him toward that crucial ability to associate sounds with their written forms. Play sounds are also helpful in making him become aware of the separate sounds within words, which is essential for later reading.

Rhyme books are great now. The resulting awareness of sounds and the ability to rhyme is an important precursor of reading. In fact, inability to rhyme is a marker of poor readers.

His increasing understanding of language and longer attention span now make it possible for him to enjoy simple stories. Reality is still very important. He is not yet ready for fantasy, as he is still building up and consolidating his knowledge of the world and could easily become confused.

As before, the best stories are those that relate to his own experiences, as we have seen how much that helps him to attach meaning to words. These predictable patterns and sequences of activities reinforce his knowledge of how the world works, particularly as you can talk to him about how the events in the stories relate to his own experiences. When he understands the basic sequences of events, it is easy for him to attach meaning to any new words that come into the sequence.

As before, reading the same stories over and over again is key to your child's understanding of the words in the book.

Made-up stories about himself, possibly supplemented by photographs, are still enormously popular, and he would find it huge fun to match the photos to the real objects in his home.

Some of the many wonderful books that meet these criteria are

A FIRST PICTURE BOOK OF NURSERY RHYMES
Elizabeth Harbour

MOTHER GOOSE
Michael Hague

SO MUCH
Trish Cooke

ANIMAL CRACKERS
Jane Dyer

THE JOLLY POSTMAN
Janet and Allan Ahlberg

GOING TO THE DENTIST (and other "First Experiences" titles)
Anne Civardi and Stephen Cartwright

CAT IS SLEEPY
Satoshi Kitamura

MY VERY FIRST MOTHER GOOSE
Iona Archibald Opie and Rosemary Wells

TELEVISION AND VIDEOS

The three rules of earlier times still hold.

• It is important to limit your little child's viewing to half an hour a day.

• It is also very important that you watch with him, so that the experience becomes an interactive one and you can help to relate what he sees to his own experiences.

• Make sure that the content relates to the world as he is coming to learn about it and not about fantasies like flying elephants, for which he is not yet ready.

Now that he is able to follow a little story, programs that depict children and animals in situations he would recognize can be fun. As with books, repetition is good, and series where the same characters do and say the same or similar things can be much enjoyed.

Cause for Concern

Below are circumstances in which it would be advisable to seek professional advice about your baby or little child's language development. (Please remember, though, that rapid progress in one area can result in a temporary delay in another.)

It is important to recognize, too, that no checklist can be a substitute for a professional opinion. If you are in any doubt, even if the reason for your concern is not mentioned here, do take your baby or little child to see a speech and language therapist as soon as possible.

Your little child may need some help

- if you notice that he doesn't seem to understand the names of lots of everyday objects like furniture or cutlery;
- if he never links two words together;
- if he doesn't show intense concentration on an object or activity of his own choice;
- if he doesn't want to help you in your activities; or
- if he doesn't show any pretend play.

The BabyTalk Program

THE RIGHT TIME

Thirty minutes a day, every day

As his play skills develop, you can continue to boost his confidence by affirming and admiring what he can do and gently helping him to do more difficult tasks so that he doesn't become frustrated. This can require treading quite a fine line! I remember a little child called Shaun who came to the clinic with his father at twenty months of age, as he had not yet begun to use any words. For some reason, his father thought that children even as young as this should be left to find things out by themselves. While the two of them were playing together, Shaun found a screw toy that was just too tight for his little hands to manage. He tried and tried, with no success, and within a few minutes, he was weeping with rage and frustration. I couldn't resist intervening, and the moment I slightly loosened the nut for him, Shaun was all smiles, and he learned a lot from the toy. I also remember, however, a little girl called Antonia, whose mother couldn't bear her to experience any frustration at all and solved all Antonia's problems before she knew she had them. For example, when Antonia played with a puzzle, her mother would show her where a piece went before the child had a chance to try herself.

Keep the room quiet.

THE RIGHT PLACE

Please ensure that noise and distractions have not crept back. Check to see that there is no significant noise coming in from the surroundings and that you are unlikely to be interrupted. Your little child still needs to experience times when listening is easy and lots of fun.

As you have done before, have a selection of toys available so that your little child has a wide choice of materials for both investigative and pretend play. It helps to keep the toys in the same places so that he can readily find what he wants, and make sure that they are all assembled and complete. Little children at this age have no tolerance at all for the jack-in-the-box that doesn't pop up or the puzzle with a piece missing.

Arrange the toys so that there is a clear area of floor and some surfaces for him to play on. A floor and walls covered with pictures and toys, however attractive, can actually be overstimulating and make it difficult for him to focus.

HOW TO TALK TO YOUR LITTLE CHILD

Share the same attention focus

It is still vital that you and your little child continue to share the same focus of interest and attention, and it is likely that this will be very well established by now through your habitual awareness of each other.

Your little child will often let you know clearly what the object of his interest is, often by means of speech, which removes much of the guesswork needed at earlier times. When he points and smiles and says, "Dere cat," there is little doubt about what is interesting him. He will be quick to let you

Make sure all the toys are working and complete.

know if you haven't worked out correctly what is on his mind. If, for example, you responded to "Teddy drink" by offering teddy a drink, and he actually meant that he wanted you to hand him teddy's cup, he will soon show you by elaborate pantomime what he actually meant.

Perhaps the most important change at this time is that, due to his rapidly expanding world knowledge and command of language, what is in his mind is not always the here and now. He loves to try to tell you about exciting things that have happened, often over and over again. My daughter, aged twenty-one months, was totally enchanted by her first visit to the zoo and told everyone she came across, "Mommy giraffe . . . baby giraffe . . . and dicky bird said 'hello'!" You can now expand a little on what he has said, and add a little to help him to recall more of what has happened. If, for example, he was talking about some children he saw playing in the park, telling you all about it in a mixture of little sentences and longer ones padded out with jargon, saying, for example, "Johnny hit ball. All fall down," you could say, "Yes, Johnny hit the ball. He fell down. His mommy picked him up. We all went home for lunch."

At other times his mind will be on what is going to happen in the near future. He may say, "Johnny go park. See bunnies." Again you could expand on this by reminding him of other things he might see in the park, such as flowers, and the swing and slide. These conversations provide opportunities for him to hear and come to acquire more complex grammatical forms like past and future tenses, which of course don't occur when you are talking about the here and now. They also enable you to use and him to follow more complex constructions, like "If it's raining, we can't go to the park."

At this stage, carefully used rhetorical questions can help him to think through and remember events. "I wonder what we'll see in the park today?" may stimulate lots of memories of past visits to the park. Be sure to answer your question yourself if he doesn't answer.

He'll also want to start talking about his feelings. "Mary's got ball. Johnny mad," for example, could lead to an interesting conversation.

As your joint experiences and conversations about them increase, your little child will come to know, as we all do, what knowledge we can expect our conversational partner to have. Knowing that he and his mother have been amused by a particular jack-in-the-box, he can safely assume that the mention of "popped up" will make her laugh, whereas another adult who had not seen the toy would need much more explanation. The more that the adults around have followed the little child's focus of attention, the more quickly he will be able to make the right assumptions about what other people know, which is so important in conversation.

I have seen many children in the clinic for whom this has not happened, and it makes conversation very difficult indeed. I remember a little girl called Sara, who came into the room the first time we met, and said, "He bigger and bigger and bigger and broke," and it took me a long time to work out that she and the other children in her playgroup had been blowing up balloons until they burst. She didn't realize that as I hadn't been there, I didn't know that she was talking about balloons.

It is important that you are very much aware of the moment when he switches out of these conversations back into the here and now. Never try to keep them going, however much you are enjoying them. At this stage, the little child's mind can change direction quite suddenly.

This is a time of transition in terms of attention development. There will still be times when his attention switches from one thing to another rapidly. As before, make it clear to him that that is fine, and again as before, comment on each focus of interest, however rapidly it changes.

At other times, he will give long spells of focused attention to objects or activities that have caught his interest. As you have done before, give a running commentary that relates as closely as possible to what is actually on his mind. For example, "What a big car. It's going up . . . up . . . up . . . the hill . . . It's at the top . . . and down it comes!"

Avoid questions entirely except for those rhetorical ones that may arise in conversations about past or future events. We want him to be listening intently to what you say, rather than trying to work out the answer to a question.

It is still important, as before, to avoid instructions entirely. As we have seen, his attention level now makes it possible for him to listen to instructions that are an inherent part of a game such as "Where's your hand?" while dressing him. These are fine in daily living activities now, but in your playtime, a running commentary is still what he listens to most easily and with the greatest enjoyment. He experiences you as adding to his pleasure in what he is doing, instead of interfering with his activities. (Of course, if he shows an interest in scribbling, there's nothing wrong with saying, "Get the crayons from the shelf.")

Please don't be tempted to try to get him to shift the focus of his attention at this stage. He is just reaching the age when he will be able to do this at an adult's request, but it will soon be much easier for him, and it is better to wait for him to reach this point on his own.

I have seen many in the clinic, up to seven or eight years old, whose attention is like quicksilver, and who go through the contents of several toy boxes in the space of half an hour, failing to learn or benefit from any of the materials in them. I saw a little three-year-old girl called Dana. Her daycare worker had noted that only occasionally was she able to follow adult direction, and the woman was deeply frustrated that she did not always do so. As I came into the room, she was holding Dana's head and trying to make her focus on a counting task. Each time she took hold of Dana's head, the little girl's eye gaze flicked immediately in a totally different direction! I don't know which of the two of them, Dana or the caregiver, was the more frustrated.

The authors of a 1986 English study into the effects of joint adult and child attention commented, "When adults use an unknown piece of language in attempts to direct the child's attention to something else, the child must shift the focus of his attention and try to determine the adult's focus. You could say that adults are better at following the child's focus than the child the adult's."[4]

An interesting study in Canada showed that children whose mothers were intrusive in their play had lower language levels than children whose mothers allowed their children to play as they chose.[5]

Bring in lots of new words now, while following his interests. Don't be worried about using long or complicated ones. As long as you are using them in that situation, he will find it great fun. I used the word "catastrophe" recently to a little boy of close to two as his airplane fell out of the air. He laughed delightedly and tried to imitate me.

> *Use lots of new words.*

Help him to continue to enjoy listening

A quiet background is the most important factor in listening, but it is still important to give your little child opportunities to find listening easy, enjoyable, and a lot of fun. Try to put one or two new noisemakers into his toy box, such as dried peas in a can or musical toys, so that he will be encouraged to play with them.

Use songs and rhymes whenever possible. Dancing to music is also now a lot of fun!

It might be fun to include books where you could use different voices, for example soft and loud ones for the different characters, as well as those to which you add play sounds.

Drawing your little child's attention to the sounds made by his chosen activity, such as the sound of the bubbles when he's involved in water play or the squelch made by clay or Play-Doh as it's handled, makes the shared focus even more interesting for him.

Use short sentences in your playtime

By the end of this age period, you are likely to have noticed that he understands a great deal of what you say. As a consequence, you will naturally start to talk to him in considerably longer sentences. It's fine to do this outside your playtimes, but it is very helpful to limit the length of sentence you use within them.[6]

> *Find sounds to make listening fun.*

Try to keep largely to sentences that contain not more than three important words, such as "Johnny's going to the park later." If your sentences get much longer than this, your little child will take longer to sort out the sounds within each word. He is also likely to fail to notice all the little words in your sentences, as he's busy focusing on following their meaning.

I saw a two-and-a-half-year-old girl named Susie. She had been sent for repeated hearing tests because she left out so many of the unstressed sounds and syllables in her speech, which can, of course, happen when a child has a hearing loss. Susie's hearing was found to be fine, and everyone was puzzled about her speech problem. When I heard the way in which her mother was speaking, particularly when I discovered that it was nearly always noisy at home, all became clear. Susie's mother was speaking in enormously long sentences, and in a soft voice. Poor Susie just hadn't had a chance to notice all the little quiet sounds and syllables, as she was having to work so hard to follow the meaning of what her mother was saying. As soon as her mother realized what was causing the problem and changed the way she spoke, Susie's speech began to improve, and within a few months it was normal for her age.

Continue to speak a little more slowly and loudly than you would to an adult, with lots of tune in your voice. This is still the most attractive kind of speech for little children to listen to, and the one that makes it easiest for them to hear and notice exactly what is in each word in terms of speech sounds.

Pause between sentences, to give him time to take in what you have said. A boy called Patrick was recently brought to me because his speech was not at all clear. He was one of a wonderful family of eight children, whose mother managed to give all her children plenty of attention. Not surprisingly, she spoke at high speed and never seemed to pause to take a breath! Once we managed to slow her down and find "alone" time, his speech rapidly improved.

Continue using names rather than pronouns. You may think he knows them all already, but it won't hurt, and it may help him a lot if he is not yet sure of how the sequence of sounds goes within that particular name or doesn't know it as well as you think he does.

Expand a little on what he has said

At this stage, the most helpful thing is to say back to him what he has said with a little expansion. For example, if he said, "Daddy go," you could reply, "Yes, Daddy's going to work." Or if he said, "Want drink," you could say, "You want a drink? Here's a drink." Similarly, if he said, "Teddy fall," you could say, "Yes, teddy's fallen"; if he said, "Mommy goed shops," you might say, "Yes, Mommy went to the shops."

Expanding on what he says in this way is related to increasing sentence length (*not* just echoing) later on.[7, 8, 9] It is extremely helpful in giving him information about grammatical structures, and also in maintaining joint attention. (Do be careful that you never ever give him the impression that you are correcting him. Keep to that golden rule of always starting with a "yes.")

One of my children at this stage said "bit" for "biscuit" and got quite angry when not everyone understood what he meant. I made a point of using lots of little sentences containing the word, like "Nice biscuits," "Biscuits for tea," "I like biscuits," and so on, and it was not long before he noticed all the sounds in the word. Again, please be extremely careful that you never ever give him the impression that you are correcting him.

Show him what you mean

It can still be helpful to use gestures so that your little child knows exactly what you are referring to, particularly when you think that you may be using a new word. It also helps to show him exactly what you mean—for example, showing him how a toy goes "round and round" as it does so, or telling him, "We'll open the drawer and put the pencil in" while doing it.

> *Speak a little slower and louder, with lots of tune.*

> *Never give him the impression that you are correcting him.*

> *Use gestures alongside the words.*

Continue to make play sounds to go with things that happen

Play sounds continue to serve a number of useful purposes, so please keep them up. They enable the little child to hear separate speech sounds, such as the "sshshsh" as you are sweeping or "gugug" as water runs away. At this stage, it's particularly helpful to add them to appropriate pictures in books, giving him an early message that there can be links between sounds and pictures.

Continue to use lots of repetition

As you know, your little child still needs to hear words many, many times in order to recall all the sounds in them accurately enough to say them correctly.

He has also reached a period of rapid comprehension, and the more different contexts a word is heard in, the more quickly it is fully understood. A little child, for example, who only heard the word "dog" when his family dog appeared, would take longer to realize that the word applies to a large number of four-legged animals who share certain characteristics than a child who had heard the word used to refer to other dogs in other settings and situations.

The number of different contexts the word is heard in is also important in helping the little child to form concepts. Different sentences such as "Dog's eating," "He's chasing the dog," "Dog's too hot," "Dog's very friendly," and so on also help to give him a clear picture of what kind of animal this is.

> *Add sounds to pictures in books.*

Children who only hear words in limited contexts can fail to fully understand their meanings. I'd been asked to see a little boy called Mark, who had had a long and serious illness and had as a consequence missed out on a great deal of play and language experience. I went to see Mark in school, and the following conversation that he had had with his teacher was reported to me:

MARK: I want to see Mrs. G [another teacher].
HIS TEACHER: Mrs. G is busy.
MARK: I want to see Mrs. B [another teacher].
HIS TEACHER: Mrs. B. is busy.
MARK: I want to see Busy.

> *Repetition is very helpful when using new words.*

Mark was clearly showing that he had not heard the word "busy" in enough different contexts to know what it means, and even what kind of word it is, referring to it as if it were a name. He will only be able to learn the full meaning of that word when he has heard it in many contexts, such as "Mark's busy with his bricks," "Daddy's busy cooking dinner," or "Mommy's busy writing."

Say back to him what he means
There will still be lots of times now when you know exactly what he means, but he hasn't the language to express it fully verbally and needs to use gesture and pantomime, padded out with babble. Saying back to him what he meant to say is an immense help. For example, he may be looking out of the window, waving his arms about excitedly, and saying, "Birdie, birdie, birdie," and you could say, "Yes, there's lots of birds. They are all flying. They're flying together."

Questions
As we have seen, it can now be helpful to ask a few rhetorical questions when talking about something that has happened or is going to happen, in order to help him to recall events more easily. Please limit the number of these questions to a few per conversation, and always answer them yourself if he does not soon show a sign that he is going to do so.

Don't ever ask him "test" questions in order to get him to answer. If you are in doubt about whether to ask a question, ask yourself if you know the answer. If you do, don't ask the question! He knows that this is not natural communication and will just become stressed if he does not know the answer.

DON'TS FOR THIS AGE GROUP

However tempted you are, please never ask him to say or copy words or sounds, and make sure that nobody else does. If your little child mispronounces a word, gets his sentences in a muddle, or leaves out sounds or syllables, he just needs to hear the word or sentence clearly again. He never benefits from a message that he has not said something right.

It remains important indeed that you never comment on how he has said something or on the fact that he has said it. This, as he very well knows, is not part of normal communication and only serves to make him feel self-conscious. As before, always respond to his communications, in whatever way he makes them.

Twenty-four to Thirty Months

A two-year-old knows the meaning of lots of words and is already able to understand long and complicated sentences. She now realizes that names fall into categories, such as family members and clothing, and that action words relate to particular situations. This ability to fit words into categories, coupled with her ever-increasing knowledge of the world and how it works, enable her to deduce more and more easily the meaning of the new words she hears. It would not be difficult, for example, for her to understand the word "aunt" in the context of family names, or "catch" in a ball game.

She comes to understand the names of smaller and smaller subcategories, such as "elbow" and "knee" and "collar" and "buckle."

Her number of concepts increases greatly, and she will now acquire those of relative size, as in "bigger" and "smaller," of color, and even of number, although at this stage, the latter only extends to "one."

Perhaps her greatest achievement by the end of this time is that she truly does understand language out of context. She would be able to respond appropriately to "We're going shopping" without any clues such as her mother putting her coat on.

She can also now follow questions more easily and responds appropriately to "where," either looking toward the object named or trotting to fetch it.

In terms of speech, most little children are using many two-word sentences and occasionally three-word sentences. These, however, are still considerably telegraphic. "Johnny goed shop," for example, is a kind of sentence often heard at this stage.

Spoken vocabulary usually increases very fast, and the little child can add as many as ten words a day. She begins to use pronouns more correctly, adds many more verbs, and now uses prepositions like "in" and "on." This increase in vocabulary enables her to put words together much more easily. By the end of this age period, many little children are using three-word sentences much of the time, and they are becoming a little less telegraphic. Some can even name a color correctly now and repeat two numbers (although without fully understanding the concept).

The little child gives and acquires information and expresses her feelings, but now also asserts her independence with statements such as "Me do it!" She frequently asks questions like, "What's that?" and wants a "yes" or "no" answer to her queries, such as "Dat Julie's hat?" Her knowledge of what other people do and do not know helps her considerably. She knows, for example, that her mother could answer the question "Where's Grandma?" whereas the salesclerk could not.

Despite her knowledge of the rules of conversation, she is still very much learning to be a talker. Adults need to do much of the work, particularly in situations outside the one-on-one playtime in which an adult is always following the focus of her attention. They need to wait for moments when her attention is not engaged and explain what the conversation is to be about. "Grandma wants to know what we bought at the store" for example, would cue her in nicely. Her contributions can be disjointed at times, even when given such help, particularly if her mind does not stay on the topic of conversation.

There will also be times when not only does she fail to respond to questions, but even ignores your comments. I was with a delightful little boy named Henry recently, who had just been swimming with his mother. His grandmother wanted to hear all about it and launched into a string of questions. I could see that Henry was fully occupied with a book he had just picked up and wasn't even aware that Grandmother was talking to him. After a few minutes, he put the book down and began spontaneously to give her the information she wanted.

Language and General Development

TWENTY-FOUR TO TWENTY-SEVEN MONTHS

At the beginning of this age period, the little child is already able to understand long and complicated sentences. Her knowledge of the sequences in her daily life, and of the way in which words fall into categories, now enable her understanding to increase faster and more efficiently. Knowing, for example, that there is a category of names for clothing helps her to understand a new word like "tights" very easily in the context of dressing. Her experience of ball games and knowledge that things move at different speeds would lead her to understand the word "slowly" in that context. All the events of her daily life are wonderful learning situations.

She is interested in small parts of a whole and understands, for example, "eyebrow" and "knee" in terms of body parts.

Spoken vocabulary is often around two hundred words at the beginning of this time and continues to increase quickly. Some little children add as many as ten new words a day. At the beginning of this period, most are using mainly two-word sentences, with the occasional one containing three. The two-word sentences most often consist of the names of people or objects, together with an action word, such as "Baby sleep" or "Ball gone." She understands more verbs now and may point correctly to pictures of children doing different things.

The little child will often talk to herself, chattering away about what she is doing as she plays and coming out with sequences of little sentences not addressed to anyone in particular. It's as if she's practicing putting words together. As Arnold Gesell puts it, the child at this age "talks while he acts and acts what he talks."[1] She is often most fluent when she is talking about interesting things that have happened to her, but at this stage, usually talks of them in the present tense. "Go park," for example, could mean that she went to the park earlier. She can also use these little sentences to ask for help with her personal needs; my daughter often said "Sticky fingers" when she needed to wash her hands.

The little child now begins to use more and more three-word sentences, constructed in a number of ways. Some are expansions of two-word sentences she has been using for some time. "Julie car," for example, might now become "Julie big car." Two-word phrases can also be put together, again often those she has been using for some time. "Mommy wash" and "wash hair" might be combined into "Mommy wash hair." Others may be constructed from single words, such as "Me want dinner" or "Teddy hit ball." The little child's speech is still telegraphic, but will gradually become less so over the next few months. Word order will also become grammatical. Pronouns are more often used correctly, and the little child begins to refer to herself as "I."

She starts to ask more complex questions now. She'll ask "Where Mommy?" or "What dinner?" to get information and attention. If asking doesn't work, however, she'll still pull and grab to get her meaning across.

The little child is also developing in other areas as well. She can now walk in any direction, and even on tiptoe. She can rise from a kneeling position without using her hands, boost herself onto a piece of apparatus with considerable agility, climb on a chair to reach an object, and even stand on one foot. This greatly increased control makes it easier for her to concentrate on what is happening and being said, whereas balance and control of her body used to take a great deal of her attention.

She has more sense of herself as a separate person now, and of the needs and feelings of other people. She likes to assert her independence by doing tasks like hand washing with the minimum of adult help. (At other times, particularly when she is tired or unwell, she will revert to extreme dependence.)

Social contacts with her peers are still few and brief. The little child does, however, show the beginnings of cooperation in that she may begin to share her toys occasionally.

In terms of understanding, the little child now recognizes the meaning of many more verbs and can point to pictures of children doing a wide variety of different things when they are named for her.

She also understands questions better and will respond appropriately to "Where?"

She recognizes more categories, such as those of food, cutlery, and animals. She knows, for example, that family members have names like "Grandma" and "Sister," and this makes it easy for her to associate meaning with a new name, like "Aunt."

Her greater understanding of the world is shown by the fact that she can also identify objects by their use, distinguishing between "the one you eat" and "the one you wear."[2]

She can understand words for some colors and words relating to size, like "big" and "little." In terms of numbers, she may have a concept of two or even three by the end of this time period.

Her greatest achievement at this stage is to understand language without the support of clues such as the time of day or the actions of other people— she really does understand the words. You may notice that she pulls out her shoes as soon as you mention that you are going shopping, whereas before, she did not do so until you had gotten out your car keys.

The little child is much more skillful in both asking and answering questions, and in expressing her feelings. Whereas previously she might have pushed away the hand of an adult who was trying to wipe her sticky fingers, she may now announce firmly, "Me do it." She extends her use of language to discover the meaning of new words. "What dat?" may be her favorite phrase to learn about the world around her.

She'll begin to use "ing" endings on verbs to mark the present tense, or an "s" to denote that it is the plural form.[3] The clarity of the little child's communication is also enhanced by her use of prepositions and the more accurate forms of words, such as "no" instead of "not" in a sentence like "No more dinner." Word order is coming more and more into line, as she becomes aware of how adults construct grammatical sentences.

Although she is making enormous strides in terms of verbal communication, she still has a long way to go in terms of becoming a skilled conversationalist. She may appear to be one in your daily playtimes, as this is the situation in which she can use all her communication skills most easily, but in most other situations, she still needs a lot of help. There will be many times when she doesn't respond to conversational overtures, even when these take the form of comments. The main reason will be that her attention is still single-channeled, and in the general situation, she is not always sharing joint attention with an adult.

In terms of body and mobility development, the little child can now jump using two feet together and climb over as well as on nursery apparatus. She can at last kick a ball, albeit gently and lopsidedly. She also begins to be able to pedal a tricycle, another great achievement. She can push a toy along with good steering now.

Her hand-eye coordination is improving rapidly. She can complete a simple puzzle with accuracy and build a tower of six blocks. She can add a caboose to a train and make a bridge from three blocks. Her pencil control is better too, and she can copy a cross. She can also match primary colors and sort objects according to whether they are big or small.

Socialization continues too. The little child will now join in play with one other person. She is often cooperative, and if she refuses to do something, you can start to bargain with her. You could say, for example, "Cookies after lunch, not now" and find that she accepts this. She is likely to be willing to help put things away and to try dressing herself, even if she does tend to put some of her clothes on backward. She may now feed herself with a fork as well as a spoon, wash and dry her hands without much help, and go to the bathroom alone, if you've begun potty training.

In summary, by the time she is thirty months old, your little child is likely to

- use as many as two hundred words;
- talk to herself about what is happening;
- ask "what?" and "where?" questions;

- put three words together; and
- refer to herself as "me" or "I."

LISTENING ABILITY

It is likely that if you have been following the BabyTalk program, your little child will have no problem listening to whatever she wants to and tuning out what she doesn't, as long as the setting is quiet.

She will now have a wide knowledge of the origin and meaning of the sounds she hears and might ask what causes a particular noise.

If at any time she doesn't seem to listen as well as she did, do have her ears checked. Infections of the ears, nose, and throat are very common in preschool children and can result in a mild hearing impairment. This could set back listening skills even in children who have had no earlier problems. Listening becomes difficult and confusing, and the little child will focus on looking and touching rather than on listening.

Attention Span

For the first time the child may able to be directed by adults—but only in certain circumstances.[4] Spells of intensely focused concentration will continue, though she might respond to your voice drawing her attention to something. It is essential to recognize that she still cannot listen while she is doing something else. She is also easily distracted, and an extraneous noise or other event will stop her from listening to you.

Many children whose environments have not enabled their attention to develop do not reach this stage for many years and continue to fluctuate between spells of extremely short attention spans interspersed with inflexible focus, in which they cannot listen at all to what is being said. This can easily continue into primary school, with disastrous effects on educational progress.

Maurice was four years old when I first saw him—very handsome and big for his age, but delayed in his speech development. He emptied two toy boxes item after item in the space of a few minutes, listening not at all to his mother's suggestions for play. He then fixated on a train, pushing it around a track, still clearly not listening to his mother at all. She reported that this kind of play was typical for Maurice, and that she was at her wits' end trying to get through to him.

Fortunately, attention will develop as soon as appropriate changes are made to the child's environment. I explained to Maurice's mother about her son's attention stage, and as a result, made sure that he experienced one-on-one quiet times with her in which she would talk to him about whatever his attention was focused on. He began to make progress immediately. When I saw him three weeks later, he was able to stop what he was doing and listen to his mother and was also understanding much more of what was being said.

This stage, in which the little child can, in certain circumstances, accept adult direction, needs to be handled with great care and considerable sensitivity. If an adult is so delighted that her child can follow directions that she begins to give her too many of them, both she and her child will be frustrated.

If you have a real need to direct your little child, there are three important rules to follow:

• If you want her to change from one activity to another—for example, to stop playing and come to the table—she needs plenty of warning. Expecting her to change activity suddenly can be a rich source of tantrums during the "terrible twos."

• She can only take in a direction if she is focusing on you, and not when she is busy. It's best if the direction is made fun, such as a game of "Here comes pudding, open your mouth" as the spoon approaches.

• It helps if the direction comes just before the task, for example, "And next come your pants" just before this happens in a familiar dressing sequence.

One amusing fact is that she now starts to give herself directions. You might, for example, hear her say, "On it goes . . . and that one . . ." as she plays with her blocks.

Play

Both investigative and pretend play really flourish in this time period, and the latter now develops into true imaginative play. The little child loves adults to be involved in her play and welcomes suggestions that can help her to extend the range of all kinds of play. (It's very important, however, to be sensitive to the times when she really wants to "do her own thing.")

INVESTIGATIVE PLAY

The little child's explorations of play materials and toys and what she can do with them knows no bounds. New control of her body and improved hand-eye coordination enable her to make impressive leaps. She is likely to continue engaging in many of the activities she enjoyed in the previous age period, but in more dexterous and sophisticated ways.

She can kick and catch a large ball, but may find a box easier to kick. Many children can, for the first time, pedal a tricycle.

The little child can build a tower of six blocks competently, placing each very carefully on top of the last. She becomes more skillful at handling crayons and pencils and can imitate horizontal strokes. She enjoys other art materials, such as chalk and paint. She can string beads with dexterity and now for the first time tackles scissors. If she is shown how to hold them, she can snip paper, which she'll love. She is quicker in her manipulation of toy tools, like a screwdriver or hammer, and will play with them for longer periods than she did earlier.

Little children of this age are immensely interested in matching and sorting. These activities give her valuable knowledge of the world of materials, by enabling her to compare different sizes, shapes, and colors and to develop many concepts like "full" and "empty," "rigid" and "flexible."

Most little children of this age love puzzles and will persevere with them for much longer periods now.

PRETEND PLAY

This stage is characterized by a passionate interest in the domestic activities the little child sees around her, like housework and gardening. The little child watches intently for quite long periods and begins to remember and imitate what she has seen, delighting in bringing these actions into her play. (You may notice at times at the beginning of this age that she doesn't always get it quite right. I remember a little girl in my clinic playing at setting the table and solemnly putting the napkins on the chairs.)

At an earlier stage, the little child used objects in single actions, like pretending to brush her hair or drink from a cup. She now remembers not only single acts, but whole sequences, and might, for example, sit down, pretend to put on her glasses, and pick up the newspaper. She might reenact a whole dish-washing sequence when playing with water, fetching the plates and cutlery, washing them, drying them, and putting them away. She may put a hat on her doll, place her in the stroller, and take her for a walk. All this mimicry is extremely important in helping your child to distinguish herself from other people by becoming more and more aware of how it feels to be doing what they do, as opposed to what she does.

Another development is the changing roles of teddy and dolly. At an earlier time, the little child brought dolly or teddy into the play, but they were passive partners in her games. They now become active.[5] Teddy may, for example, hand back his cup for another drink, or dolly may jump up to catch the ball.

Your child loves adults to be involved in her play and to help give her new ideas she can incorporate into her own play sequences. Examples of this would be suggesting that dolly might like a drink after her bath, or giving her a kiss as she is tucked in bed.

IMAGINATIVE PLAY

The little child is beginning to experience herself much more as a separate person and to understand the feelings and needs of other people. As a result, she often starts to imagine that she *is* another person and to enact imaginative sequences of events that are not merely what she has observed. She is most likely to take on the role of her mother or father or other people she most frequently observes in her daily life, and when she does so, dolly or teddy often become her. While pretending to be her mother, for example, she might pick up her shopping bag, put teddy in the stroller, and pretend to go to the store. These imaginative sequences all help her to find out what it is like to be that person, and to do the things they do. Role reversal—for example, taking turns being the shopkeeper and the shopper—is great fun for your toddler.

The little child also enjoys prolonged imaginative play with models and plays more extensively and imaginatively with dollhouse and furniture, or zoo or farm animals. She may also pretend to feed a picture of a doll.

By the end of this time period, the little child may even invent people, like other shoppers in a shop or imaginary people visiting a zoo.

Her constructions become so elaborate that she may want them to remain in place overnight so that she can continue her game the next day.

TELEVISION AND VIDEOS

Please keep to the rules:

- Limit the time your little child spends watching television or videos to half an hour a day.
- Watch with her so that you can discuss what you see together.
- Avoid fantasy. Your little child still has a long way to go in terms of understanding how the world works.

The same criteria apply to choosing videos and television programs as to choosing books. She will still love familiar characters doing the kinds of things that she does, and she will adore repetition in terms of getting to know the same characters and seeing them enact familiar sequences of events.

Rhymes and music will have a powerful appeal, and so will humor at this stage, particularly of a slapstick variety.

THE TOY BOX

The suggested additions to the little child's toy box are divided into those that are likely to encourage investigative and pretend/imaginative play, but your little child may surprise you with the ways she thinks of using the toys.

Investigative Play
Different sizes and colors of paper
Paint and brushes
Chalk
Plastic scissors
Tricycle
Picture bingo
Puzzles
Boxes

Pretend and Imaginative Play
Cash register and money
Pots and pans and play oven
Gardening or housework equipment

THE BOOKSHELF

Please continue to share a book every day with your little child. Nothing, as we have seen, stands her in better stead for reading later on.

Do not, whatever you do, try to teach her to read. Your goal right now is to share a lovely interactive time together as you introduce her to the magical world of books. She will absorb all the vital information—such as the fact that you read from left to right, that words relate to pictures, and above all that books are enormous fun.

Your little child will still love stories about the familiar sequences of events in her daily life. These can lead to discussions about past and future events just as her play sometimes does.

The books can be a little longer now, combining an interesting story with bright, attractive pictures. The little child will enjoy following characters over a series of several books. Soon they'll be like old friends. She'll love discussing their feelings and motives, as well as their activities. It is helpful if the content of the stories lends itself to large numbers of sentences containing three important words, for example, "Grandma lost her hat" or "He blew out the candles."

Rhymes are still very helpful to her. Make sure that you use a lively voice and emphasize the rhythm.

She likes concepts like "big" and "small" and "one" and "many" and would love books in which these are illustrated.

There are many wonderful books meeting these criteria, some examples of which are shown below. (She doesn't need a huge number of new books at this time, as she loves the frequent repetition of familiar stories.)

ELLA AND THE NAUGHTY LION
Anne Cottinger and Russell Ayto

WHAT DO YOU DO WITH A POTTY?
Marianne Borgardt

THE NEW BABY
Anne Civardi and Stephen Cartwright

ZA-ZA'S BABY BROTHER
Lucy Cousins

BE GENTLE!
Virginia Miller

OLIVER'S VEGETABLES
Vivian French and Alison Bartlett

I LIKE IT WHEN . . .
Mary Murphy

She will enjoy programs that include concepts such as size and number.

She will enjoy little stories, and as when she is being read to, will like to hear a lively voice and dramatic rendering.

Causes for Concern

Below are circumstances in which it would be advisable to seek professional advice about your baby or little child's language development. (Please remember, though, that rapid progress in one area can result in a temporary delay in another.)

It is important to recognize, too, that no checklist can be a substitute for a professional opinion. If you are in any doubt, even if the reason for your concern is not mentioned here, do take your baby or little child to see a speech and language therapist as soon as possible.

Do take your little child to see a speech and language therapist

- if she is not showing an increase in the number of words she is using;
- if she still mainly uses single words rather than two together;
- if you often can't understand what she has said;
- if she does not seem to want you to play with her;
- if she does not show any pretend or imaginative play;
- if she doesn't seem to understand what you say to her unless you make it very simple; or
- if her attention span is still very short most of the time.

The BabyTalk Program

THE RIGHT TIME

Explain why she can and can't do things.

Half an hour a day

I hope that you are enjoying your daily playtimes so much that there is no question of letting them lapse. They will continue to do so much for your little child, not only in terms of her language development, but also her play, attention, and emotional development.

Many studies both in the United States and in the United Kingdom have shown that a high proportion of children with delayed language development have emotional problems.[6, 7, 8] This is hardly surprising, as it is not difficult to imagine the frustration of being unable to understand what is being said, or to make yourself understood.

The connection between language and emotional development is of particularly great importance at this age, often referred to as "the terrible twos." Children at this age are beginning to perceive themselves as independent people, and in the process to assert themselves, frequently refusing to do what they are asked. Much of the inevitable frustration can be avoided by explaining to the child why she cannot do something and negotiating with her. (It really is best to avoid saying "no" unless it is absolutely necessary.) Clearly you can do this more easily with a child who has a good understanding of speech. Conversely, a child with limited understanding often feels as if she lives in a world where adults arbitrarily prevent her from doing what she wants. It isn't difficult to see how easily behavior problems can arise.

Children's interaction with one another is also affected by the degree to which they can understand and use language. It has been found that children's popularity is affected by their level of understanding of speech. A child who comes vividly to mind is Dan, a four-year-old who was brought to see me because he was only talking like a two-year-old. His mother reported that she was extremely distressed at Dan's inability to make friends. She had tried to help by having other children for playdates and taking them out on interesting trips, but the day always ended in fighting and tears. Once Dan and his mother started on the BabyTalk program, Dan's language skills quickly began to catch up, and his mother noticed that he and other children began to discuss what they were going to do and to negotiate and establish rules instead of fighting. Dan's popularity began to improve as soon as this started to happen, and six months after I first saw him, both his language and social interaction were normal for his age.

As we have said before, the undivided attention of a beloved adult makes a little child feel affirmed and therefore confident, and relieves her of the enormous stress of trying by any means (often sadly by being naughty) to obtain it. I have seen many children who have calmed down to an amazing extent when they started on the BabyTalk program, even before they had had enough input to increase their understanding of speech. One such was a three-year-old named Teddy, who was so tense when I first saw him that he gave the impression that he might explode at any moment. His movements were so tremulous that his coordination was very poor. His behavior was becoming worse in an attempt to gain his mother's attention, and she was becoming so frustrated that she was cutting herself off more and more from him. The difference in Teddy was astonishing once he realized that he was to have a daily playtime with his mother however he behaved. His naughty behavior began to diminish after just a few days.

There is much you can do to enrich and enhance your little child's play. She is at the stage when adult suggestions sensitively given can do a great deal to help her make imaginative leaps in her pretend play, and also to find out many wonderful ways in which play materials can be used.

The results
Referrals to speech and language therapy peak at this age, and I am always sad when I see the children who have not been played with. Their experience is already so much more limited than those who have had the benefit of an adult who was interested in their play. One little dark-haired girl called Mandy clearly had lots of toys at home, as she knew basically what they were for, but the ways in which she played with my toys were extremely limited. She approached the dollhouse, for example, and just piled the furniture into it at random. The dolls were just pushed around, and there was no real play at all. We set up the BabyTalk program for her. Her mother, while being careful always to let Mandy choose their play activities, now showed her how the toys could be played with. She showed her, for example, how it was fun to put the dollhouse furniture in the same places that their real furniture was in at home, and how many different objects could be used to make imprints in Play-Doh. Mandy just loved these playtimes and within a few months

was playing in a much more appropriate way for her age.

Another little boy called Scott had been left in the care of many different baby-sitters, none of whom had really played with him. He handled my toys listlessly and without any evident enjoyment when he first came to the clinic and clearly did not expect any adult involvement in his play. I saw him

Make sure it's quiet during your playtimes.

again two weeks after his mother had established a daily playtime with him, and the difference gave me great pleasure. Scott handed his mother toys several times, looking at her expectantly, and avidly took up the play ideas she gave him. The two of them were clearly beginning to have real fun together.

Regular playtimes together build a bank of shared experiences that provide wonderful conversational topics. These conversations do so much for the little child's language development and her understanding of the world.

THE RIGHT PLACE

Make sure that the setting is still quiet and that you are unlikely to be interrupted.

Make sure that the toys are intact and are kept in the same place so that your little child knows exactly where they are and doesn't need to be distracted by searching for them.

Have a clear area of floor or tabletop so that she has plenty of room to play. Some of her pretend play may need a considerable amount of space. She may want her creations to be left up overnight.

HOW TO TALK WITH YOUR LITTLE CHILD

Continue to share her attention focus

As children get older, more and more of their conversation is not about the ongoing situation, but instead is about experiences they have had, and plans for the time ahead. This is very helpful for language development, as it enables the adult to use and the child to understand complicated sentences, such as "When we get to the park . . ." or "While we were out shopping, we saw . . ." Talking through past experiences also helps her to remember the sequence of events in her daily life.

Children who have not been given these conversational opportunities clearly show in their play that they are not at all sure about the meaning and purpose of their experiences, and consequently they live in a very confusing world. A little girl called Andrea came to my clinic for the first time the day after she had been taken to a restaurant. She playacted paying the waiter as soon as she arrived, and then handed him the bread rolls. The whole play sequence was chaotic, and it was plain that nobody had explained to her either before or after the event what it was all about.

Make sure that these conversations about nonpresent events are always initiated by her and conclude the moment her attention switches. Let her govern entirely how much of your conversation is about the here-and-now during your playtimes.

Bring in lots and lots of new words. Don't be afraid of extending her vocabulary. As long as you are following the focus of her interest, she will absorb them easily. As before, always show her exactly what you mean by using gesture and relating what you say to exactly what is happening at that moment. You might say, for example, after building a tower of blocks, "It's toppling over—oh dear—it toppled over" as it did so.

This shared attention focus, as we have said before, is the most vital precursor to all subsequent communication and cultural learning. An interesting English study[9] points to the skills of shared attention at this stage as laying the groundwork for understanding the thoughts and feelings of others at four to five years of age.

Help her to continue to enjoy listening

It's important that your little child continues to have lots of experiences where listening is easy, attractive, and lots of fun.

Repetitive rhymes and action rhymes like "The wheels on the bus" are great teaching tools that will help her later with learning to read. She will still love rhymes made up about herself that go with a traditional tune.

Coughing and sneezing are fun at this age. She'll find a pretend bout of sneezing hilarious.

Keeping your voice lively and tuneful should now be the natural way you speak to her, and you will also be speaking a little slower and louder than you do to an adult. A little pause between sentences helps her to listen easily to what you have said.

As before, it is often great fun to draw her attention to sounds made by her focus of attention, like the sound made when you open or close a jack-in-the-box. She will also still love other play sounds.

Say back to her what she means

Your little child now has a great deal to say, but still has not quite enough language to say it with. As before, when she mispronounces a word, make a point of using it in several little sentences—for example, "Yes, it's a gorilla. Gorilla's huge. A huge gorilla."

If her sentence is muddled or incomplete, model for her what she wanted to say. If she said, for example, "Daddy goed work," you could reply, "Yes, Daddy went to work."

As before, it is *extremely* important that you always make this part of the natural conversation. The golden rule is "Always start with a 'yes.'"

You may now run into what can be a very distressing situation when you don't understand what

> ## Don't let your sentences get too long.

she has said. I usually say something like, "I'm sorry—I didn't quite hear that" and if necessary, I encourage the little child to point and show me what she means.

Keep your sentences short during playtime

The best way to speak to your little child during BabyTalk playtime continues to differ from the way in which you speak to her the rest of the time. Her understanding is extensive now, and you really can chat away outside these times if all has gone well. Your little child herself, however, is still likely to be mainly using two- to three-word sentences that are a bit telegraphic, and she's also likely to have lots of immaturities in her pronunciation. These can easily combine, as we've seen, to make little children at this stage quite difficult to understand, particularly for people who do not know them well.

To help her through this stage as quickly as possible, it is helpful to keep your sentences short during your playtimes, while bringing in lots of new words. Try to limit some of your sentences to those containing not more than three important words, such as "Teddy's fallen off his chair," "On your chair, teddy," or "Don't fall off again."

I saw a bright little girl called Mary in my clinic recently. Her vocabulary and the way she was putting sentences together was fine, but I found her difficult to understand, because her speech sounds were confused. Her mother could understand her perfectly and didn't realize how difficult it was for other people. She was talking to Mary in long sentences, and it was evident that all Mary's attention was taken up with following their meaning. Once her mother began to give Mary a clear model of what she was trying to say, and to speak to her in short sentences for part of the time, Mary's speech quickly became much more understandable.

Continue to use repetition

Repetition is still helpful, particularly when you think you may be using a word she doesn't know. Bringing it into several different little sentences will quickly establish her understanding of it. You might say, for example, "I'm slicing. Slicing the potatoes. There—slices of potato."

Extend what she says

We have already talked about the fact that it is enormously helpful to give your little child a clear model of what she meant to say, when either her words or

Expand a little on what she has said.

her sentences are not quite clear. At other times, extend what she has said, as you did in the previous age, adding a little more information. You might, for example, reply to "Mommy went shops" with, "Yes, Mommy went shopping. She bought some new shoes."

Both of these responses are wonderful for building your little child's understanding. They give her lots of information about both grammar and the meaning of words in the form easiest for her to take in.[10, 11, 12]

Do remember the golden rules at all times when using these techniques. Always start with a "yes," and never ever give her the impression that you are correcting her in any way.

DON'TS FOR THIS AGE GROUP

As before, make absolutely sure that nobody *ever* corrects your little child's speech or asks her to say or copy words or sounds. Our role as adults is to talk to little children in the most appropriate way. We don't want to give her the message that we don't like the way she speaks.

Questions

A few questions are now permissible in addition to the rhetorical ones we have discussed before. Include some that can help her to remember sequences of events. Saying, for example, "Something came after the big swan—remember?" might help her to remember that she also saw some ducks. Do limit the number of these questions, and always answer them yourself if she doesn't.

Never ask her questions in order to get her to answer. This again is not part of normal communication, and she knows it.

<table>
<tr>
<td>

Make suggestions to develop her play.

</td>
<td>

Limit the amount of "negative" speech that you use. You will still need to move her bodily away from or toward things. There is plenty of time later to explain why some things are forbidden, and why she must do others whether she likes it or not.

Try to limit your use of the word "no" as far as you can. We as adults don't like to hear it, and neither do our little children. Talking more positively will help eliminate the number of tantrums you encounter.

</td>
</tr>
</table>

PLAY

Happy to be together

Your little child is almost certain to want you to join in her play, because you have been having so much fun together.

As you have done before, when you are playing together, make sure that you keep mainly to a running commentary that is related to her immediate focus of attention, as this is still a wonderful language learning situation.

Though your little child is just moving into the stage when she can be adult-directed in some situations, it is better not to do this at all in your play session yet. The optimum learning situation still involves following her choice of activity. I have seen many children whose parents became bossy as soon as they noticed that their little child was able to follow their directions. One such was Nigel, a dark-eyed, curly-headed four-year-old who was brought to see me because his speech was unclear. He approached the toy box, and as soon as I began to speak, put his hands over his ears. When I later saw him playing with his parents, it became clear why this had happened. They both (and sometimes at the same time) gave Nigel streams of directions like, "Come and look at this," "Now do this jigsaw," "Finish it," and "Right, now build with the blocks." The whole family became increasingly cross.

Although it's important not to overdo the directions, it can, however, be enormously helpful to make some suggestions to extend your child's pretend play. For example, if you were playing together at going to the doctor, you could show her the prescription pad, or if you were in the role of shop-keeper, show her how the cash register works.

Show her all the different ways in which play materials can be used. It could be fun, for example, to show her how you can build a double tower once she is adept at building a single one. It's best when showing her a new activity to start it and then to withdraw and let her try it out for herself. She'll let you know if she needs you. Just make sure that your suggestions are really only suggestions, and never turn into directions.

It has been found that children whose mothers showed a high level of intrusiveness had significantly lower language attainments than did a group whose mothers followed their children's lead.

OUTSIDE YOUR HALF HOUR

- Always talk through her daily routines.
- Explain to her why she cannot do certain things and must do others.
- Help her to join in your conversations by telling her clearly what is being talked about.

Thirty to Thirty-six Months

At the beginning of this age period, your child understands the names of virtually all the objects and people in his environment, all common verbs such as "eat," "sleep," and "play," and many adjectives like "big" and "small." He can follow complicated sentences from the words alone, without the help of clues given by the situation. He no longer needs to see his mother's library books to know that they are going to the library.

By the time he reaches the age of three, he is fully aware of the meaning of different question forms and responds appropriately to "why?" and "how?" questions. He also understands prepositions and will look in the appropriate places for something he has been told is "on" or "under" another object.

The number of words he can absorb from one sentence is another important step forward. Whereas at the beginning of this time he could only cope easily with sentences containing two important words, such as "*Teddy* wants his *hat*" or "Your *shoes* are *upstairs*," by the end of this time period, he can follow and remember a sentence containing three simple verbal commands such as "Go into the kitchen. Open the big drawer and bring me the ball of string."[1]

This ability, together with his growing understanding of how animals, people, toys, and events interact with one another and with him, enable the little child to listen to a simple story with great enjoyment.

For the first time he can deduce the meaning of something that is not stated directly. By the time he's three, he can understand that "later" means that he can do something in the near future but not immediately.

Words have a powerful influence over his behavior. If he were pedaling his tricycle, for example, and his brother shouted "Faster!", he would redouble his efforts.

His spoken vocabulary now increases very quickly, and he begins to use more and more grammatical markers like tenses and adverbs, several verb forms, and some plurals. His sentences lengthen too, and parents will notice that their little child is using complex ones. By the end of this time period, he may be using sentences containing four or five important words, such as "I'm going to the zoo to see lions and tigers." These sentences become steadily less telegraphic, and by the age of three, are hardly so at all.

Another major advance is that the little child now links two sentences together for the first time, either by "and" as in a sentence like "We went to the shop and bought some ice cream" or by "because," as in "Mommy was mad 'cause I spilled my juice."

He can now describe interesting experiences he has had in the recent past, and also name and talk about his scribbles, which are unlikely to be at all recognizable by adults. He can give more information, such as his first and last name if he's been taught to do so, and correctly answer the question "Are you a boy or a girl?"

By the time he is three, conversation is very different. The little child can initiate a conversation with ease, saying, "Listen, Mommy," or "I want to tell you . . ." Turn-taking in conversation is very well established, and by the end of this time, he can even handle interrupted turn-taking. He'll wait, for example, for his mother to complete what she was saying after breaking off to answer the phone.

He's well aware of how to respond appropriately to the contributions of his conversational partner, understanding when he is being asked a question or what to do if his partner has not fully understood what he has said.

The little child's awareness of what others know increases steadily, making it much easier for him to converse with people in the wider environment. He knows, for example, that if he wants the salesclerk to understand what fun he had in the water, he first has to tell her that he has been taken to the beach.

Speech is being used for an even wider range of purposes. He can now use it to express his problems as well as his feelings and needs. He might say, "I can't do it," "I lost the ball," or "I was frightened." He also uses speech when he wants to resist, with sentences like "I don't want to," or "I won't." Speech expresses humor too, and he will enjoy telling little jokes.

The little child still talks to himself a lot, and rather than just describing what he is doing, as he did at the beginning of this time, by the time he is three, he will be using speech to clarify his concepts and ideas. He may, for example, say something like, "These are all big ones—they're Johnny's. These are little ones—they're for the baby."

Words can now also help him to think about his behavior and how he is regarded by other people. He is keen for approval and will ask questions like "Is that right?"

By the time the little child is three, he has fully realized the significance of asking questions in the pursuit of information and may do so endlessly. Some of his questioning may seem like a game, and a great way of holding the adult's attention, particularly when he asks the same things over and over, but it is usually the outcome of a genuine wish to understand and to clarify the meaning of information.

Language and General Development

THIRTY TO THIRTY-THREE MONTHS

The number of words the little child understands continues to increase rapidly in this time, and as a result, he can follow more and more complex sentences. He comes to recognize not only virtually all common object names and action words, but also now the most common adjectives like "thick" and "thin," "tall" and "short." He also begins to understand prepositions, and will look in the right place for an object he has been told is "in" or "on" another object.

The little child is making important advances in realizing what information other people already have and what is new to them. He is aware, for example, that the milkman knows that he likes milk and the mailman knows that he gets regular postcards from his grandma, but that each does not have the information of the other.

He begins to use lots more grammatical markers now, although with considerable inaccuracy at first. He begins to use verbs like "can" and "will" and a variety of forms of the verb "to be" such as "is," "are," and "am." Mistakes like "him is going" are, however, frequent at this stage.

He starts to use articles, but not always in the right places. You might hear, for example, "A car's going" or "I want the cookie."

A final "s" to indicate plurals may be used, and pronouns like "he" and "they" are spoken accurately. The little child also begins to use "can't" and "don't" in the middle of sentences, as in "I can't do it" or "I don't want to go to sleep."

These developments not only serve to make the little child's sentences less telegraphic, but also enable him to use language in interesting new ways. He can make up imaginative little stories like "The train came out of the tunnel . . . and it went up the hill . . . and it fell over."

If his conversational partner doesn't understand him, he may not only repeat what he had said, but may now also change it to help his partner to understand his meaning.

The child at this age soon realizes the great power behind the word "why," both in obtaining information and in keeping the conversation going. As a result, he uses it frequently.

The little child is gaining more control over his large body movements. Not only can he hop with two feet together, but he can now jump down from a bottom step. He can pedal his tricycle more easily, kick a ball a little more forcefully, and march in time to music, which he finds a lot of fun.

He can match geometric forms such as triangle and square and fold a piece of paper in half. He recognizes tiny details in pictures and loves to point them out to an interested adult.

The little child can do much more for himself now. He can use a spoon and fork together and remove and put on simple articles of clothing. He even needs little help undoing and doing up buttons himself.

He will imitate a long sequence of actions he has seen an adult carry out, and usually does so correctly. He might pour the cereal, then add milk and sugar, and finally spoon it to his mouth.

By the end of this age period, he starts to join in play a little with other children, in games like chasing or kicking a ball.

THIRTY-THREE TO THIRTY-SIX MONTHS

By this time, he fully understands a wide range of prepositions, verbs, and adjectives and can even identify people by the actions they are engaged in, replying correctly, for example, to questions like "Which one is sleeping?" He can understand and remember instructions containing three important words, rather than only two. He would be able to respond appropriately to something like "Take the book off the shelf and give it to Daddy."

He has acquired many concepts now, about animals, people, and toys. He knows not only about their colors, shapes, and sizes, but about what they do and how they interact. As a result, simple stories depicting his everyday life become fascinating, and he follows them with great enjoyment.

The little child knows still more about what knowledge other people have and what is new to them. He might say to a stranger, "That's my baby in there—he's called Joey." He would be well aware that family members would not need to be given this information.

By the age of three, the little child will not only understand complex sentences, but may be using sentences containing up to three or four important words like "Mommy went shopping to buy trousers for work" or "Daddy's going to town in the car later." He even joins two together now, which is a great new departure. He may say something like "We went to the park and I dropped my tractor." His sentences are rarely telegraphic now, but many still contain a number of errors in grammar. After all, he has not been using these markers very long. Verbs are frequently still inaccurate, and sentences like "He wented out" are common.

He may use more correct plurals, both regular and some irregular, such as "trains," "houses," and "children." He may start to use "tag" questions like "isn't it?" or "doesn't it?," saying, for example, "Smoke comes out of the chimney, doesn't it?"

All these new skills now enable the little child to use language freely to relate interesting experiences he has had in the recent past and to describe in lots of detail what he sees in pictures. He can also now begin to tell little stories, although these are usually limited to one or two sentences. He might say, "The car went down the road and met a tractor. They had a big crash."

He is a much more skilled conversationalist now, and adults need to do much less of the work. He can start a conversation with a statement like "Mommy listen," and take turns skillfully, noticing, for example, that his partner has paused to think and waiting for her to continue.

He is very well aware of his conversational partner's intentions and understands whether he is being asked a question or being asked to clarify what he has just said. Conversations become much longer now, as he can take a number of conversational "turns."

By the time the little child is three, language has become his vehicle for thought, as it will be for the rest of his life. He talks to himself a lot when he is not having conversations with other people, as if he is practicing putting his thoughts into words. His questions become endless and can drive the adults in his life to the point of exhaustion. His interest in this wonderful world is boundless, and he now has the key to finding out all about it.

He may relish telling little jokes like, "Why did the chicken cross the road? To get to the other side!"

Once again, the little child's increased control over his body and the fact that many motor activities like walking and running are carried out automatically mean that he can give more attention to conversation and question-and-answer sessions.

He can walk upstairs one foot at a time and walk backward and sideways while holding a toy. He can throw a ball overhead and catch it between extended arms and can at last kick a ball forcefully, which makes him very happy. He can pedal his tricycle not only in a straight line but also around wide corners. He seems altogether much more aware of his body in relation to his surroundings, knowing for example what size space he can fit himself into and how to climb under and over obstacles, ducking to go under a barrier or clambering over a low fence.

He uses his hands more skillfully now. He holds a pencil near the point, with two fingers and thumb, and attempts for the first time to draw a person, producing a circle and two lines to represent legs. He is likely to be able to copy a shape, match six colors and name one, and count by rote to five.[2]

The little child can copy a bridge built from blocks and build a tower of nine to ten blocks. He can fold paper twice, cut with scissors, and put lids on and take them off containers with considerable dexterity.

He now begins to combine play materials. He will play with cars and blocks together, making a road or a garage. He may put a driver into the engine of a train, or boxes into a truck.

He is well versed in the routines of daily life. He can help to set the table and pour from a pitcher with little spilling. He drinks from an open cup with few accidents and can dry as well as wash his hands without help. He may dress himself, but may still put his shoes on the wrong feet.

He is becoming more interested in other children and what they are doing. He begins to play with them a little and awareness of the rules of turn-taking begins to emerge. He learns, for example, to wait for his turn on a swing or slide or to kick a ball.

The little child will play alone for short spells now, but needs to be constantly watched and to know that an adult is nearby. He loves to involve adults in his imaginative play.

By the end of this age period, your little child is likely to

- listen with great enjoyment to stories;
- understand little instructions with three important words, like "Open the box, take out the car, and give it to Daddy";
- talk about what is happening in a long monologue;
- take part in a conversation about something that has happened; and
- give his full name when asked.

Listening Ability

As in the previous time period, it is likely that your little child will have no difficulty in focusing on what he wants to listen to and tuning out all other sounds when he is in a quiet setting.

His knowledge of the meaning of the sounds in his environment is becoming more extensive, particularly now that he can ask questions about the noises he hears.

Attention Span

Your child's attention development has not changed greatly from the last age period. He can in some situations shift his attention focus from what he is doing to listening to an adult speaking to him and then return to his original focus, but never when he is deeply engrossed.[3] He can still only focus on one thing at a time and is still highly distractible. Even if he has stopped what he was doing in order to listen to you, he will immediately stop listening if something else occurs like a sudden noise or someone coming into the room. As in the last time period, if you need to talk to him about something that is not related to his immediate focus of interest, choose your moment carefully.

Warn him before changing an activity—for example, "We'll have to fetch Tim from school in a minute." If possible, wait until his attention is focused on you before you speak, and if you have to give him a direction, do so immediately ahead of the task, saying, "Coat on" as you hold his coat out to him.

Play

The little child's increased control of his body and hand-eye coordination enable him to do much more with the different play materials available to him. He develops greater skills in using scissors and drawing materials. In the course of his investigations, he continues to learn a great deal about colors, shapes, sizes, and textures. Pretend play also flourishes and includes very extensive role playing in which he likes to reverse the roles, taking turns with an adult, for example, at being dentist and patient.

He mostly plays alongside other children, but does now begin to involve them in his pretend play, turning it into a social activity. Another child might be involved in a pretend tea party and be instructed to drink from his cup.

The little child's extensive language skills now take him on imaginative flights of fancy. He can even confuse what is real and what is imaginary. I was amused recently when a friend described how her little boy Charles frightened himself with his own made-up story. He started talking about how a little boy went walking in a forest, and how it grew dark and he became lost. Charles began to get quite frightened, until his mother reminded him that it was only a story, which she quickly steered to a happy ending.

Your contribution to your child's investigative play is extremely important at this stage. It provides him with the proper information regarding his play materials. You can show and tell him all the different things he can do with his toys.

Take your child on little adventures. He will love to reenact a trip to the zoo or the park later on. He also needs time to watch others in his home engaging in activities like cooking or gardening. It's also wonderful for him if adults playing with him take on all the many roles he asks them to. As before, make suggestions about how the roles could be extended. He could be shown how the librarian stamps the books, and perhaps even given a play stamp.

It is enormously helpful for the same adult to play with the little child on a regular basis. She will know all about the games that have gone before, and when an activity is being repeated or extended. She will also of course know about the real experiences the little child has had and wants to reenact in his play.

INVESTIGATIVE PLAY

The little child now enjoys lots of active play, such as pedaling his tricycle and throwing and kicking balls. Sand and water are extremely popular with him, and he will play with these in more complicated ways, often using them as background for a play activity rather than just investigating their properties as he did before. He will enjoy sailing boats in the water or making roadways in the sand for his cars. He enjoys large play equipment such as a swing and a slide in the park (which should be used under close adult supervision), and becomes increasingly interested in playing near other children.

He still loves matching, sorting, and grading colors, shapes, and sizes and becomes increasingly skillful at doing so.

His cutting with scissors is more accurate, and he now becomes interested in copying an adult folding paper. He can do this vertically and horizontally, but interestingly, his visual perception is not yet mature enough for him to do so obliquely!

Construction materials like large Legos can be used in a variety of different ways, such as for making roads and houses. Like sand and water, these materials are now being used as means to an end rather than investigated in order to discover their properties.

PRETEND AND IMAGINATIVE PLAY

The little child will engage in very long sequences that represent accurately the activities of adults he's been observing for some time. He may pretend to wash teddy's clothes, put them out to dry, iron them, and then put them back on teddy.

He is still interested in role playing and now loves to dress up to make this more realistic. He will love to totter about on high heels being Mommy, or smoke a pretend pipe like Grandpa. He would find a fireman's or mailman's outfit enormous fun.

He reenacts less frequently occurring events now, such as going to the barbershop, and brings more and more detail into his play. He might not only pretend to cut someone's hair, but also carefully brush the "cuttings" off his client's shoulders.

The objects the little child uses to represent others can be less realistic now; a piece of string would serve as a stethoscope, for example. By the time he's three, he can do without any props at all. He may have an imaginary dog at the end of a piece of string, or talk to imaginary passengers when he's pretending to drive a bus. Many little children have an imaginary friend at this time.

He plays much more imaginatively with models and begins to combine them in order to elaborate his play. He may build a long road for his cars, or a runway for his airplanes. A tractor may be made to push a wagon, and a driver and passenger put into a bus or train. The train may now break down and need rescue, or stop at many different stations, representing all the places he has been. Farm and zoo animals may have all sorts of adventures, such as getting out and becoming lost and eventually returning safely to their homes.

Dolls and teddies are involved in much longer play sequences, and may, for example, be undressed, bathed, fed, and dressed in pajamas.

Glove puppets can be lots of fun now, and they may take on distinct personalities, enjoying all sorts of wonderful adventures.

TELEVISION AND VIDEOS

As you have done previously, please limit your little child's television or video watching to half an hour a day, and preferably watch with him so that you can discuss what he has seen and give him any necessary explanations.

Your choice of programs can again be determined by the same principles you apply to your choice of books. He will enjoy those in which characters who become familiar do the kinds of things that he does himself and will still relish lots of repetition of both scenes and activities. He will like some imaginative stories now, but as with books, be careful that he does not become frightened.

Rhymes and music will continue to appeal, as will slapstick humor, and he will also enjoy programs that address the kind of concepts he is interested in now, like those of size and color.

As before, *please do not be tempted to teach him to read yet*. Tell him about the pictures and read him little stories. When he initiates it, talk to him about the characters and events in the books and how they relate to his own experiences. These conversations will often be about past and future events, and they give wonderful opportunities for language input.

It is still the shared enjoyment of books that matters, and as we discussed in the last section, your little child is learning a great deal about how books work in terms of the conventions of print and illustrations. All this vital groundwork means that at the right time, he is likely to learn to read quickly and easily. Conversely, many children who are taught to read before they are ready are put off books for life and have a huge struggle learning to read.

When you read to him, bring in lots of drama by using a lively voice and perhaps using different voices for the different characters. (You can, by the way, still change the words or the stories a little at this stage, if you think they are too long for his attention span or that a change of wording would help his understanding.)

His language skills now enable him to follow a simple story, and his grounding of knowledge about how the world actually works is now adequate for him to differentiate between the real and the imaginary to a sufficient extent to enable him to enjoy some fantasy now.

Be careful that your little child doesn't become frightened by imaginary events. Make sure that you always help him to know what is and what is not real by discussing this, and if he does become frightened, change the story, particularly by ensuring a happy ending!

Again, there are many wonderful books that meet the criteria for this stage.

ARTHUR'S CHICKEN POX
Marc Brown

THE WIDE-MOUTHED FROG
Keith Faulkner

LADYBUG ON THE MOVE
Richard Fowler

FUZZY YELLOW DUCKLINGS
Matthew Van Fleet

I LOVE YOU, BLUE KANGAROO
Emma Chichester Clark

THE TALE OF BEAR
Helen Cooper

WHEN MARTHA'S AWAY
Bruce Ingman

HARRY THE DIRTY DOG
Gene Zion and Margaret Bloy Graham

Causes for Concern

Below are circumstances in which it would be advisable to seek professional advice about your baby or little child's language development. (Please remember, though, that rapid progress in one area can result in a temporary delay in another.)

It is important to recognize, too, that no checklist can be a substitute for a professional opinion. If you are in any doubt, even if the reason for your concern is not mentioned here, do take your baby or little child to see a speech and language therapist as soon as possible.

Your little child may need some help

- if he frequently doesn't seem to understand what you have said;
- if he often doesn't seem to know what other people already know (for example, when he uses names, is he aware of whether the other person knows who the person is?);
- if he often says things that seem to you to be irrelevant;
- if he still uses sentences of only two or three words;

- if he doesn't use any little grammatical markers like an "s" at the end of a word to mark a plural;
- if he never asks questions;
- if he shows no interest in stories;
- if he shows no interest in playing with other children;
- if people outside the family find him difficult to understand; or
- if his attention span is still very short most of the time.

The BabyTalk Program

THE RIGHT TIME

Daily play

Keep up your daily half-hour playtimes! He still needs you to be very much aware of his attention level, and as we have seen in the section on play, you can do a great deal to enhance his development. In particular, your regular availability as a play partner is a wonderful gift to your little child. His emotional development will benefit immensely from this undivided attention, and you will boost his confidence by encouraging and praising him. These times also give you opportunities for discussing your daily lives, including any new rules he needs to follow. Explaining the reasons before implementing a rule can minimize tantrums.

(He's at the age when little children sometimes test the rules by deliberately silly behavior like refusing to do something or claiming they can't do something you know they perfectly well can. If you do have to reprimand him, try always to criticize the behavior and not your little child. It's much better to say "That was a silly thing to do" rather than "You're a silly boy.")

These playtimes will also give you an opportunity to answer his endless questions for as long as he wishes to continue with them. It can be difficult to do this in the hurly-burly of everyday life, but he will learn so much from being able to pursue an inquiry for as long as he wishes. Playtimes give him wonderful opportunities to practice his newly acquired conversational skills.

I remember a little three-year-old called Guy, who was brought to see me because there were concerns that he would not be able to make himself understood in the playgroup he was about to enter. It transpired that Guy had three extremely talkative sisters, and throughout his life had had few opportunities to spend time alone with one adult. As a result, he hadn't engaged in any kind of extended conversation and had not learned the basic rules like how to start a conversation, or how to take turns. He constantly interrupted other members of his family, which made them angry, and often didn't listen to their replies. Once we established daily one-to-one playtimes for him with his mother, Guy quickly began to learn these skills. He entered the playgroup three months later and settled in without any problems.

One-on-one attention

Yet another reason that these playtimes can be so important for some little children is that it is a common age for a new baby to come upon the scene. Feelings of jealousy and displacement can be greatly alleviated by these times alone with one adult. Wait until your partner gets home and can mind the baby, or bring in a friend or relative for half an hour a day if necessary.

This time can be a particularly important one if your little child has experienced a distressing event like the split-up of his parents or the loss of a family member. It is important that he has the opportunity to talk about the event and how he feels about it and to ask questions about it. In particular, it gives you the opportunity to reassure him that what has happened is in no way his fault, which is something that little children often tend to assume.

Please do not be tempted to turn your playtimes into teaching sessions. Your little child is now likely to be showing interest in concepts like color, number, and shape, and many adults think that teaching these puts their child at an educational advantage. Do not waste your precious time together doing this. Bring the names of these concepts into the conversation only as they arise naturally, such as naming "the blue car and the yellow car" as you play racetrack or "the long brick fits next to the short one" as you build.

I have seen many children who could name lots of colors and shapes and who knew the alphabet and recited it like robots, but didn't know what the objects were that they were describing or what to do with them. Their parents had taught them these concept names almost to the exclusion of normal conversation.

One such child was Dan, a three-year-old who was brought to see me because his language development was very delayed, and whose most frequent phrase was "I can't." His mother had had the notion that children acquire skills much more quickly if they are taught them, and she had spent hours each day trying to teach Dan to walk when he was five months old, and had started to teach him the letters of the alphabet and the names of colors, numbers, and shapes before he was a year. Dan had become an extremely aggressive and frustrated little boy, whose development was showing delay in most areas. Once his mother started to move from her agenda to his, following his interests and commenting on them instead of teaching him, he quickly relaxed and started to learn. His behavior soon started to improve as well, and his language development caught up with his age level within a few months.

Another such boy was Tom, whom I first saw when he was nearly three. He had an uncle with learning difficulties and his parents were so anxious that Tom not be the same that they spent every available moment teaching him to count and to say the alphabet. Like Dan, he hadn't the least idea what these letters and numbers meant, and because of all the time the teaching had taken, he had missed out on a huge amount of play and conversational experience. He said very little spontaneously, and instead, frequently echoed what he had heard. His attention was at the fleeting level, and he showed hardly any pretend play. Happily, he also made huge progress very quickly once his parents stopped teaching him and became aware of his attention focus.

Conversations that arise naturally enable the little child to acquire the vital understanding of what prior knowledge different people have, and what they need to be told in order to join in the conversation. We all need this information to a high degree if we are to communicate successfully with one another. Conversations also help him to understand the different ways in which we all use language, such as commenting, questioning, and requesting clarification.

Your little child will need to have a wide variety of toys and play materials available, including those for investigative and pretend/imaginative play. As you did before, make sure that the toys are intact and are kept where your little child can easily find them. He may well want to combine different toys and play materials now, like using blocks to make a road for his cars, or people to put in a train, so do keep this in mind when you assemble his toys.

Make sure too that there is adequate floor and table space for him to play, and if possible let him leave constructions like roadways or runways up overnight. I remember Paul, a friend of my elder son, at this age. He and my son spent a whole afternoon building a farm, with walls and houses for the animals. They were very proud of the display. Unfortunately, Paul's father did not allow the boys to leave their construction up, insisting that they dismantle it almost immediately after it was completed. At the end of the afternoon, when I arrived to collect my little boy, both children were in tears.

HOW TO TALK WITH YOUR LITTLE CHILD

Continue to share his attention focus

Although your little child can now in certain situations follow a direction from you, it is still much better during your playtimes to follow his lead. You will find that you are now having lots of conversations about interesting things that have happened to him in the recent past and things you are planning for the near future, but as before, always let him determine entirely how much you talk. Always stop a conversation as soon as his attention switches to something else, whether this be another topic of conversation about past or future events, or whether it is about something in the here and now.

Although your little child is becoming competent in many ways, his attention is still entirely single-channeled. He really can only think about one

> *Continue to follow your little child's focus of attention.*

thing at a time, whereas it is likely that many thoughts not connected with the here and now go through your mind in the course of your playtime.

I have seen so many parents who did not understand this and complained about their children's concentration. One such was a little girl called Maria. Her mother spent lots of time playing with her, but wanted the two of them to complete each play activity and tidy it away before starting on the next one. I watched the two of them thoroughly enjoying a tea party game one day. After a while, and just after her mother had introduced another character, Maria lost interest in the game and moved toward the paints. Her mother insisted that she sit down at the tea party again, but it was clear that the little girl was neither enjoying it nor listening at all to what her mother was saying to her, instead constantly looking toward the paints.

Lucy was another little three-year-old who had the opposite problem. Her parents both played with her at the same time and wanted her to complete a large number of activities in the limited time they had with her while her baby brother was asleep. Poor Lucy had barely completed an activity when it was whisked away, giving her no time to admire the result of her efforts!

Have a conversation

Conversing with your little child will become much easier for you as this time period progresses. Many of your conversations are likely to be extensive now and will include not only discussions about things he and other people have done, but also now the reasons for doing them and the feelings associated with them. The opportunities for a rich language input are boundless. You can use as many new words as you like now, and do not be frightened of doing so. As long as they are used in the context of his interest and attention, he will very quickly come to understand them. As before, repetition is very helpful when you think that a word may be new to him. Put the word into several different little sentences such as "It's a tarantula. Look—the tarantula's running. What a big tarantula."

> *Use lots of new words.*

Make your response part of the natural conversation.

You can also use a wide variety of grammatical structures. Don't worry now about simplifying your sentences—just use whatever sentence form seems appropriate. Your little child is acquiring these grammatical markers very fast now, and as long as they are used in the context of his chosen focus of attention, he will rapidly increase his knowledge.

Say back to him what he means

As we have discussed earlier, your little child is busily beginning to use more grammatically complex sentences. It is still helpful indeed, when you notice that your little child has not got a sentence quite right, to say it back to him correctly. If he said, "We wented to the park," you could say, "Yes, we did— we went to the park. We went this morning."

Make sure that your response is always part of the natural conversation, and never gives him the impression that you are correcting him. Don't forget to start with a "yes."

Your little child will still almost certainly be mispronouncing some words, as we do not expect the whole speech sound system to be in place until the age of seven. As before, it is helpful to say back to him clearly words he has mispronounced, in several short sentences. If he said, "It's a big simney," you could say, "Yes, it is big—it's a very big chimney. The chimney nearly reaches the sky!" This gives him the best possible chance of noticing all the sounds in words and the order in which they appear.

Say back clearly what he has said.

Expand on what he says

We talked in the last section about how helpful it is to expand on what your little child has said. He might say, "The clown had a funny hat," and you could say, "Yes, he did. It had a bobble on the top. The bobble waggled about and made us laugh." You are likely to find that these expansions lead to interesting conversations.

Questions

You are likely to find yourself asking more of the kind of questions we discussed in the last section, which are designed to help the little child remember the sequences of events he has experienced. The question "Do you remember what the dentist did after he cleaned your teeth?" could lead to a useful recapitulation of the morning's events. It's still important to limit the number of questions, though,

> *Don't ask questions in order to get him to speak.*

and always to answer them yourself if he doesn't. For example, if that particular sentence were greeted with a silence, you could say, "He gave you your coat and a sticker to put on it."

Once again, never ask questions in order to get your little child to answer. I remember an enchanting three-year-old called Mike who was brought to our clinic because he was having difficulty putting words into sentences. His mother was asking him a constant stream of questions designed to force him to put words together, like "Is that a big bus or a little car?" and "Are these your black socks or your white gloves?" Mike steadfastly refused to answer and began to ignore the presence of other people altogether. As soon as his mother started to turn most of her questions into comments relating to his focus of attention, he became the greatest fun to play with. He had lots of imaginative ideas and a wonderful sense of humor.

It's fine, of course, to ask questions to which you do not know the answer, such as "Would you like milk or juice?" This kind of question may now include those asked in order to clarify what's in your little child's mind, such as "Do you want teddy to have the next turn or me?"

P L A Y

Developing play skills

In terms of investigative play, the first essential is to provide him with lots of appropriate materials, such as chalk or different colors and sizes of paper for drawing, and toys that can be used with water, sand, and Play-Doh. Show

> *Help him to extend his play.*

your child what exciting things can be done with all these materials, like drawing with white chalk on black paper, or tracing his hand or foot. Of course, you will pick the moments when he looks to you for such suggestions. He's likely to try to do more difficult things now, like cutting and folding paper, or building complicated structures, and often a little help, tactfully given, can be very welcome. As you did before, you will find it best to extend the skills he has already. When he can cut relatively skillfully with scissors, you could show him how doubling the paper over before cutting makes an interesting shape. It's best to show him an activity or extension to an activity and then retreat, leaving him to have a try himself. He will not hesitate to let you know when he wants you to be involved again.

There may also be opportunities to help him understand turn-taking in play. By the end of this time period, he is likely to enjoy matching games like picture dominoes. Learning to take turns becomes a natural part of the game.

You can be of just as much help to him in terms of his pretend/imaginative play. Again, providing materials like dress-up clothes or some of your old jewelry or shoes can stimulate wonderful games. You are likely to find yourself in all sorts of roles like the dentist or the hairdresser, as he seeks to find out what these people do and why they do it. He will love to reverse the roles with you, too. As before, you can add suggestions like showing him how the barber sweeps the hair clippings from the floor or the dentist makes the water swirl around in the basin. (Of course, you will never persist if he is not interested in your suggestions.)

When he plays with model toys, like farm or zoo animals, you can also help to extend his play by offering suggestions and new scenarios—for example, that a train breaks down and the engineers come to repair it. (It's important to make sure, however, that such suggestions are within his experience and are therefore meaningful for him.)

When he starts to combine materials, like making a road for his cars out of blocks, you will also find opportunities to elaborate the game, like adding traffic lights or a crossing.

Your little child may bring pretend people into his play by the end of this time period and will be delighted if you join in with his imaginings. You could even help him to extend the personalities of these people, and of course you will be very interested in the activities of his imaginary friend if he has one!

> *Keep lots of tune in your voice.*

Make sure that he continues to enjoy listening

It is still helpful to ensure that your little child has plenty of opportunities to enjoy listening, particularly to voice. Those repetitive rhymes and action rhymes we've been talking about for so long are still wonderful for this, such as "Ring around the rosie," "Row, row, row your boat," "Here we go round the mulberry bush," and "The wheels on the bus." He'll relish silly songs and chants now and, as before, jokes made around coughing and sneezing. Exaggerated expressions of surprise and horror will also amuse him mightily!

Please continue to speak to him a little slower and louder than you would to an adult, with lots of tune in your voice. This is still the most attractive kind of speech for him to listen to. Keep your play sounds up too when playing or reading.

Don't let your sentences get too long during playtimes

As we have seen, the little child now understands an enormous number of words. There is still, however, a limit to the amount of information he can deal with in one sentence (although he may understand every individual word in a long one). Keep the sentences limited to three main concepts, like "Grandma is going on a bus to the store."

There is another important reason for limiting your length of sentence in your playtime. The little child is beginning to use lots of the little grammatical markers like "s" at the end of a word to mark plurals,

> *Don't let your sentences get too long.*

and different forms of verbs. This is really no small task to sort out. Think of all the variations of the verb "to be," for example, which include "am," "is," "are," "were," "will be," and so on. He needs time to observe and absorb them all. When we use very long sentences to little children, they do not have much chance of noticing all the grammatical markers. Many of these are in fact in the unstressed part of the word. It would be very easy, for example, to miss the ending of the word "walked" in a long sentence.

DON'TS FOR THIS AGE GROUP

Never correct his speech, and make sure that nobody else does either. His pronunciation is likely to be immature for some time yet, largely because he has not yet noticed where every sound goes in every word, and also because he hasn't quite attained the necessary coordination of tongue and lips to enable him to produce the more difficult sounds. Correcting the little child only serves to give a message that we don't like the way he speaks. As we have said before, the most helpful thing is to enable him to hear us saying the words clearly.

Don't set out to teach him

Provided that you spend time with your little child and follow his agenda in terms of your activities, he will now acquire vocabulary, grammatical structures, concepts, and the rules of social interaction effortlessly and naturally.

Were you to set the agenda and decide to teach him specific words or concepts, his learning would be nowhere near as fast and would be far less meaningful and interesting for him. I have seen many children who were in a state of considerable confusion about colors, shapes, and numbers because their parents had set out to teach them. The children had picked up their parents' anxiety for them to learn, and had, as a result, found learning difficult. Conversely, I have seen other children who knew every color by the age of two because they were particularly interested in them and their parents had noticed this and used the names incidentally while following their child's lead in play.

OUTSIDE YOUR HALF HOUR

- Let him do things for himself whenever possible (but be there to help if he is becoming frustrated!).
- Explain to him why he must do some things and cannot do others.
- Give him lots of opportunities to watch you and other adults carry out domestic routines like cooking and gardening.
- Talk him through his daily routines, telling him what is happening.
- Let him use large play equipment in the park.
- Give him opportunities to play near other children.
- Give him opportunities to act out his experiences, for example by playing at going to the barber or the dentist.

Three to Four Years

In the space of only four short years, your child will have acquired a vocabulary of thousands of words that she can both understand and use, along with all the basic sentence types that there are in the language. She will continue to increase her vocabulary throughout her life, as we all do, and will find more and more complex ways of putting sentences together, but she is now a fully verbal, communicating human being.

As we have seen, the little child understands a wide range of different kinds of words, including names, verbs, adjectives, and prepositions and has made the jump to being able to follow sentences containing three important words rather than just two. Her vocabulary may include less commonly heard words like "sharing," "slicing," and "pliers." She may also understand the meanings of indirect comments like "in a moment."

By the age of three and a half, she can follow sentences that have four important words, such as "The blue blocks are on the top shelf." She begins to understand similes and would be most amused, for example, to hear that someone had a nose like a strawberry. She also begins to be able to understand some metaphor, knowing that if she hears that someone is "under the weather," this means that they are not well. The little child's much greater awareness of words now means that she notices immediately if the words of a familiar song or story are changed, and she protests strongly.

At the beginning of this time period, the little child uses sentences containing three or even more important words and also begins to use some grammatical markers like a final "s" to indicate plurals. She links sentences by "and" and " 'cause" (because). As is the case with understanding, she also now takes big steps in her spoken language.

By the time she is three and a half, she uses much longer sentences, which include still more grammatical markers, including more plurals, correct use of the pronouns "he," "she," "you," and "they," and a variety of different negatives like "can't" and "won't." She links sentences together using "when," "but," "if," and "then." She may say, "I'm having ice cream when we go shopping," "I like it but it's too hot," "We'll go to the park if Daddy comes soon," or "We're going to the park and then home for a snack." These developments now enable her to express her meaning exactly and in great detail.

By the time she reaches the age of four, she uses all the basic grammatical structures in the language. Her spoken vocabulary is near five thousand words, and her speech, although still immature, is usually clear enough to be understood by strangers. She can now give a lengthy account of recent events and tell long stories in which fact and fiction get quite confused. Questioning is at its all-time peak and can seem endless to the adults around her.

When she reaches the age of four, the vocabulary she understands includes words that are less frequently heard, like "solid" and "furry," and the length of sentence she can follow contains five important words, such as "The big dog is in front of the farthest gate."

Language is well established as a means of thinking, and the little child can be heard working things out and solving problems as she chatters to herself. She might say, "That piece goes there . . . but if it does, there will be no room for that one," or "I know, I'll have to turn that one around," or "I'm going, Johnny's going—and Joey can come too if he has finished his snack."

At the beginning of this period, she was already a skilled conversationalist and could initiate, maintain, and repair breakdowns in conversation. Language had begun to be a vehicle for thought, and a way in which humor could be expressed. She had also made the wonderful discovery that questions bring information.

Language now becomes more a tool for thinking, learning, and imagining. The little child uses it for virtually all the purposes that adults do, albeit some in a rudimentary way. By the age of four, language becomes extremely important in helping the little child to develop and maintain her social relationships, both with adults and with her peers. She can, for example, negotiate and bargain, making comments to another child like, "I'll have this one first, and you have that. Then we'll switch." She can explain rules as in statements like "The counter starts there, and then goes this way" and make threats such as "I won't play with you anymore." She can also tease, saying things like "You can't have it . . . no, you can't . . . yes, you can!"

She also uses language to discuss her own actions and what she thinks of them. She can be critical of herself, saying, for example, "That was silly." She can also congratulate herself with comments like "I did a great drawing today."

Language and General Development

THREE TO THREE AND A HALF

At the beginning of this age period, the little child understands a wide range of verbs, adjectives, and prepositions and can follow sentences containing three important words, like "Teddy's on the biggest chair."

She has begun to understand the meaning of indirect comments like "in a minute" and has acquired a considerable amount of awareness of what other people do and do not already know, which helps her to converse with a wider range of people.

By the time she reaches the age of three and a half, she also understands words that are much less commonly heard, like "delivery" and "horrible," and can follow sentences containing four important words, like "Baby's yellow cup is in the kitchen." She begins to enjoy similes and even metaphors if she has heard them used.

Most of the little child's understanding, however, is still strictly literal. I was amused recently by a story a friend told me. She had taken her little boy Charles to his grandmother's house, and his grandmother opened the door to them, saying, "I'm having such a fight with my bedspread." Charles fell about laughing, saying "You can't fight with a bedspread!"

The little child's great interest in and awareness of words means that it is no longer possible for an adult to change the wording of a song or story without being greeted with strong protests.

She does not always listen fully to the answers to her questions, being more interested in how they fit in with her own thoughts. You might be giving a detailed explanation of how bulbs develop into flowers, in reply to a question, only to be greeted with the inane response, "There are lots of flowers in the park."

By the time she's three and a half, she starts using complex sentences with more correct grammatical markers, including past tenses, present tenses, and plurals both regular and irregular, like "babies" and "women."

She now uses the pronouns "I," "you," "we," "she," and "they" correctly, and her questions are worded in the right order. She will say, for example, "What are you doing?" rather than "What you are doing?" as she would have earlier. She uses a variety of negative forms, including "can't" and "won't," and links more sentences together with conjunctions. For example, she could say, "I want that one, but it's too hot," "We'll go out if it stops raining," and "I'm going on the swing, then I'm going on the slide."

These developments enable her to use language freely to express herself, and she now does so clearly and in considerable detail. She would have no difficulty in asking for "the big cookie with the chocolate on the top." She has become a skilled conversationalist, initiating, maintaining, and repairing breakdowns in conversation. She has strategies for initiating conversation, with opening questions like "Do you know what?" and is much more able to communicate with strangers and her peers. She is very well aware of the conventions of conversation, knowing when she is being asked a question, or how to clarify something she has said.

When playing with a partner, she may carry on both sides of a conversation. She might say to herself, "I'm putting this here," and then turn to her partner and add, "and you put that one there."

She can participate in pretend conversations and switch from one kind of voice and way of speaking to another, using a deep gruff voice for a giant and a high one for a little child.

As always, language is not the only area in which there are great advances and developments. The little child at this age loves vigorous outdoor activities. She can kick a large ball and can also throw a small one several feet. She can hop, jump from a second step, and run smoothly now, without slowing down to go around wide corners. She can also run while she is pushing or pulling toys along.

By the time she is three and a half, the little child can cut along a line fairly well with scissors and trace a double diamond. She can copy the letters "V," "H," and "T." She becomes still more independent in caring for herself and can eat with a knife (if permitted) and fork and wash and dry her hands, arms, and face.

She relishes adult approval and will try to conform to the household rules by helping to tidy up her toys and sharing them with others.

THREE AND A HALF TO FOUR

By the time she reaches the age of four, she knows the meaning of many thousands of words, including all the basic types like nouns, verbs, adverbs and adjectives, and prepositions. She understands words that are infrequently heard, like "liquid," "forest," "eagle," "pasting," and "woolly."[1] Even more important, she now can follow sentences containing up to six important words, such as "Let's put both the big teddies under the long shelf" or "The big blocks are in the red box behind the door." There is very little everyday speech that she will not follow, and consequently she will be listening to and acquiring the meaning of new words and grammatical structures for much of the time, and not only when she is being spoken to directly.

By the time she reaches the age of four, the child's spoken vocabulary is around five thousand words. She has also acquired the ability to use all the basic grammatical structures of the language (although she still makes mistakes from time to time). All that remains for the future is to acquire more vocabulary and to use grammatical structures in more complex ways.

The extent to which she can use language to plan and problem-solve is evidenced by her use of sentences like "I think we'll let Tommy come too" and "I want to play outside, but it's going to rain."

The little child's speech is usually easy to understand now, despite some continuing immaturities. She is likely still to substitute an easier sound for a more difficult one, like "tare" for "chair," and to simplify difficult clusters of sounds, as in "sibble" for "scribble." It may be another two years or even more before these are all correct. Some children do not pronounce the difficult sounds "r" and "th" correctly until they are seven years old.[2]

The little child at this stage seems to revel in her new linguistic abilities and becomes very talkative indeed. She can give coherent accounts of recent events and future plans and can tell long stories in which fact and fiction are considerably confused, reflecting her difficulty in separating the two. She may make up wonderful excuses and fabrications that she comes to believe herself! She may assure you that a giant came down the chimney and knocked over her juice. She can give identifying information, including her full name and address.

Questioning is at its peak. The questions differ now from those of earlier times in that rather than relating to simple cause and effect ("Why is that wet?"), they relate to her desire to understand both nature and the social world. Questions like "Why did that lady give . . . ?" or "How do birds fly?" are age-appropriate.

The little child is a skilled conversationalist, helped by her greatly increased social awareness. She is competent at initiating conversation, by calling a name or using a phrase like "I want to tell you something," and finishing by changing topic or starting a different activity. She notices straightaway when her partner is looking puzzled and quickly repeats or rephrases unclear words or sentences before she is asked. Her timing of conversational "turns" approximates that of adults. She chooses, for example, an appropriate time to join in other people's conversations, waiting for a pause in which to do so and keeping to the topic under discussion. She will continue to take turns for longer in a conversation and may nod or say "yes" to acknowledge what her partner has said. She may even adapt her speech to suit different conversational partners. She could speak very simply to a baby, for example, and politely to an authority figure like a playgroup leader, being careful to use "good morning" and "please" and "thank you"—which may get forgotten at times at home and with her peers.

Her knowledge of what prior knowledge her conversational partners have is extensive, but not yet complete. She could still forget that her preschool teacher didn't know that she went to the beach on the weekend, even as she launches into a lengthy description of the waves.

She can bargain, saying to another child, "You can go first on the slide, and I'll go first on the swing," and negotiate—"I'll give you all these blocks if you let me choose what we build." She will also threaten, with statements like "I'll take them all away if you don't let me have a turn!" She can use language to state rules, as in "You put the piece on this square first," and even as a means of establishing an alibi, with a comment like "It must have been Johnny—I was outside." She will appraise her actions verbally too—"That was good" or "I didn't get that right."

The little child loves to play with language. She adores jokes and loves to use language to clown, for example chanting, "It's raining, it's pouring, the old man's snoring" repeatedly as she waves her arms vigorously in the shower. Malapropisms like "It's roaring with pain" for "It's pouring with rain" make her giggle.

Physically the little child becomes more skillful in terms of the active outdoor activities she loves. She can run to kick a ball, which now goes in her chosen direction, can catch a ball bounced to her, and can begin to use a large bat. She can run on tiptoe and turn sharp corners when she is running. She loves to climb ladders or trees. She can hop on one foot, skip, and pick up small objects from the floor by bending from the waist. She can jump from standing or running and can even turn a somersault. She is an expert bike rider now, maneuvering with dexterity at considerable speed.

The little child holds a pencil in the same way as adults do and steadies the paper with her other hand. She draws a person with head, legs, arms, eyes, and trunk and also a simple house. She can copy a cross. She is able to fold a piece of paper three times and crease it and can build a tower of ten blocks. She may be able to count to ten by rote, although she is far from understanding the concept of more than three as yet.

She is almost entirely independent in terms of dressing and undressing, only needing help with difficult fastenings. She can spread jam or jelly with a knife and brush her teeth herself. She loves to go on little errands—to mail a letter or water the garden.

By the time she is four, the little child tends to be a bundle of energy, extremely active and exuberant, and she finds it hard to sit still. She can be self-willed, and her behavior tends to go out of bounds at times. She may be quite impertinent, saying things like "I don't like you, and I won't do what you say." She can, however, cope at times with not getting her own way.

The little child becomes a considerable show-off and loves to become the center of attention by using mimicry, jokes, and teasing.

In terms of language development, by the time she reaches the age of four, your little child is likely to

- be understood by people who are not familiar with her;
- give a connected account of recent events;
- give her address and age;
- ask endless questions;
- listen to and tell long stories;
- use language to bargain and negotiate; and
- use social terms like "please" and "thank you."

Listening Ability

If you have been following this program, your little child will have no difficulty in listening in a quiet environment. It is still more difficult for her than for an adult, however, to listen when it's noisy, so don't be surprised if she responds to you more slowly outside your quiet playtimes.

Attention Span

The little child for the first time becomes able to shift her attention focus by herself from what she is doing to someone speaking. She no longer needs an adult to cue her by calling her name, but rather she will notice on her own and shift her attention from what she is doing in order to listen. This shift of focus is not quick; she often takes some time to register that someone is speaking and to stop to listen. The more she is concentrating on what she is doing, the longer she takes to shift her attention focus and the more quickly she returns to the task at hand.

Her attention is still single-channeled. She cannot, until the end of this time period or even beyond it, listen to someone talking about an object or action unconnected with what she is doing.

The little child still needs warning when there is to be a change of activity, plus time to make a shift of attention focus. It is helpful if any necessary directions are given not far ahead of what she is being asked to do. Instructions like "Wash your hands before lunch" are still best given shortly before she is required to wash up.

Play

Play becomes a cooperative social activity at this stage. The little child now delights in playing with her peers, although she will also still play alongside them at times. Her newly acquired skills in language enable her to discuss and agree to plans and rules. She learns to take turns, to explain herself, to listen to others, to negotiate, and to understand their points of view.

The little child has a good working knowledge of the properties of the toys and play materials available to her and the language skills with which to think about them imaginatively and creatively. Individual differences in play preferences begin to emerge. Lifelong interests, in art, music, or science, may begin at this stage.

Investigative play

The little child enjoys active outdoor play. She loves to ride her tricycle and to run, jump, and kick balls.

She still loves sand and water play and likes to pour these materials to and from different containers. More often now, however, she takes part in more complicated play—with vehicles and play people. The little child continues to learn a great deal about size, weight, texture, and volume from these materials.

She starts to enjoy a wider range of modeling materials, such as clay or Play-Doh, and will use them constructively to make objects for her games, like food for a doll's tea party or structures like pens for her farm animals. She starts to experiment with the materials too, discovering, for example, that patterns can be made by pressing different objects onto them.

She now also likes using "junk" materials constructively, building boxes and tubs into wonderful constructions, both indoors and out.[3]

The little child relishes being involved in real activities like gardening and cooking. Her joy at producing cookies or jelly or watching a bulb she has planted flower is boundless. She will also marvel at silkworm or butterfly cocoons and the transformation of tadpoles into frogs.

Pretend and imaginative play

Pretend play develops into social play in which different children take different roles, for example, that of a shopkeeper and people taking turns making purchases.[4] This occurs in short spells initially, as the children still have much to learn about how to organize and maintain such play. Cooperation is a very new skill. There is not yet much of a plot or a sequence of events to the play—that will come later.

When there are no other children available, the little child will, as before, act out experiences she has had—like going to the doctor—and will love adult involvement in such play. She may now also act out events from a story or television program, such as pretending to be a runaway train or a monster. She likes realistic props like a shopping bag, cash register, and play money.

Pretend play with roadway, garage, farm, or zoo becomes more elaborate, and will often be enjoyed by two or more children at the same time. One child might be in charge of the farmer and load up the tractor, while another will see that the animals are returned to the field.

Little children at this age start to enjoy playing simple competitive card games such as Go Fish and board games like bingo. Simple party games like musical chairs can be played, and the children become interested in learning the rules, and enforcing them when necessary!

THREE AND A HALF TO FOUR

Investigative play

By the time she reaches the age of four, she loves to test herself to the limit, jumping as high and as far as she can and doing stunts like riding her tricycle in a standing position.

Her manipulation of creative materials is much more coordinated than it was earlier. She enjoys painting and drawing and also loves to use many different media, for example printing with potato cuts and other materials, making rubbings and collages, cutting out and pasting.

She will use "junk" like yogurt cups, lids, tubs, and boxes to create wonderful constructions like a fire station or a castle. Her interest in cooking and gardening is undiminished. She likes to do more difficult puzzles, and uses construction material like Legos to make elaborate structures. She likes smaller construction materials and will use them, for example, to make buildings to go with her airport.

Play with construction materials like blocks or bricks becomes cooperative and several children may collaborate on a building. Of course, there is not always harmony and agreement, and squabbles are not at all infrequent. Children at this age are often alternately cooperative and aggressive both with one another and with adults. They can, however, show considerable sensitivity to others, particularly to siblings and playmates who are in distress.

Cooperative games now become very popular, such as follow the leader and Simon says, as do simple card and board games.

Materials like large boxes and blocks can be transformed into a shop, a plane, or anything else needed for a game.

Little children at this stage are fascinated by sprouting peas and beans, in watching bulbs flower and tadpoles and butterflies grow. They love to watch birds eating bird food from a feeder and become greatly interested in caterpillars and spiders.

Pretend and imaginative play

Group pretend play really develops at this age. The little child makes social advances and acts out a whole sequence of events, like going to the hairdresser or barber, or even something from a book or television program. Imaginary themes start to come in, like stories of dragons or monsters. A decision may be made to have a pretend fire, rescue all the people in the building, and put out the blaze. This extended pretend play may at times include fantasy—for example, a fire engine coming from the sky to the rescue. The play can be enhanced by dressing up, and the little child may try to act, changing her voice and movements to fit different characters.

A playhouse can be lots of fun for all sorts of domestic play and offers opportunities to take many roles.

Dolls are often involved in imaginary play, like being train passengers who experience a crash and are taken to the hospital.

TELEVISION AND VIDEOS

At this age TV and videos can be a good source of information, learning, and sheer fun. As with books and play, little children show more marked individual preferences, but certain programs are pretty universal.

The little child will love stories, particularly about characters who become familiar to her by appearing in a series of programs. She likes to predict what will happen next. Imaginary events can be fun, but remember that she still has a lot of difficulty separating fact from fiction and may need some help. The word "pretend" is a useful one now. Remember too that her understanding is literal and she could become confused by figures of speech like "The giant's feet were like tree trunks."

THE TOY BOX

As always, the suggestions for additions to the toy box are divided into those that are likely to be used for investigative, pretend, and social play.

Investigative and Creative Play

Clay

Finger paints

Felt-tipped pens

Sponges for painting

Stamps and other materials for printing

Tissue paper

"Junk" such as cardboard tubes, boxes, yogurt cups, pipe cleaners, shoelaces

Large boxes for outside constructions

More difficult puzzles

Plants and bulbs

Bird feeder

Silkworm or butterfly cocoons

Tadpoles

Pretend and Imaginative Play

Realistic dolls that can be involved in prolonged imaginative sequences

Playhouse

Model houses, trees, and people for sand play

More dress-up clothes, such as those for a fireman or doctor

Hobbyhorse

Farm or zoo play set

Floor road map

Social Play

Simple card games like Go Fish and Old Maid

Bowling

Board games like picture dominoes, bingo, Chutes and Ladders, or Candyland

THE BOOKSHELF

The little child can fully discover the delights of books as a means of obtaining information, as food for the imagination, and as highly enjoyable entertainment.

As in play, children's individual preferences will begin to emerge more strongly, and it may be helpful to go to the library to discover what she really likes before buying. My daughter and my elder son loved anything and everything I read to them, so I was surprised when my younger son showed a strong preference for specific stories.

Though she'll still enjoy stories relating to her everyday life, she can now enjoy imaginative stories. It's important to recognize that little children at this stage may have difficulty in separating fact from fiction, as their experience of the world and its wonders is still limited. They need adult help, particularly with stories that are potentially frightening. Although they are just beginning to recognize figures of speech, their understanding is strictly literal, and they may therefore be confused by analogies that are not explained clearly to them. A sentence like "a blanket of snow" may perplex her, as she is unable to see the connection between her cozy blanket and the cold outside.

Traditional stories like *The House that Jack Built*, *The Three Little Pigs*, and *Goldilocks and the Three Bears* are favorites. Little children love the repetitive words and sound patterns, and these stories all have elements that arouse surprise and humor over and over again. You may find that when your little child has heard them many, many times that she wants to take her turn telling *you* the story!

She is likely to enjoy factual books about nature, particularly those aspects she knows. If she has seen frogs, she would love a book about how they develop from tadpoles.

Little children at this stage love to look at detailed pictures and pick out familiar parts of them. She is also likely to be interested in books about concepts like color, number, similarities and differences. Rhyme books are also great fun.

You may well find that she is now interested in the print, as she will have realized that the words on the page actually correspond to the words read to her. She may even recognize that a letter stands for a particular sound. If she spontaneously recognizes a word or letter and tells you what it is, that's great—but once again, please don't set out to teach her. It's not time yet.

There is a wealth of lovely books for this age group, and those suggested below are a tiny sample. As we said earlier, children already show strong individual tastes by this age. Follow the golden rule, and always give her the choice.

Make sure that you continue to share a book every day!

Stories Relating to Everyday Life

WHAT MAKES ME HAPPY?
Catherine and Laurence Anholt

WHAT'S THAT NOISE?
Francesca Simon and David Melling

TODAY I FEEL SILLY
Jamie Lee Curtis and Laura Cornell

Stories with an Element of Imagination

THE SNOWMAN
Raymond Briggs

ALLIGATOR SHOES
Arthur Dorros

COZY IN THE WOODS
K. K. Ross and Jane Dyer

CAN'T YOU SLEEP, LITTLE BEAR?
Martin Wadell and Barbara Firth

Factual Books

ANIMAL HOMES
Debbie Martin, Judy Tatchell, Alan Baker, and Jane Rigby

BUGS AND SLUGS
Judy Tatchell

1001 THINGS TO SPOT ON THE FARM
Gillian Doherty

FARMYARD TALES
Heather Amery

Books about Concepts
I CAN COUNT
Ray Gibson

FUN WITH NUMBERS
Ray Gibson

MOUSE PAINT
Ellen Stoll Walsh

SO MANY BUNNIES
Rick Walton and Paige Blair

STARTING TO COUNT
Jenny Tyler and G. Round

MY MANY COLORED DAYS
Dr. Seuss

SIZES
Jenny Tyler and G. Round

Rhymes
EACH PEACH PEAR PLUM
Janet and Allan Ahlberg

Rhymes and music will be very much enjoyed, and she will love jokes and slapstick humor even more than she did previously.

The little child tends to be extremely interested in nature at this time, and this is really where television and videos come into their own. They can show her things that are not possible either in her daily life or by means of other media. She can see many marvels—for example, a flower opening as she watches or the transformation of a chrysalis to a butterfly. She can also see animals in their natural habitats in many different parts of the world. (Watch with her, and be prepared to answer plenty of questions.)

Although at this stage television and videos have much that is of great value to offer, it is still important that you limit the amount of time your little child spends watching them. An hour a day really should be it. The powerful stimulus of the television screen will keep her attention for considerable lengths of time now, but do remember that the television doesn't answer questions, or explain the meaning of words, or even tell the little child what is fact and what is fantasy.

Causes for Concern

Below are circumstances in which it would be advisable to seek professional advice about your baby or little child's language development. (Please remember, though, that rapid progress in one area can result in a temporary delay in another.)

It is important to recognize, too, that no checklist can be a substitute for a professional opinion. If you are in any doubt, even if the reason for your concern is not mentioned here, do take your baby or little child to see a speech and language therapist as soon as possible.

Have your little child assessed by a speech and language therapist

- if she often looks puzzled, as if she doesn't understand what you have said, or doesn't do what you have asked her to;
- if she doesn't concentrate on anything for more than a few minutes;
- if she doesn't use grammatical markers like verb endings and plurals;
- if her speech is very unclear;
- if she can't recount something that happened when you were not present;
- if she doesn't ask lots of questions;
- if she doesn't want to play with other children; or

- if she shows or tells you that she is aware of her nonfluency or seems to be struggling to get the words out.

The BabyTalk Program

THE RIGHT TIME

Once a day, every day

Your little child has moved into the stage where play with other children becomes increasingly important. She will gain enormous benefit now from spending some time in a playgroup or preschool setting, and from children coming to visit your home. She will still benefit from her time alone with you, so please keep it up. You can do much to introduce her to creative activities and to help her to extend her play. Your regular attention gives her both great emotional security and the opportunities to discuss necessary prohibitions and requirements, greatly reducing frustration for both of you. It goes without saying that she will still relish the opportunity to have a captive adult to answer all her questions.

Over half of all children between the ages of three and four go through a period of "nonfluency" in which they repeat syllables or words many times. This happens because there is an enormous amount going on in their heads and they don't yet have enough language to express it all. The repetitions occur when the little child is trying to figure out how to put what she wants to say into words. She is totally focused on this thought process and unaware of the repetitions. This stage is completely normal and will pass within a few weeks or months, as her language skills develop. Parents can leap to the erroneous conclusion that their little child has started stuttering. They start saying things to the little child that are meant to be helpful, such as "Say it again slower" or "Take a deep breath before you speak." The little child, who was blissfully unaware of what was happening, is made aware and begins to try to stop the repetitions. This can actually *lead* to struggle and a stammer. So remember, never, ever draw the little child's attention to how she is speaking.

The only additional thing that can be helpful at this stage is to slow your speech down a little if your child is a rapid speaker. This will automatically slow her down without her being at all aware of it.

I'm thinking of Michael, an enchanting curly-headed three-year-old, whose mother had asked me to see him as a matter of great urgency. She told me that she was panic-stricken, as Michael had started stammering. She had two brothers who stammered, and she was very much aware of what a disability this could be. She had been trying to help Michael by reminding him to speak slowly, but felt that if anything, he was repeating more and more frequently. In my office, Michael launched himself at the toy box and began chatting away. He clearly had a great deal to say, and several times repeated a word up to fifteen times. It was evident that he was completely unaware of this and was totally relaxed, unlike his mother.

Michael's mother was immensely relieved to hear that he was going through a totally normal stage. She phoned me a few weeks later and told me that Michael's nonfluency had virtually stopped, all by itself.

THE RIGHT PLACE

As long as the two of you are alone together somewhere that is quiet, you can vary the setting for one-on-one communication. Your little child may, for example, love to spend time with you in activities such as gardening or setting up window boxes, putting out bird food, or cooking. A walk or trip somewhere can be wonderful, too.

If you are at home, make available to her materials for creative activities, like paint or clay, as well as some for investigative play and some for pretend.

HOW TO TALK

Follow her focus of attention

It is still important to follow her lead all the time in your playtimes. As before, it's important to let her determine entirely the extent to which your conversation focus is about the here and now and how much can be a discussion of past and future events.[5]

> *Never draw her attention to how she speaks.*

When you are focused on the here and now, avoid directions entirely, instead doing what I hope is natural to you by now and giving a running commentary on what is happening, when you are not actually engaged in conversation.

Do not be tempted to go a step further and start to teach her. She will learn so much more when she is given information incidentally as it relates to what she is interested in at that moment. She will be able to show you when she is interested in concepts like color and number by her choice of books or her conversation. Two studies, one from 1970 and one from 1989, both showed that children whose parents played with them did better on later school-related tests than those whose parents had tried to teach instead of play.[6, 7]

This reminds me of a little three-year-old boy called Ben, who was brought to my clinic because he was only using two- to three-word sentences, and even those were not at all clear. Three weeks after I first met him, and after lots of discussion with his father—who had had great difficulty abandoning his desire to teach Ben—I watched the two of them having a wonderful play session together. Ben had chosen a bag of large blocks of different shapes and wanted to make a complicated roadway with them. As he placed the blocks, his father commented on what he was doing, mentioning the shapes of the bricks incidentally, saying for example, "That's a good idea. The square brick fits nicely beside the rectangular one," and "The round one makes a very good traffic light." Ben, who had been very confused about the names of shapes, was using their names correctly within less than an hour!

PLAY

Developing play skills

Provide your child with appropriate toys and play materials, and show her all the wonderful different ways in which she can use them. Interest in activities your little child has been doing for some time can be enhanced by providing new materials, such as felt-tipped pens for drawing or sponges for painting. Add paste to paint to change the texture, so that you can make patterns in it with

Admire her efforts.

twigs, comb, or toothbrush. Give her clay for modeling, perhaps with different cutters and shapes to
press into it. Make rubbings of tree bark or other materials by putting paper on them and rubbing it with a
crayon. You could show her how to make a scrap-
book by cutting out pictures from magazines, or a col-
lage by crumpling tissue paper and gluing it onto
colored paper. (Remaindered wallpaper lining is a

cheap source of plentiful paper! And newspaper print shops will often give
you the ends of the rolls they take off the presses.)

An American study in the 1980s showed that merely providing appropriate play materials was enough to encourage advanced development in later
childhood.[8]

Clearly, if an adult not only supplies the materials, but also shows the little child how these can be used and helps her to do so, the child will benefit.
The two of you can have great fun experimenting with creative activities.
And think of the wonderful words that could be used in a tree-bark-rubbing
activity—"splintery," "flaky," "embossed," "outstanding," and "relief."

Praising and admiring what she produces does wonders for her confidence. She will love to see her pictures on the wall and her constructions on
the windowsill.

Your little child will love it if you play simple board games and card
games with her, and you can be of great help to her in explaining the rules
before she plays them with other children.

Your little child will love it if you make lots of suggestions in order to extend her play, such as showing her, when she's playing at being a firefighter,
how they slide down a pole to get into the fire engine, and how they coil up
the hoses. A shopping game could be extended by showing her where the
stock is kept at the back of the shop and how the shelves are refilled.

Always resist the temptation to take over, however many wonderful ideas
you might have. Never forget the golden rule of letting her lead. An American
study showed that parents who are too intrusive in their child's play actually
hinder their development.[9]

> *Make sure she still finds listening fun.*

If you have a little group of children in your home to play, make sure that they have adequate space in which to play and at least half an hour in which to do so. Provide materials like boxes, cartons, and blocks so that they can create structures such as boats or planes.

You can also be very helpful in sorting out disagreements, as the children do not yet have very extensive skills in doing this themselves.

Make sure that she continues to enjoy listening

Your child will now thoroughly enjoy singing, dancing to music, and clapping to the rhythm. She will also adore repetitive rhymes like "Old MacDonald had a farm" and "There was an old lady who swallowed a fly." Book time, too, gives her wonderful opportunities for listening. When a group of children are around, games like musical chairs and hot potato, which depend on listening, can be played.

Make funny noises to go with drawing and scribbling, like "wheeeee" to a circular scribble and "di domp di domp" to a zigzag one.

Your little child is still not too old to enjoy play sounds associated with water play and play with vehicles. "Shshshshsh" and "gugugugug" as water comes from the tap and runs away are always very amusing!

SENTENCE LENGTH

You no longer need to think about sentence length. Just chat away! Your little child will now be able to tell you if she doesn't know a word, ask what it means, or let you know if she wants you to repeat what you have said. It is still helpful to put a word that you think probably is new into several sentences, like, "It's an antelope. I think antelopes like to eat leaves. Antelopes seem even more graceful than some other kinds of deer."

There is no need to continue to speak slowly (unless your little child is going through the stage of nonfluency) or loudly or tunefully. She will already be interested in language and fully aware of how interesting it is to listen to!

She will make some mistakes with grammar, and there are likely to be some immaturities in the way she pronounces words. It is helpful, when this happens, to say back clearly what she has said. Never ever forget the rules. Always make your response part of the natural conversation, and always start it with a "yes."

Continue to expand on what she has said

As you did in the last age period, expand on what she tells you, adding some more information. She might say, "We went to the bouncy castle," and you could say, "Yes, we did, and teddy fell on his nose. Poor old teddy—he really did have a big bang on his nose!" It is also helpful to add more information in response to her questions (watching carefully, of course, to make sure that she is still interested). If she asked you, "Why is that bird carrying a twig?" you could explain about nest-building. These conversations will now be driven much more by her. She is likely to be asking endless questions, wanting explanations, and making it clear when the information she receives is not enough.

Questions

Carefully selected questions can help the little child to think and to work things out. If she's having difficulty with a puzzle, for example, you could say, "What would happen if you turned that piece upside down?" Or if she were building with blocks, you could say, "What did putting the big one under all those little ones let us do?" Please do not ask many of these, and as before, be sure to answer them yourself if she doesn't.

Never ask her questions in order to get her to answer. Little children, however poor or good their language development, always know what you are up to and very quickly become inhibited. I met a delightful little boy named Charles for the first time recently. As we met, I commented on what he was doing, and in no time we were enjoying a lengthy conversation, in which he revealed delightfully advanced language development. His mother was amazed. She had defined Charles as a shy child, as he usually took a long time to start talking to adults he did not know. I let her in on my simple secret—that I had commented to Charles on what was happening and had not asked him any questions. This led her to think of an elderly relative who had always initiated conversations with her by crossing her arms, fixing her eyes on her, and saying, "What's your news?" Charles's mother recalled exactly how she had felt and suddenly understood why he preferred comments to questions.

Some don'ts for this age

• Never correct your little child's speech. Remember—if her words or sentences are not clear, the helpful thing to do is to let her hear you say them clearly.

• Never draw her attention to the way in which she is speaking. This is particularly important if she is going through the stage of nonfluency. Always respond to what she is communicating, and not how she is doing so.

OUTSIDE YOUR HALF HOUR

• Give her time and space in which to play.
• Let her do things for herself when she wants to.
• Be aware of her attention level.
• Give her opportunities to play with other children.
• Give her opportunities for active play outside, if possible.
• Help her to discover the wonders of nature.

Now That Your Child Is Four

As we have seen, the little child has basically mastered the language by the time he is four, having a wide vocabulary and understanding and using all the basic sentence types in the language. He now continues to add to his vocabulary and to his knowledge of grammatical structures, and to utilize language in mature ways.

He now uses language to solve problems, like how to reach a tree house, and to make play plans both for himself and for groups of children. The little child becomes more and more skilled not only in communicating his ideas, but also in bargaining and negotiating, making deals, for example, about the allocation of turns in having the lead role. He also becomes more adept at describing his experiences and what he thinks and feels about them.

He takes part in long, complicated conversations and becomes increasingly able to adapt the way he speaks to the situation and the listener, being very clear, for example, that teachers are spoken to differently from little brothers! He is better at remembering the rules of politeness and needs to be reminded to say "please" and "thank you" less often. He becomes persistent in engaging an adult's attention when he wants to begin a conversation, and is better at picking the best moment to join into other people's conversations, waiting for a pause rather than interrupting.

He enjoys language enormously in terms of riddles and jokes and loves to listen to long and complicated stories.

Despite all this wonderful progress, however, his immaturity shows in a number of ways. It is still absolutely normal in the fifth year to make grammatical errors such as "goed" instead of "went," and most children still have immaturities in their speech sounds, using "f" for "th," "th" for "s," and an "r" sounding rather like a "w." The little child still doesn't always know the extent of other people's knowledge of his conversational topic and may leave them a little baffled as to what he is talking about. He also may fail to respond to his conversational partner's topic if his mind is elsewhere.

General Development

By the time he is five, he is able to dance to music and to play ball games with great agility. He loves to draw, and his drawings become more recognizable. Some little children begin to write a few letters spontaneously at this age.

His attention, at last, becomes two-channeled, and he is now able to continue what he is doing while listening to someone speak to him, without needing to stop and look at the speaker.[1] This happens in short spells at first, which gradually become longer. Arriving at this stage means that the little child is now ready for school, in that he will be able to listen to instructions about what he is doing, which is essential for learning in a classroom situation. (This ability, however, will not be fully established for another year.)

The little child loves very active play now and handles a bicycle and ball competently. He also loves to engage in the artistic and creative activities begun in the previous year and makes more elaborate constructions with blocks and other building materials. Pretend play continues to be a highly social activity, with lots of joint planning and cooperation. Rules are made, and usually kept to. Imagination continues to flourish, and he often acts out stories he has encountered in books and television programs.

How You Can Help

I hope that spending time every day alone with your little child is so much fun that I don't really need to suggest that you continue to do so. As in the last year, this doesn't have to be in a special playtime, but can be spent involving him in activities of yours like cooking or gardening, or taking him swimming or to storytime in the library. These sessions continue to give you wonderful opportunities for answering his questions and discussing with him the events in his life and how he feels about them. This is of particular importance if there has been a distressing event like the separation of his parents, the death of a family member or even of a beloved pet, allowing him to express his feelings and find reassurance.

Continue to share a book with him every day. Your little child will have developed his own individual taste in books now, so allow him to choose his own library books.

There are still things you can do to make sure that his language development continues to flourish. As was the case last year, you do not have to worry at all about restricting either the vocabulary you use or the complexity of your sentences. But continue to expand on what he has said. He might say, "We're going to the park after lunch," and you might reply with, "Yes, we are, and William and his mommy are coming too, and then they are coming back to our house for a visit."

If you notice a grammatical error, it's still helpful to model the correct version for him as part of the conversation, as you have done before.

The same goes for mispronunciations. If your little child said, "That bird has gray fevvers," you could say, "Yes, he's got gray feathers on his head, and I think I can see red feathers on his tail."

It's helpful to be alert for the times when he overestimates what someone else knows. My little friend Charles's mother had to remind him recently that I didn't know whether Joe was a child or an animal when Charles was telling me all about how Joe fell in a puddle.

Make sure that your child has enough time and space in which to play and, increasingly, opportunities to play with other children.

Limit his television watching to an hour a day. He can enjoy and learn much from children's programs now, and they can stimulate his imagination and enable him to witness wonders of nature that he cannot see in real life. He still, however, has an enormous need to play, to interact and converse with people, and to act out the events of his daily life so that he comes fully to understand them. He just hasn't got more than an hour to spare. As before, he will need you to watch with him and answer his questions and explain things that puzzle him.

And Now to School . . .

The most important event of this year is likely to be starting school. After doing the BabyTalk program, your little child is likely to have developed the attention, listening, and language skills that will enable him to enjoy school.

As I have mentioned, there is a huge controversy at present about the most appropriate timing for formal teaching of reading, writing, and numbers. My experience leads me to think that later is better for many children, but most parents have no option about when and where their children start school. The important thing for you as a parent is to make sure that your little child has plenty of opportunities to play at home and lots of enriching experiences—like visits to the swimming pool, the park, and the library. He may, of course, want to read, write, and work with numbers at home during this time, and there is no problem with that, but he needs balance. Just make sure that he always has the choice.

Some schools let you take your little child to have a look round before he starts. Talk to him a lot about what will happen at school, and make sure that you have time to answer all his questions. He will love to hear stories about when you started school. Above all, remember that your little child is extremely quick to pick up your attitudes, and if you believe that starting school will be a positive and fun experience for him, so will he.

APPENDIX 1
A WARNING ABOUT LABELS

I have worked with children suffering from rare neurological impairments that cause long-term speech and language difficulties. These tend to run in families, and affected children need intense speech and language therapy, and many require special educational provision as well. I discuss them here, because in our opinion—based on our extensive experience—we have found that many children today are being inappropriately labeled with these disorders.

"Specific language impairment" is the clinical term for severe and persistent language learning difficulties in the absence of other impairments such as hearing loss, autism, or learning difficulties.

"Dyspraxia" is another neurologically based disability that causes children to experience delay in language development, with associated difficulties in coordinating the movements of tongue and lips to make the series of speech sounds needed to produce words. They have difficulties in planning and organizing their body movements—for example to fit themselves into a small space, or to work out how to reach a toy by moving and climbing onto a chair. Affected children often appear generally clumsy and uncoordinated, and their play can be very disorganized.

"Attention deficit hyperactivity disorder" (ADHD), which shows a particularly strong family history, is a disability evidenced by difficulty in controlling attention and in staying on task. The children are extremely distractible. Some are helped considerably by medication.

Deirdre and I have seen many children who have been given these labels, including some whose parents have been advised to teach them sign language and to anticipate special educational needs. For a tiny number, this was absolutely appropriate. But for the great majority, the problems could have been prevented by help in early life working with listening and attention skills, and with understanding words. This majority, when their parents followed our program, rapidly reached normal limits, some ending up in the highly gifted range, both linguistically and in terms of general intelligence as measured by standardized tests, and all in a few short months.

I met Sonia when she was just over three years old. She was a very attractive little girl, with huge blue eyes, the youngest of three children. She had had a number of assessments in different parts of the country, as her parents were anxious about her slow speech development. She had been labeled "dyspraxic" as well as severely language delayed, and special education was being discussed. Sonia was indeed clumsy, having no idea how to hold a pencil or scissors, and could not organize herself, for instance, to stand on a box to reach a toy. She understood and used only a few single words.

At first sight, Sonia did indeed look like a child with serious difficulties. It emerged, however, that she had spent nearly all her life to date with a nanny, who, although affectionate and caring, hardly ever spoke to her, and sat her in front of children's videos for most of the day. After just three weeks on the BabyTalk program, Sonia began to understand and use two- to three-word sentences. Her skills in drawing, building, and cutting also developed rapidly once she had opportunities to engage in these activities and was shown what to do. It is clear already that she will have no long-term educational problems. I was delighted to hear from her mother recently that at the age of five, she is now reading books normally read by six-and-a-half-year-olds and is happy in school.

Another child who had been classified as affected by "specific language impairment" turned out to have an amazingly original and creative mind.

When I first met him at three years old, Ben had the understanding and use of language typical of a child of only sixteen months and was being taught to use sign language. Almost unbelievably, six months into the BabyTalk program, he was taxing us all with questions like "What is time?" and "How do your bones get inside your skin?" By the time he was four, he had the language skills of a seven-and-a-half-year-old!

APPENDIX 2
COMMON QUESTIONS FROM PARENTS

These are some questions commonly asked by parents who are doing or thinking about doing the BabyTalk program with their little children. I hope that you might find the answers helpful.

I have to go back to work when my baby is six months old. Will this be a problem?

I very much hope that by then you will have gotten into the habit of enjoying half an hour a day one-on-one with your baby, and that it won't be too difficult to keep it up when you are back at work. That half an hour a day can make the most enormous difference to your baby's development. If you can also share the BabyTalk principles with whoever is going to be your baby's main caregiver, so much the better. But even if this is not possible, rest assured that you will still be giving him valuable time to develop.

My wife is going back to work, and so I am going to be the main caregiver for our baby. Are there any worries about this?

Not at all! I have worked with lots of fathers who are in charge, and all of them have done a wonderful job. The only difference I have noticed from working with mothers is that fathers find it much more difficult not to "teach" their little children and not to ask them questions. I hope that you will try hard to follow the program in these respects and resist the temptation. If you do, I'm sure that you will be successful, and above all that you will have lots of fun in the process.

I am a single parent with two older children. It will be difficult to find time alone with the baby.

I do sympathize and recognize how very difficult this can be. I do believe, however, that it is worth going to a lot of trouble to enlist the help of a friend, neighbor, or relative to take care of the other children for a short time. It may also perhaps be possible to change your baby's routine so that he is awake at times when the other children are at school or playgroup. Even if this is not possible every day, your baby will still benefit a great deal from any time you can give him on his own. That precious half hour a day can make such a difference.

We are going to have a nanny for our baby. What should we take into account?

If your nanny is to spend a substantial amount of time with your baby, it is important that her first language is the same as yours. Share the BabyTalk program with her, so that she knows the principles, even if you will be doing the actual half an hour a day (as I hope you will).

If it is not possible to have a nanny who shares your language, encourage her to talk and sing to your baby in her own mother tongue. Your baby will then have an opportunity to acquire more than one language. It is important that if you have to change to a different nanny that the subsequent one speaks the same language as the first. I have seen a number of children who have been cared for by a succession of nannies who spoke different languages and who were making little progress in any of them.

I will have to put my baby into daycare while I work. Will it matter if they don't follow the BabyTalk program? I've heard the staff there asking the

children lots of questions, for example, and I have come to realize how much better it is not to do so!

When your little boy goes into the nursery, it is even more important that you do the program consistently with him at home every day if you possibly can. Little children are luckily very adaptable, and as long as you enable him to experience all the program at home, he will still get great benefit from it, which will not be undermined by the different approach taken in the nursery. He will benefit from all the play materials and toys at daycare, and later on from the company of the other children. You might in time tactfully come to be able to share your views with the daycare staff.

I have a three-year-old who seems jealous of the fact that I have time alone with his little brother. He never gets any such time as the two of them go to bed at the same time, and the baby is always awake when Michael is not at playgroup. What can I do?

Try putting the baby to bed a little earlier or letting Michael stay up a little longer so that he does have some time alone with you. All children benefit so much from undivided attention from an adult, and I believe that this could help a great deal with his jealousy of your baby. You are likely to find that Michael loves the part of the BabyTalk program for his age level.

My husband and I are getting divorced. Is there anything we can do to minimize the effect on our three-year-old daughter?

You cannot, of course, prevent your little girl from being upset by such a sad event. I believe, however, that by continuing to spend one-on-one time with her and giving her the opportunity to talk about her feelings and to ask questions, you will be helping her a lot. You will be able to help her to understand to a limited extent what is and is not going to happen. It is also important to recognize that children tend to assume that such events are their fault, and to reassure her repeatedly that this is not the case.

I am Italian, my wife is English, and we live in London. I should like my little boy to learn Italian, but I am worried that hearing two languages might confuse him. Am I right about this?

Babies and young children who have the chance of learning more than one language can do so easily in the right circumstances and are fortunate in having the opportunity. They only become confused in two situations. One is if the two languages are mixed together to a great extent, that is, with several words of each language within the same sentence. The other is when a caregiver uses a language that he or she did not acquire in childhood. An important part of the BabyTalk program is to modify the way we speak to babies and little children, and it is well known that it is extremely difficult to do this in a language other than the mother tongue or one acquired in early childhood. Adults would also be unlikely to know the traditional rhymes, songs, and stories in a language not acquired in childhood, and these are a rich part of the heritage we share with our children.

My advice to you is to speak in Italian to your little boy whenever you are alone together, and for total perfection, you can do the BabyTalk program with him in Italian and his mother in English.

REFERENCES

Introduction

1. T. Walpaw, J. Nation, and D. Aram, "Developmental Language Disability—a Follow-up Study," M. Burns and J. Andrew (eds.), *Selected Papers in Language and Phonology,* no. 1.

2. T. Fundudis, J. Kolvin, and R. Garside, *Speech in Retarded and Deaf Children* (London: Academic Press, 1979).

3. P. Silva, "The Prevalence and Stability of Language Delay from Three to Seven Years," *Folio Phoniatrica* 35, no. 3-4 (1983).

4. N. Richman, J. Stevenson, and P. Graham, *Pre-school to School—A Behavioural Study* (London: Academic Press, 1982).

5. C. Drillien and M. Drummond, "Developmental Screening and the Child with Special Needs" in *Clinics in Developmental Medicine*, vol. 86 (London: Heinemann Medical Books, 1983).

6. S. Ward, "An Investigation into the Effectiveness of an Early Intervention Method for Language Delayed Children," *International Journal of Disorders of Language and Communication* 34, vol. 3 (1999), pp. 243-64.

7. D. Wechsler, *Wechsler Intelligence Scale for Children,* 3d. UK ed. (Sidcup, Kent: The Psychological Corporation, 1992).

8. J. Rust, *Wechsler Objective Language Dimensions* (The Psychological Corporation, Harcourt Brace & Co, 1996).

9. J. Rust, S. Golombok, and G. Trickey, *Wechsler Objective Reading Dimensions* (Sidcup, Kent: The Psychological Corporation, 1992).

10. L. M. Dunn, and C. Whetton with D. Pintilie, *British Picture Vocabulary Test* (Windsor Berkshire: NFER Nelson, 1982).

11. B. Skinner, *Verbal Behavior* (New York: Appleton Century Crofts, 1957).

12. N. Chomsky, "A Review of 'Verbal Behavior' by B. Skinner," *Language* 35 (1959), pp. 26-58.

13. N. Chomsky, *Aspects of the Theory of Syntax* (Cambridge, Mass.: MIT Press, 1965).

14. N. Chomsky, *Knowledge of Language: Its Nature, Uses, and Origin* (New York: Praeger, 1986).

15. S. Pinker, *The Language Instinct* (London: Penguin, 1994).

16. K. Kaye, "Towards the Origins of Dialogue," H. R. Shaffer (ed.), *Studies in Mother-Child Interaction* (New York: Academic Press, 1977).

17. C. Trevarthen, "A Descriptive Analysis of Infant Communicative Behaviour," H. R. Shaffer (ed.), *Studies in Mother-Child Interaction* (New York: Academic Press, 1977).

18. L. Vygotsky, *Thought and Language* (Cambridge, Mass.: MIT Press, 1962).

19. E. Hoff Ginsberg, "Methodological and Social Concerns in the Study of Children's Language Learning Environments," *First Language* 12 (1992), pp. 251-55.

20. J. Huttenlocher et al., "Early Vocabulary Growth," *Developmental Psychology* 27 (1991), pp. 236-48.

21. G. Wells and W. Robinson, "The Role of Adult Speech in Language Development," C. Fraser and K. Scherer (eds.), *The Social Psychology of Language* (Cambridge University Press, 1982).

22. M. Tomasello and J. Todd, "Joint Attention and Lexical Acquisition Style," *First Language* 4 (1983), pp. 197-212.

23. A. Fernald and P. Khul, "Acoustic Determinants of Infants' Preference for Motherese," *Infant Behaviour and Development* 10 (1987), pp. 279-93.

24. K. Nelson, "Towards a Rare Event Comparison Theory of Syntax Acquisition," P. Dale and D. Ingram (eds.), *Child Language—An Interactional Perspective* (Baltimore: University Park Press, 1981).

25. E. Lenneberg, *The Biological Foundations of Language* (New York: Wiley, 1967).

26. B. Thorpe, *Birdsong—The Biology of Vocal Communication and Expression in Birds* (Cambridge: Cambridge University Press, 1961).

27. J. Law, *The Early Identification of Language Disabled Children* (London: Chapman and Hall, 1989).

28. M. Sheridan, "Children of Seven Years with Marked Speech Defects," *British Journal of Disorders of Communication* 8 (1973), pp. 1–8.

29. M. Bax, H. Hart, and S. Jenkins, "The Assessment of Speech and Language Development in Young Children," *Paediatrics* 3 (1980), pp. 19–26.

30. P. Macintyre and R. Umansky, "Speech and Language Screenings as Predictors of Communicative Problems in Young Children," *Folio Phoniatrica* 35, no. 3–4 (1983).

31. L. Bliss and D. Allen, "Screening Kit of Language Development," *Journal of Communication Disorders* 17 (1984), pp. 133–41.

32. M. Nash in *Time* magazine (24 February 1997) reporting on the work of researchers at the Baylor College of Medicine Houston; Harry Chugain, Wayne State University Belmont; Corey Goodman and Carla Shatz, University of California Berkeley; Stanley Greenspan, George Washington University; and Eric Kandel, Columbia University.

33. J. Cooper, M. Moodley, and J. Reynell, *Helping Language Development* (London: Edward Arnold, 1978).

Birth to Three Months

1. A. DeCasper and W. Fifer, "On Human Bonding," *Science* 208 (1980), pp. 1174–76.

2. R. Aslin, "Visual and Auditory Development in Infancy," J. D. Osofsky (ed.), *Handbook of Infant Development* (New York: Wiley, 1987).

3. W. Fifer and C. Moon, "Psychobiology of Human Newborn Preferences," *Seminars in Perinatology* 13 (1989), pp. 430–33.

4. D. Messer, *The Development of Communication* (Chichester: Wiley, 1994).

5. R. Cooper and R. Aslin, "Preference for Child Directed Speech in the First Month After Birth," *Child Development* 61 (1990), pp. 1584–95.

6. P. Eimas et al., "Speech Perception in Infants," *Science* 171 (1971), pp. 303–6.

7. A. Slater, D. Rose, and V. Morison, "Newborn Infants' Perception of Similarities and Differences Between Two and Three Dimensional Stimuli," *British Journal of Developmental Psychology* 2 (1984), pp. 287–94.

8. R. Fantz, "Pattern Discrimination and Selective Attention as Determinants of Perceptual Development from Birth," A. Kidd and J. Rivoire (eds.), *Perceptual Development in Children* (New York: International Universities Press, 1966).

9. E. Melhuish, "Visual Attention to Mothers' and Strangers' Faces and Facial Contrast in One-month Olds," *Developmental Psychology* 18 (1982), pp. 299–331.

10. I. Bushnell, F. Sai, and J. Mullin, "Neonatal Recognition of Mother's Face," *British Journal of Developmental Psychology* 7 (1989), pp. 3–15.

11. B. Berthenthal et al., "The Development of Infant Sensitivity to Biomechanical Motions," *Child Development* 56 (1985), pp. 531–43.

12. A. Melfzoff and K. Moore, "Newborn Infants Imitate Adult Facial Gestures," *Child Development* 54 (1983), pp. 702–09.

13. A. Melfzoff and A. Goprick, "The Role of Imitation in Understanding Persons and Developing a Theory of Mind," S. Baron-Cohen, H. Tager-Flushberg, and D. Cohen (eds.), *Understanding Other Minds—Perspectives from Autism* (Oxford: Oxford University Press, 1993).

14. L. Camras, C. Malatesta, and C. Izard, "The Development of Facial Expression in Infancy," R. Feldman and B. Rime (eds.), *Fundamentals of Nonverbal Behavior* (New York: Cambridge University Press, 1991).

15. T. M. Field, R. Woodson, and C. Cohen, "Discrimination and Imitation of Facial Expressions by Neonates," *Science* 218 (1982), pp. 179–81.

16. C. Trevarthen, "A Descriptive Analysis of Infant Communicative Behaviour," H. R. Shaffer (ed.), *Studies in Mother-Infant Interaction* (London: Academic Press, 1977), pp. 227–70.

17. L. Camras, C. Malatesta, and C. Izard, "The Development of Facial Expression in Infancy," R. Feldman and B. Rime (eds.), *Fundamentals of Nonverbal Behavior* (New York: Cambridge University Press, 1991).

18. B. Stern et al., "The Infant's Stimulus World During Social Interaction," H. R. Shaffer (ed.), *Studies in Mother-Child Interaction* (London: Academic Press, 1977).

19. G. Bremner, "Object Tracking and Search in Infancy," *Developmental Review* 5 (1985), pp. 371–96.

20. A. Slater et al., "Movement Identity and Identity: Constancy in the Newborn Baby," *British Journal of Developmental Psychology* 3 (1985), pp. 211–20.

21. P. Slater, "Visual Perceptual Abilities at Birth," B. de Boysson-Bardies et al. (eds.),

Developmental Neurorecognition—Speech and Face Processing in the First Year of Life (Boston: Dordrecht, 1993).

22. G. Bremner, "Object Tracking and Search in Infancy," *Developmental Review* 5 (1985), pp. 371–96.

23. P. Eimas and P. Quinn, "Studies on the Formation of Perceptually Based Basic Level Categories in Young Children," *Child Development* 65 (1994), pp. 903–18.

24. P. Hepper, "An Examination of Fetal Learning Before and After Birth," *Irish Journal of Psychology* 12 (1991), pp. 95–107.

25. E. Hoff-Ginsberg, "Methodological and Social Concerns in the Study of Children's Language Learning Environments, *First Language* 12 (1992), pp. 251–5.

26. J. Huttenlocher et al., "Early Vocabulary Growth: Relationship to Language Input and Gender," *Developmental Psychology* 27 (1991), pp. 236–48.

27. E. Bates, I. Brotherton, and L. Snyder, *From First Words to Grammar* (Cambridge: Cambridge University Press, 1988).

28. D. Messer, *The Development of Communication* (Chichester: Wiley, 1994).

Three to Six Months

1. D. Hay, A. Nash, and J. Pederson, "Interactions Between Six-month-old Peers," *Child Development* 54 (1983), pp. 557–62.

2. K. Hirsch-Pasek et al., "Clauses are Perceptual Units for Children," *Cognition* 26 (1987), pp. 269–86.

3. M. Ruddy and M. Bornstein, "Cognitive Correlates of Infant Attention and Maternal Stimuli Over the First Year of Life," *Child Development* 82 (1982), pp. 53–183.

4. M. Ruddy and M. Bornstein, "Cognitive Correlates of Infant Attention and Maternal Stimuli Over the First Year of Life," *Child Development* 82 (1982), pp. 53–183.

5. A. Fernald and P. Khul, "Acoustic Determinants of Infants' Preference for Motherese," *Infant Behaviour and Development* 10 (1987), pp. 279–93.

6. J. Werker and P. Mcleod, "Infant Preference for Both Male and Female Infant Directed Talk," *Canadian Journal of Psychology* 43 (1989), pp. 230–46.

7. A. Fernald, "Four-month-olds Prefer to Listen to Motherese," *Infant Behaviour and Development* 8 (1989), pp. 181–95.

8. M. Papousiek, M. Bornstein, and I. Nuzzo, "Infant Responses to Prototypical Melodic Contours in Parental Speech," *Infant Behaviour and Development* 13 (1989), pp. 539-45.

9. J. Ryther-Duncan et al., "Infant Versus Adult Directed Speech as Signals for Faces," Poster at Biennial Meeting of SRCD, New Orleans, 1993.

Six to Nine Months

1. K. Bzoch and R. League, *Receptive-Expressive Emergent Language Scales* (Granville, Florida: Pro-Ed Inc., 1991).

2. S. Bochner, "The Development of Vocalisation of Handicapped Children in a Hospital Setting," *Australian and New Zealand Journal of Developmental Disabilities* 12 (1986), pp. 55-63.

3. J. Bruner, *Child's Talk: Learning to Use Language* (New York: Norton, 1983).

4. C. Trevarthen, "Communication and Co-operation in Early Infancy," M. Bullowa (ed.), *Before Speech* (Cambridge: Cambridge University Press, 1979).

5. D. Messer, *The Development of Communication* (Chichester: Wiley, 1994).

6. K. Bzoch and R. League, *Receptive-Expressive Emergent Language Scales* (Granville, Florida: Pro-Ed Inc., 1991).

7. M. Turvey, R. Shaw, and W. Mace, "Issues in the Theory of Action," J. Requin (ed.), *Attention and Performance,* no. 7 (Hillsdale, N.J.: Lawrence Erlbaum Associates Inc., 1978), pp. 557-95.

8. R. Baillergeon, "The Object-Concept Revisited," C. Gramrud (ed.), *Visual Perception and Cognition in Infancy* (Hillsdale, N.J.: Lawrence Erlbaum Associates Inc., 1993).

9. E. Lenneberg, *The Biological Foundations of Language* (New York: Wiley, 1967).

10. R. Griffiths, *The Abilities of Babies* (London: University of London Press, 1954).

11. J. Mandler, P. Bauer, and L. McDonagh, "Separating the Sheep from the Goats," *Cognitive Psychology* 23 (1991), pp. 263-98.

12. C. Murphy and D. Messer, "Mothers, Infants and Pointing," H. R. Shaffer (ed.), *Studies in Mother-Infant Interaction* (London: Academic Press, 1977).

13. G. Collis, "Visual Co-orientation and Maternal Speech," H. R. Shaffer (ed.), *Studies in Mother-Infant Interaction* (London: Academic Press, 1977).

14. K. Bzoch and R. League, *Receptive-Expressive Emergent Language Scales* (Granville, Florida: Pro-Ed Inc., 1991).

15. C. Trevarthen, "The Development of Intersubjective Motor Control in Infants," M. G. Wade (ed.), *Motor Development in Children* (Dordrecht: Reidal, 1986).

16. C. Trevarthen, "Communication and Co-operation in Early Infancy," M. Bullowa (ed.), *Before Speech* (Cambridge: Cambridge University Press, 1979).

17. A. Nelson, "Constraints on Word Learning?," *Cognitive Development* 3 (1988), pp. 221–46.

18. K. Clarke-Stewart, "Interaction Between Mothers and Young Children," *Monographs of the Society for Research in Child Development,* no. 153, vol. 38 (1973), pp. 96–7.

Nine to Twelve Months

1. M. Carpenter, K. Nagell, and M. Tomasello, "Social Cognition, Joint Attention and Communicative Competence from Nine to Fifteen Months," *Monographs of the Society for Research in Child Development* 4, no. 255 (1998).

2. C. Trevarthen, "Signs Before Speech," in T. A. Sebeok and J. Umiker-Sebeok (eds.), *The Semiotic Web* (Berlin, Amsterdam: Mouton de Gruyter, 1990).

3. K. Bzoch and R. League, *Receptive-Expressive Emergent Language Scales* (Granville, Florida: Pro-Ed Inc., 1991).

4. S. Ward, "The Predictive Accuracy and Validity of a Screening Test for Language Delay and Auditory Perceptual Disorder," *European Journal of Disorders of Communication* 27 (1992), pp. 55–72.

5. K. Nelson, "Structure and Strategy in Learning to Talk," *Monographs of the Society for Research in Child Development,* No. 38 (1973).

6. J. Cooper, M. Moodley, and J. Reynell, *Helping Language Development* (London: Edward Arnold, 1978).

7. M. Adamson and T. Bakeman, "Affect and Attention: Infants Observed with Mothers and Peers," *Child Development* 56 (1985), pp. 582–93.

8. D. Hay and H. Posse, "The Social Nature of Early Conflict," *Child Development* 53 (1982), pp. 105–113.

9. S. Pinker, *The Language Instinct: The New Science of Language and Mind* (London: Penguin, 1994).

10. J. Bruner, "Early Social Interactions and Language Acquisition," H. R. Shaffer (ed.), *Studies in Mother-Child Interaction* (London: Academic Press, 1977).

11. K. Kaye, *The Mental and Social Life of Babies* (Chicago: University of Chicago Press, 1982).

12. E. Hoff Ginsberg, "Methodological and Social Concerns in the Study of Children's Language Learning Environments, *First Language* 12 (1992), pp. 251-55.

13. K. Nelson, *Making Sense: The Acquisition of the Child's Shared Meaning System* (New York: Academic Press, 1985).

14. G. Wells and W. Robinson, "The Role of Adult Speech in Child Development," C. Fraser and K. Scherer (eds.), *The Social Psychology of Language* (Cambridge: Cambridge University Press, 1982).

15. M. Tomasello and J. Farrer, "Joint Attention and Early Language," *Child Development* 57 (1986), pp. 1454-63.

16. L. Baumwell et al., "Maternal Responsiveness and Infant Language Comprehension," SRCD Conference New Orleans, 1993.

17. M. Tomasello and J. Todd, "Joint Attention and Lexical Acquisition Style," *First Language* 7 (1983), pp. 197-212.

18. M. Carpenter, K. Nagell, and M. Tomasello, "Social Cognition, Joint Attention and Communicative Competence from Nine to Fifteen Months," *Monographs of the Society for Research in Child Development*, 63, 4, no. 255 (1998).

19. M. Tomasello and J. Todd, "Joint Attention and Lexical Acquisition Style," *First Language* 7 (1983), pp. 197-212.

20. V. Reddy et al., "Communication in Infancy," in G. Bremner, A. Slater, and G. Butterworth (eds.), *Infant Development—Recent Advances* (London: Psychological Press, Taylor & Francis, 1997).

21. C. Snow, R. Perlman, and P. Nathan, "Why Routines are Different," K. Nelson and A. Kleek (eds.), *Children's Language* vol. 6 (Hillsdale, N.J.: Lawrence Erlbaum Associates Inc., 1987).

Twelve to Sixteen Months

1. J. Huttenlocher, "Origins of Language Comprehension," in R. Solso (ed.), *Theories in Cognitive Psychology,* 5th ed. (Potomac, Md.: Erlbaum, 1974).

2. K. Nelson, *Making Sense: The Acquisition of Shared Meaning* (New York: Academic Press, 1985).

3. K. Bzoch and R. League, *Receptive-Expressive Emergent Language Scales* (Granville, Florida: Pro-Ed Inc., 1991).

4. D. Furrow, K. Nelson, and H. Benedict, "Mother's Speech to Children and Syntactic Development: Some Simple Relationships," *Journal of Child Language* 6 (1979), pp. 423–42.

5. J. Mandler, "The Development of Categorisation: Perceptual and Conceptual Categories," G. Bremner, A. Slater, and G. Butterworth (eds.), *Infant Development: Recent Advances* (London: Psychological Press, Taylor & Francis, 1997).

6. J. Cooper, M. Moodley, and J. Reynell, *Helping Language Development* (London: Edward Arnold, 1978).

7. M. Beeghley, "Parent Infant Play," K. Macdonald (ed.), *Parent Child Play* (New York: State University of New York Press, 1993).

8. M. Beeghley, "Parent Infant Play," K. Macdonald (ed.), *Parent Child Play* (New York: State University of New York Press, 1993).

9. C. Snow et al., "Mothers' Speech in Three Social Classes," *Journal of Psycholinguistic Research* 5 (1976), pp. 1–20.

10. M. Tomasello and J. Todd, "Joint Attention and Lexical Acquisition Style," *First Language* 4 (1983), pp. 197–212.

11. M. Della Court and B. P. Keene, "The Relationship Between Pragmatic Dimensions of Mothers' Speech to the Referential-Expressive Distinction," *Journal of Child Language* 10 (1983), pp. 35–44.

Sixteen to Twenty Months

1. J. Huttenlocher et al., "Early Vocabulary Growth: Relationship to Language Input and Gender," *Developmental Psychology* 27 (1991), pp. 236–48.

2. R. Baldwin, "Infants' Contribution to the Achievement of Joint Reference," *Child Development* 62 (1991), pp. 875–90.

3. J. Cooper, M. Moodley, and J. Reynell, *Helping Language Development* (London: Edward Arnold, 1978).

4. M. Tomasello and J. Todd, "Joint Attention and Lexical Acquisition Style," *First Language* 4 (1983), pp. 197–212.

5. P. Dunham, F. Dunham, and A. Curwin, "Joint Attention and Lexical Acquisition at Eighteen Months," *Developmental Psychology* 29 (1989), pp. 827–31.

Twenty to Twenty-four Months

1. K. Bzoch and R. League, *Receptive-Expressive Emergent Language Scales* (Granville, Florida: Pro-Ed Inc., 1991).

2. R. Griffiths, *The Abilities of Babies* (London: University of London Press, 1954).

3. A. Gesell, *The First Five Years of Life* (London: Methuen, 1954).

4. M. Tomasello and J. Farrer, "Joint Attention and Early Language," *Child Development* 57 (1986), pp. 1454–63.

5. N. Cohen and A. Barwick, Department of Research, Hinks Bellcrest Institute, University of Toronto.

6. L. Gleitman, E. Newport, and H. Gleitman, "The Current Status of the Motherese Hypothesis," *Journal of Child Language* 11 (1984), pp. 43–79.

7. C. Wells, "Adjustments in Adult Child Conversation: Some Effects of Interaction," in H. Giles, W. Robinson, and P. Smith (eds.), *Language: Social and Psychological Perspectives* (Oxford: Pergammon, 1980).

8. M. J. Farrer, "Discourse and the Acquisition of Grammatical Morphemes," *Journal of Child Language* 17 (1990), pp. 607–23.

9. R. Brown and U. Bellugi, "Three Processes Involved in Language Acquisition of Syntax," *Harvard Educational Review* 34 (1964), pp. 133–51.

Twenty-four to Thirty Months

1. A. Gesell, *The First Five Years of Life* (London: Methuen, 1954).

2. S. Edwards et al., *Reynell Developmental Language Scales* (Windsor, England: NFER Nelson, 1997).

3. R. Brown, *A First Language—The Early Stages* (Cambridge, Mass.: Harvard University Press, 1973).

4. J. Cooper, M. Moodley, and J. Reynell, *Helping Language Development* (London: Edward Arnold, 1977).

5. R. McConkey, D. Jeffree, and S. Hewson, *Let Me Play* (London: Souvenir Press, 1964).

6. R. Battin, "Psychological and Educational Assessment of Children with Language Learning Problems," R. Roes and M. Downs (eds.), *Auditory Disorders in School Children* (New York: Theime Stratton, 1987).

7. D. Johnson, *Learning Disabilities* (New York: Grune and Stratton, Inc., 1976).

8. D. Cantwell and I. Baker, "Psychiatric Disorder in Children with Speech and Language Retardation," *Archives of General Psychiatry* 34 (1977), pp. 583–91.

9. S. Baron-Cohen and H. Ring, "A Model of the Mind Reading System," C. Lewis and P. Mitchell (eds.), *Children's Early Understanding of the Mind* (London: Hove Erlbaum, 1994).

10. R. Brown and V. Bellugi, "Three Processes in Childrens' Acquisition of Syntax," *Harvard Educational Review* 34 (1964), pp. 133–51.

11. M. Farrer, "Discourse and the Acquisition of Grammatical Morphemes," *Journal of Child Language* 17 (1990), pp. 607–24.

12. C. Wells, "Adjustments in Adult Child Conversation" H. Giles, W. Robinson, and P. Smith (eds.), *Language: Social and Psychological Perspectives* (Oxford: Pergammon, 1980).

Thirty to Thirty-six Months

1. K. Bzoch and R. League, *Receptive-Expressive Emergent Language Scales* (Granville, Florida: Pro-Ed Inc., 1991).

2. R. Griffiths, *The Abilities of Babies* (London: University of London Press, 1954).

3. J. Cooper, M. Moodley, and J. Reynell, *Helping Language Development* (London: Edward Arnold, 1978).

Three to Four Years

1. L. M. Dunn and C. Whetton with D. Pintilie, *British Picture Vocabulary Test* (Windsor, Berkshire: NFER Nelson, 1982).

2. J. Cooper, M. Moodley, and J. Reynell, *Helping Language Development* (London: Edward Arnold, 1978).

3. R. McConkey, D. Jeffree, and S. Hewson, *Let Me Play* (London: Souvenir Press, 1964).

4. J. Singer and D. Singer, "Combinatorial Play, Conceptual Development and Early Multi-Word Speech," *American Psychologist* 2 (1990), pp. 184–90.

5. M. Tomasello, *Joint Attention as Social Cognition: Origins and Role in Development* (Hillsdale, N.J.: Erlbaum, 1995).

6. P. Levenstein, "Cognitive Growth in Pre-school Children Through Verbal Interaction with Mothers," *Journal of Orthopsychiatry* 40 (1970), pp. 426–32.

7. M. Bornstein, "Maternal Responsiveness: Characteristics and Consequences," *New Directions for Child Development* 43 (1989).

8. H. Gottfried and I. Caldwell (eds.), *Play Interaction* (Lexington, Mass.: Lexington Books).

9. D. Singer and J. Singer, *The House of Make-Believe* (Cambridge, Mass.: Harvard University Press, 1990).

Now That Your Child Is Four

1. J. Cooper, M. Moodley, and J. Reynell, *Helping Language Development* (London: Edward Arnold, 1978).

ABOUT THE AUTHOR

DR. SALLY WARD is a speech and language therapist. She is a member of the Royal College of Speech and Language Therapists and a member of the British Society of Audiology. She lives in England.